As I've gotten older, I've come to realize that life does not travel in a straight line. In fact, it has ever flowing twists and turns challenging our very soul to find positivity. Most times this requires looking within ourselves to alter our perspective from hopelessness to gratitude. Sometimes, in the thick of it all, that perspective is more easily gained from others who have learned from their own experiences and look to pass on that knowledge to show others that there is always, always something to be grateful for. I hope to be the light that guides you to heal your soul and find peace through a positive perspective.

"It is profound how a few little words can so powerfully impact ones very soul! Lisa Mate captured my heart on many occasions with her regular messages and posts.... Sometimes of inspiration, sometimes expressing life's struggles and challenges, but always full of wisdom, grace and goodness! From the simple reminder of how exceptionally blessed we each are in our own lives, to the realization of natures' beauty that surrounds us when we are not too busy "doing". Her words will sometimes melt you, sometimes make you cry, sometimes make you laugh. Her words will always make you think!" Namaste - Cindy P.

"From the first "Mindful Moments" entry Lisa made, I knew it was something special. If her day is overwhelming for her, she manages to convey such positive outlooks and even leaves the reader with a sense of calm and tranquility. I owe that to her incredible sense of optimism and hope. If you're having a rough day, the inspiration in her prose will leave you in peace and looking forward to the next "Mindful Moments" - Robert M.

i

D1086873

"Your Mindful Moments opened our eyes to the life you live in a world with Autism. You made me laugh and cry and brought me joy. I'm glad I helped to encourage you to write this amazing book. You have been an inspiration to us all." - Betty S.

"The moments in this book are, as said, mindful. Not only are they mindful, but they are the most genuine of moments that any person could learn by. These moments have reminded myself of my own struggles, and have helped me to come to the realization that all things in life will have their ups and downs no matter the person. We find our peace and serenity in the things around us and Lisa has exposed the things that most of us take for granted. May this book bring you laughter, sadness, happiness, peace and this gentle reminder—We are all human and have flaws. All we can do is be mindful of those moments and push to find the silver lining in all things that challenge us. From a genuine person with the most amazing outlook on life, please enjoy all of the Mindful Moments here. Death is inevitable, lead the best life you can no matter what your moments may be." - John G.

"I can't tell you how much I appreciate your "Mindful Moments" posts. The post with William and Rocket made me weep. I don't always comment but I need you to know that your honesty has helped me put perspective on many of my own struggles. What you refer to as "transparency", I see as just plain generosity. Your struggles and solutions with William can be so daunting— but your love for him overpowers it all. Huge respect, my friend and thank you." - Karen S.

"I have enjoyed Lisa's "Mindful Moments" posts from the beginning. I don't think I've ever known a kinder more positive person that Lisa. She has helped me apply her thinking to my rough times. Lisa is also a wonderful mom to William. The stories about the difficult times that William had as he has grown up are very interesting. There's always a positive message and a happy ending. Lisa always finds solutions that work perfectly. I admire Lisa and I appreciate her posts. I always look forward to the next edition." - Ken F.

"I don't even know where to begin. First, it's an incredible honor to be in your sphere of influence. You push us all to be better. Do better. And just be a darn good human. You make the world a better place and I am forever thankful that our paths have crossed and to be on this journey together." - Anonymous

Mindful Moments: A Pandemic Memoir of Positivity and Gratitude

Lisa Mate

BookLocker
Trenton, Georgia

Copyright © 2021 Lisa Mate

Paperback ISBN: 978-1-64719-868-8
Ebook ISBN: 978-1-64719-869-5

All rights reserved. No part of this publication may be reproduced, stored in a retrieval system, or transmitted in any form or by any means, electronic, mechanical, recording or otherwise, without the prior written permission of the author.

Published by BookLocker.com, Inc., Trenton, Georgia.

Printed on acid-free paper.

BookLocker.com, Inc.
2021

First Edition

Library of Congress Cataloguing in Publication Data
Mate, Lisa
Mindful Moments: A Pandemic Memoir of Positivity and
Gratitude by Lisa Mate
Library of Congress Control Number: 2021920414

DEDICATIONS

My deepest gratitude goes out to the difficult decisions and situations I have been faced with throughout life for without them I would not have gained renewed positive perspective. I find that within everything that happens FOR, not TO, us is a lesson to be learned and growth to be had.

To my wonderful husband Boston, Steve, for his patience, someone who listens quietly, always has a plan and a helping hand, supports my crazy ideas, tolerates my singing and dancing and incessant positive outlook. My life has been forever gifted with your love and support. You are appreciated more than you know.

My heart is filled with pride and gratitude for everything my children, Caitlin and William, have taught me about life; not sweating the small stuff and finding the joy within the simplest of life's true gifts around us. That special abilities are a gift which teaches the most important, lifelong lessons about dedication and love. Thank you for loving me and my goofy personality. I love you both with all of my heart and soul.

To my parents who loved, guided and watched an insecure, wall flower of a little girl grow up to be an independent, secure adult growing from single parent, to business owner to fierce special needs advocate. Without your guidance I would not have had the courage to forge ahead in my endeavors. I am grateful for mom with her 94 years of experience seeing all of our accomplishments and know that dad is always watching over us with pride. You are both forever in my heart.

To my brothers, Tom, Rob and Dave, you are all so very special to me and have helped me to grow in your own unique ways. Your dedication to those you love, have loved and aided throughout your lives is a true testament to the kindness you hold in your hearts. Always remember how special and loved you all are and I will forever be your "Dorito breath" little sister.

In conclusion, without the love, validation and encouragement of my Aunt Betty (Dolly) this book may not have come to fruition. Thank you for believing in me without hesitation. You are loved.

CONTENTS

Lisa Mate

March 17, 2020 – schools closed with switch to remote learning.

March 20, 2020 – all non-essential businesses shut down.

Hospitals, gas stations and food stores were considered essential and kept open and available. Most of us stayed home, isolated and online food and supply sales skyrocketed. Sanitizing supplies, PPE and toilet paper literally flew off the shelves. A state of panic ensued.

As we navigated through the fear of the unknown, isolated from everyone outside of our homes, the situation became overwhelming.

My business shut down with no unemployment available, at that time, for the self-employed.

My Autistic child began struggling emotionally from the lack of routine, declining social interaction and drastic change to life as we knew it.

We all did our very best to find our new normal. It became emotional survival.

I felt myself drowning in anxiety and stress while watching the entire world crippled with sickness, death and the unknown.

While parenting, I became a teacher, therapist, friend and confidant to my special needs child. All of that while trying to navigate a closed business with clients desperately looking for answers as much as we all were.

I decided that I needed to hold myself accountable. I wanted to feel "normal", bring our experiences to commonality and show the positive you can create in the most difficult of times. I decided to use social media in order to share our personal daily struggles but to end each day on a positive note with hope for a better tomorrow. After all, weren't we all having our own personal struggles and needed a gentle nudge to switch our perspective to positivity? Didn't we all want to feel that we were not alone in our struggles and that there was a light to be found at the end of all of this uncertainty?

I am humbled that the inspiration and gratitude resulting from these daily accountabilities has, in turn, positively affected so many.

My goal is to tap into your emotions, empathy and make you think in order to show the world emotional freedom through a positive perspective every single day.

My prose began as "things I saw today" as I tried to focus on the positives of each day. The title was appropriately altered to "Mindful Moments".

Please join us in our personal journey of navigating through the COVID-19 pandemic and finding gratitude in all of life's ever-changing challenges.

2020 PASSAGES

3/17/2020

I want to tell you what I saw today.

I saw a post in our neighborhood FB page offering help to anyone who needs it i.e., grocery shopping, etc.

I saw kids on skateboards.

I saw kids walking outside, in small groups talking, no phones.

I saw Fur babies walking their humans.

I saw families going for walks after dinner.

I saw runners.

I saw bike riders.

I saw staff at school prepping work for parents to pick up.

I saw helpers and people making the best of an unsettling situation.

We are in this together.

Take a deep breath.

Find the Joy! ♡

Namaste

3/18/2020

This is what I saw today ....

My daughter, the light of my life. ♡

Less traffic making work travel smooth.

In the traffic, the majority, semis. That's a good thing! They're carrying needed supplies meaning we continue to thrive.

Lower fuel prices.

A Good Samaritan who stopped on the shoulder of I55 to help change the tire of a stranded motorist with traffic whizzing by.

A dog walking his human as he happily carried a stick larger than himself wagging his tail. We should all be so in the moment.

Plans for Telehealth to continue William's therapy remotely despite our challenging times. Where there is hope, there are solutions.

Spring rain to help our earth produce food, oxygen and beauty.

Birds flying, bunnies hopping and squirrels scurrying up trees living their best life.

The beginnings of perennials peaking their heads out for a first look at Spring and promises of better times to come.

A friend to talk to, to share, to help each other, to provide support. ♡

Sleep well - Namaste 🙏

3/19/2020

This is what I saw today ....

Many Mobile services on the road - traveling health care, tow trucks, heating and cooling, storm restoration, Mobile dog groomers.

An inflatable tall building height dragon - it amused me.

Older man driving his car wearing a protective mask - thankful that he had one.

Covid19 treatments in the works and vaccines for the future.

Construction companies donating their N95 masks, hazmat suits and foot coverings to the front-line medical personnel who so desperately need them.

Many thousands of converted ventilators sent out to help the severely ill.

No more confirmed cases in Wuhan.

2 men, in their late 60's. One with his 3 dogs walking him and the other with walking sticks. Walking on opposite sides of the street, toward each other - greeted each other with a smile, a few kind words and walked on getting their exercise and fresh air.

My LA Fitness instructors/friends offering their time with free online classes. My gym time was my self-care, my exercise, my escape from reality and my face-to-face friendships. The gym is closed and I haven't been there for a while but I will be online whenever a class is in my time frame and continue my home workouts for ME.

Eating healthy, getting exercise, self-care is so very important during stressful times. Make no mistake, stress lowers your immune system and will make you sick.

The realization that Covid19 media/FB post overload was causing too much stress with becoming a home school teacher of a special needs child, trying to run a business that may be shut down sooner than I care to think, managing Williams fear and anxiety and the fear of our unknown future.

I now only watch the daily White House updates and watch for local shelter in place announcements for areas my business can no longer service ... period.

These have been feelings of the days just after 9-11 when the tv HAD to be shut off, only this at a much different level of life's uncertainty and sustainability.

Time to scroll past the dozens of statistical posts, informational posts many from unreliable sources, turn off the news and find peace, serenity and balance for our personal health, peace of mind and that of our vulnerable families.

We cannot control anything but ourselves. We are 100% responsible for our decisions 100% of the time. Find your balance.

As my father always said in any stressful situation ....

And this too shall pass.

Sweet dreams my friends and good health to you - Namaste 🙏

3/20/2020

Things I saw today ....

Williams cute face at 6:30am.

Gypsy's fuzzy bum while we had our morning walk.

The quiet streets, calm breeze, somewhat peaceful while surrounding our isolation.

Ligia my friend and Zumba queen one of several instructors creating togetherness through dance virtually.

Stacy and Jennifer; thank you to the 3 of you for lightening the load on our minds through dance.

William putting down his tablet to dance with me during class.

Seeing a smile on Williams face from my goofball antics - he thinks I'm funny - he's only 11.

A much-needed conversation with the most amazing mother-in-law. Her calming voice and kind words are sunshine in my day. ♡

Fast-food drive- up lines at every corner - keeping our community working.

I wiped down the ATM with a Clorox wipe before and after my turn and gave the lady behind me a thumbs up - always pay it forward.

I saw small non-essential businesses like mine shut down in a New York minute - the fear of the unknown hit hard BUT to my surprise, after a few moments of panic, there was relief. I know weird right?!

It was going to happen, worrying didn't change it, now did it. At least there is direction now. Planning to do and an end to look forward to.

On the plus side I haven't had this much time away from work since Jr high!

I see everyone finding a new norm.

Friends posting some hysterical memes! Angela this virus has produced some great comedic relief! Preston the Zen master of the singing bowls.

Posts of "let's share photos" "who needs help" "I have supplies if anyone needs something" heartwarming.

Our nation had become more divided over recent years and oddly it took a virus to bring people back together while we are kept far apart.

Teaching appreciation of things we've taken for granted like going to the movies, going to work, school, sipping coffee at a coffee shop, bowling, eating in a restaurant, seeing friends and family, smiling, making eye contact, offering help, hugs ....

When this is over let's not forget these lessons of appreciation we're learning.

Try to be a rainbow in some else's cloud. - Maya Angelou

Be well - Namaste 🙏 ♡

3/21/2020

Who's still with me? Wanna see what I saw today? Here goes ....

THE SUN!!

My tax return signed and submitted.

A text from William's teacher asking how he's doing and saying she misses her boys also passing on more school work we can add!

An email from the school coordinator organizing a google live chat for each class to see each other and their teacher and chat for 20 minutes on Tuesday - how cool is that??!!

Also, in the works the counselors at school creating a video for the kids to watch about Zones of Regulation to make it fun for them and possible E Teaching for after break if they can make it work.

Great advice from a group for where I can reach out for financial help as a self-employed small business owner.

The ability to help my family from a distance.

My nightly chat with mom who I miss seeing very much ending in I love yous' and be safe. ♡

Fresh strawberries from our friend and neighbor delivered to my door - thank you Lucie you are loved and appreciated.

Morning Zumba class with friends - virtually - took me right out of an impending funk - dance is good for the soul.

What are your positives today?

Be well - Namaste 🙏

3/22/2020

Things I saw today ....

A clean house with team work, laundry started and home school plan for tomorrow.

Decluttering paperwork and tchotchkes.

Caring correspondence with cancelled clients - gestures of well wishes and "be healthy."

Gypsy romping and playing in the snow - she eats more than falls from the sky!

Cody spending time with William giving me some free time and showing William he's important and loved.

A beautiful blanket of fresh snow.

My family around the dinner table eating roast beast ... or a crock pot pork loin ... whatever!

Loyal Amazon deliveries.

A peaceful glimpse at the slowed world from a 2nd floor window - no cars, no walkers or joggers - everyone home as it should be. ♡

Tired - Namaste 🙏

3/23/2020

Things I saw today ....

My new daily journal arrived!! My new philosophy on life!

This cute bunny looking for Gypsy. ♡

William reading a book 2 levels higher than were sent home - sent THAT video to his teacher!

Signed William up for Adventure Academy - learning slipped in under cover of games.

William continuing to learn life skills folding his laundry that he washed yesterday.

A good sweaty workout with my LA friends! Boy does that release stress! Should've done another tonight - too pooped!

A surprise message from one of my amazing sisters in law to have cousins read books to William virtually, truly blessed.

Thoughtful friends tagging me in funny and informative posts (Landa) I'll be checking that out! Perfect timing! Hope you are doing well in WA! Tell Andrew to stay on his side of the room!

FINALLY got telehealth set up after hours of a dozen attempts - these are the times that try men's souls.

Continuing to get grooming requests from new clients who thought we were considered "curb side business" but are willing stay on a list for after. ♡

Good food in our belly's.

Chilled glass of wine.

Stay the F$*@% home!!

Namaste 🙏

3/24/2020

Things I saw today ....

A therapist making time to continue counseling virtually in the most needed of times. ♡

An alternative school planning class chat so the kiddos can see their teachers, paras and peers - even more important for special needs kiddos struggling with loss of much needed structure/routine during shut down. ♡

Watching Williams excitement and HUGE smile when familiar faces appeared before him. Silliness and constant chatter about pets and Pokémon ensued for almost an hour. Can't lie, I teared up. ♡

Another is planned for Friday! ♡

Took William on a field trip today! to the ATM, with Clorox wipes, for my last deposit for a while. Then to DD for his breakfast for tomorrow, stock up on coffee, a vanilla frosted long john in the Jeep on the ride to Auntie Paula's for a drop off/pick up! We miss you Auntie Paula! ♡

Then to our neighborhood park/path for Pokémon Go. So many out enjoying the fresh air yet keeping safe distance from strangers respectfully. Babies in strollers, dogs walking their humans, little ones running around oblivious to the world's changes, innocence. ♡

While William searched Pokémon, I was filled with curiosity searching for the next positive chalk message left on the foot path by an amazing soul. William's patience and silent angst when I grabbed my phone to shoot some inspiration. ♡

We need these interruptions in our lives to remind us WHO and WHAT is important and to stay positive in uncertain times. ♡

Receiving more emails and texts for grooming appointments than I've had in weeks being added to a waiting list for after. And I thought I'd "just" be homeschooling and decluttering the house pshhh. ♡

Chipotle Door Dash delivery making dinner easy after a busy day of wearing MANY hats. ♡

Nighttime sleep struggle for a little mind trying to process big scary things - and like so many things in recent years and more specifically recent months - this too shall pass little man. ♡

What was your interruption today?

And tomorrow the sun will rise again - Namaste 🙏

3/25/2020

Things I saw today ....

A handsome young man struggling emotionally the past 24 hrs. but focusing on his school work and cleaning up our community. ♡

That same young man has outgrown his pedal kart and wants a new one - how fast they grow - perhaps a new one in the future. ♡

Popped up, in the middle of an area of grass, a single, pretty, little purple flower calling him over to remind him of the beauty on our earth that he is cleaning up. He asked if he could touch it and ever so gently gave it a Springtime welcome pat. ♡

Continued appointment requests to add to the growing list.

Gypsy enjoying 2 walks instead of one - a good day in dog land.

My Zumba friends - always put a smile on my face - thank you Jennifer for a fun sweaty class today!

A phone call from a caring friend, Paula, thank you for the heads up today.

Shipt grocery delivery MUCH easier to find a spot for delivery tomorrow. A sign that panic has slowed, pantries are full and butts are getting wiped.

Promise of stimulus funding for most who so desperately need it and small business recovery in the talks.

And lastly, this sweet young man gazing somberly out his bedroom window before bed. When I asked what was on his mind he sighed, sadly, and said he didn't know.

I said "One of the sad things in life is that we tend to take for granted the everyday things that become routine and expected".

The expectations of seeing friends, visiting family, special teachers, going to the movies, a person who is special to us and those who have a heavy load they carry to care for many go unappreciated ... until they're no longer there."

But there's a lesson to be learned. When we have those things and people back in our lives ... and we will ... let's not take their presence for granted or underestimate how much they and our freedom mean to us. Let's find a new perspective. Turn negativity into positivity, pay it forward, show kindness, look for the helpers and appreciate our friends, family and community."

I read him a great story tonight so perfect for our times, and he doesn't have me read to him at night much anymore, "Circle of Thanks" a children's book about helping others without expecting thanks - just doing so because it's kind and the right thing to do and then that kindness comes back tenfold. ♡

And with that, after a tough day, he fell asleep. ♡

Namaste 🙏

3/26/2020

Things I saw today ....

An 11 yr. old boy's version of social distancing from the hand towels - see photos ....

A surprise project "pick me up" for William delivered to the front door from an incredibly thoughtful friend. Enclosed was a note to him saying he is "loved and prayed for" - he'll see it tomorrow; again, with the grateful tears today - thank you Sheila.

Another tough day in isolation and in his own head with a little man worried he'll never find the "right girl to love him" or have someone to tell his feelings to when he's an adult - such big things on little ones' minds with much deeper meaning, this I know.

We have a lot of time to think and reflect right now look for the positives in those reflections.

I saw a really nice, hardworking Shipt shopper bringing my groceries. In our need for human connection learning things about each other quickly through the door - seems we don't have time right now to get to know people.

I did learn that she has a son who is sick and lands in the hospital occasionally so working for Shipt allows her the ability to leave work to be with him without getting fired. Always choose kindness, you never know the struggles people endure.

Williams keyboarding getting faster and with more confidence.

I saw a little sponge of learning and finding my confidence in teaching him and learning from him things I have forgotten or didn't know. ♡

I saw that you can prep, cook and be eating a coconut shrimp dinner in less than 40 minutes (there were 2# of shrimps!) and it was delicious - when you're really tired from teaching and entertaining all day a quick dinner is a relief. ♡

Coffee, I saw coffee, thank you coffee for without you isolation would be institutionalization. ♡

Namaste 🙏

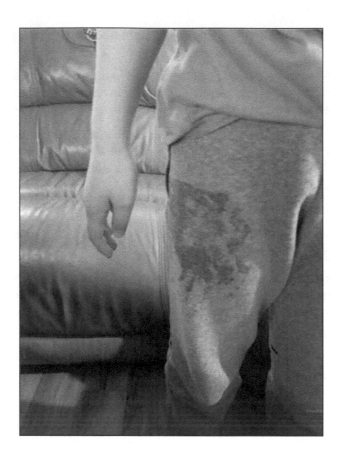

3/27/2020

Things I saw today ....

A face in our chicken - think we can get anything for it on eBay??! 😝

Two robins "fighting" or ... well it's Spring sooooooo .... 💞

Two bunnies chasing each other through the yard ... to fight ... cuz it's Spring you know .... 💞

Two Guinea Pigs chasing each other around their cage ... not cuz it's Spring, they're actually fighting. 💞

The 11 yr. old's airing themselves out.

A nice-looking Camaro in my favorite color!

William busting' a move behind me during Zumba!

Random, unsolicited hugs.

My friends smiling, encouraging faces.

Miss Emily's class enjoying some chat time - no loss for Pokémon, Beyblade and Williams photography show and tell!

The neighbor kids playing basketball in their backyard, laughing and getting exercise.

A father and very young son doing random exercises jumping, skipping, knee highs, up and down the sidewalk next to their house, made me smile.

The sun!

My couch buddy asking for a late-night camp out but snoozing by 7.

I saw friends and neighbors finding new ways to find their joy.

Namaste 🙏

3/28/2020

Things I saw today ....

Backyard Jenga in the front room! Coming soon, Jello shot Jenga for bacon-fries.

A little guitar lesson time.

Steve made dinner, yum, a very much needed break!

Chicken Tortilla soup ready for tomorrow with corn bread.

Piggie playtime with a bowl of fresh arugula, red pepper and spinach.

Unemployment confirmation in the mail, grateful to have it available to the self-employed, non-essential, out of work. ♡

Small Business Loan paperwork filled out and uploaded. ♡

Tree's live FB hangout party - we love this dude!

William sleeping peacefully, in his own bed.

Mamas tired! Hasta Manana!

Namaste 🙏

Your grandparents were called to war. You're being called to sit on your couch. You can do this.

3/29/2020

Things I saw today ....

I peeked through my blinds at 7am and this fur baby was just sitting there, looking directly at the patio doors as if waiting to say good morning, I've been watching over you, are you well, where's my coffee?

Gypsy in her favorite spot on our bed. When the blinds are open the world, or at least the street, is at her guard and disposal. ♡

"Lamb of God" concert in our front room - you're talented Cody, play it loud play it proud! ♡

Pokémon battles.

Video games.

A ride in the truck for Pokémon Go on wheels.

The boy feelin' the beat!

Decluttered and organized spice cabinet, medicine cabinet and freezer - apparently, I now have more time for more organizing.

Family - we are here for each other and will make it together. ♡

Coloring with Caitlin, like old times ♡

Chicken Tortilla Soup and corn bread to fill the tummies I love.

A good day in a crazy world. ♡

Namaste 🙏

3/30/2020

Things I saw today ....

The Puppy Bowl and the Kitty Half Time show ♡

William finished his Lego kit!

Our ducks relaxing in club Mateblatts spa. The green water is enticing, isn't it??!! - As we watched them living their best life from William's bedroom window oblivious to our human challenges, William looks at me and says, "they're so majestic!" I'm impressed at his insight and heart!

William looking out his 2nd floor bedroom window "there's no one out there" ... ♡

All clients cancelled from March 22nd through May 1st and beyond? - quite sobering but I am so grateful to have a long list to call when this is over.

My LA friends on Zoom! Thank you, Stacy!!

Hershey, one of our guinea pigs, growling at me from inside her hutch incensed by my movement in "their" space while Marshmallow scarfs all of their food oblivious to my intrusion - unique little personalities.

A generous offering of free merchandise to her friends from a friend closing her 13yr business due to Covid19 - what a kind, generous heart after such a tough decision who said "I have everything I need/want. I want to share this with you guys. No purchases, no thank yous" - I've seen so much kindness rising from despair.

Day by day, moment by moment our lives are changing.

STAY HOME!!

and find your positives and your joy - we have much to be grateful for.

Namaste

3/31/2020

Things I saw today ....

"Cars 3" at 5am!

Coffee by 5:45am - I needed my cup of patience!

Hope-Love-Smile at a neighbor on our morning walk.

A "pirate ship" in my front room, I got to sit in the "life boat."

A Treasure Map to Atlantis to find The Jewel of Atlantis to power the city of Duckburg lol - love this kid. ♡

We went "into the out" and into the in (Jeep) for drive up prescription pickup, drive up lunch and dine in Jeep and drive around Pokémon Go. ♡

I found myself wiping everything with Clorox wipes, my debit card, money, change - years ago you'd be "crazy" now you're crazy not to!

Stopped for gas, Clorox wipes in hand - wiped down the entire gas pump handle, key pad, touch screen and my card - so bizarre! But $1.85 for gas I'll take! ♡

Roped off parks. ☹

People out shopping with face masks and gloves and others STILL not getting it in stores they don't need to be in with no PPE - have you not seen the seriousness of this yet?? You are not safe, anywhere, you are not exempt, if don't NEED it, you don't need to be out - STAY THE F HOME! stepping down...

Another de cluttered and organized cabinet.

A successful Tuscan Salmon and homemade garlic cheese bread dinner. ♡

Watched William try to pick this lock - BUT he's a smart kid with common sense - "all ya gotta do is take off the key from the ring mom, then you can open it ".

Gypsy to the vet tonight with concerning issues that turned out well. A wait in the car, phone communication only until they're ready for you. No chances taken anywhere. ♡

"Never give up on something you really want. It's difficult to wait but harder to regret."

Namaste 🙏

4/1/2020

Things I saw today ....

A request for a beak and wing trim on an African Grey Parrot - now that's a first.

Federal tax return deposit.

Ability to request delivery of Williams much needed new glasses from a temporarily closed For Eyes - his eyes have been hurting for over a month - glad he doesn't have to wait much longer.

On our walk this morning William stopped many feet away from a mama Robin hunting worms in the grass so he wouldn't scare her - he waited patiently and very still.

Gypsy feeling better eating her rice and turkey and taking her meds. 🩶

Dusted off the craft box, mostly for me so I could make my hearts and William built popsicle stick buildings - he's not a fan of crafts - bummer for me, cuz I am.

After weeks of feeling lost, William finally found some things to occupy his own time - be careful what you wish for, you just might get it; guitar time (it's louder, downstairs, in the kitchen, just under the play room).

Yes, we still have his mini–Christmas Tree up and lit every night - it's calming. ♡

A little neighbor girl bouncing happily on her backyard trampoline, by herself. There are usually many friends with her - in good time.

7-hour National Geographic Critter Fixers: Country Vet and The Incredible Dr. Pol marathon through crafts, LUNCH, chillin' time and DINNER - have you seen this show??

We saw everything from guinea pig ear wax to elbow deep checking cows for pregnancy (we could all use those long gloves btw), removing stones from a male horse, birth of deformed/mutated goats, a horse needing to be put down for a dislocated torn knee, abscesses filled with oozing puss - the camera does not shy away - you get the picture.

What intrigued me was William's fascination with all of the procedures. Not being grossed out by them but inspired to do the same as Dr. Pol.

His compassion for animals and his caring heart gives me great pride every day. Despite his challenges, no matter what his future holds, he will do great things. ♡

And with that I wish you a good night, be safe and stay home.

Namaste 🙏

4/2/2020

Things I saw today ....

Gypsy from rags to riches with pretty feet sporting her heart bandana - she was so overdue and so uncooperative ☺

Although it took me 3 hours to groom her instead of 2 with the "help" of my assistant, it felt good to do something normal and rewarding and she feels cooler.

Our morning walk was quiet, peaceful and filled with the sound of chirping birds - mindfulness. ♡

Our first heart sighting (same house with the father and son exercising up and down the sidewalk recently) mine go up in a different place tomorrow.

The Kolache I ordered arrived today for Easter like mom and dad used to make every Christmas and freeze for Easter. There were always extras for friends and family. They worked together, had a system, ground their own walnuts - everything from scratch. I miss that so I'm hoping this is close - thank you Paula for bringing it to my attention. ♡

The man across the street and his daughter were out front making plans to paint an old table top with red white and blue. They cleaned it and left it to dry. Can't wait to see what they have planned. ♡

A completed project for mom from all of us to be dropped off. For those who are in it, who actually get the implications of the serious nature of this pandemic, it's so hard to be away from family especially with a holiday coming up we would typically spend together. Life is very short. When your parent is 92, isolated during a pandemic you pray that you will see them again, be able to hug them and that they won't be alone. ♡

This virus doesn't travel on its own. It's spread by people who travel with it. The scary part is the asymptomatic folks who look and feel fine but are contagious. Those of us with underlying health issues, have elderly parents, special needs children are very concerned; staying home, wearing masks, only going outside to get fresh air and a walk away from people, not getting out of vehicles because of those who aren't staying home, aren't wearing masks, aren't washing hands etc.

It's not just older folks and sick folks that are seriously sick or dying. I heard of a friend's friend, a 32 yr. old healthy eater who exercises regularly barely making it out alive.

I've seen interviews with young, normally healthy, people pleading with everyone to isolate, stay away from crowds, wear masks, wash hands constantly. I think if you have a conversation with one of these people and any healthcare worker or their family member facing this every day, it may open your eyes to reality, not what you read on FB. Don't bury your head in the sand or think you are exempt.

Until we get to zero new cases per day, life will remain as is. Today we had 758 bringing us just under 8,000 in a few weeks. We're in isolation to get those numbers down. I, for one, don't want to find out IF I'm a lucky one to recover or if I wouldn't make it. Not a risk I'm willing to take by being complacent.

Be safe, be smart, protect yourself and your family, find projects to do at home, read a book, start something you've been putting off, plant some seeds, color, paint, mow, weed, clean, declutter ... - let's make this go away sooner than later so we can get back to our new normal with those we love with us. ♡

Sweet dreams of better days ahead. ♡

Namaste 🙏

4/3/2020

Things I saw today ....

William trying to teach me to purr better, my lips don't flap like his do, he's good - isolation goals!

Many signs that Spring and Easter will arrive despite social distancing.

Village of Romeoville crediting $50 to everyone's water bill in June.

Thanks to Disney + watching Onward this morning in our jammies in bed.

Jennifer for some sweaty Zumba. Dancing surely is a lifeline during this time. Our LA instructors giving their time to give us something to look forward to. An hour to get your mind off your worries we thank you all.

FaceTime with Williams teacher, meeting her mom the "classroom grandma" who buys the kids lunch and activities for their room occasionally. Met her dog and discussed next week's E Learning Plan. Required services will also be provided i.e., counseling, OT, speech - we are preparing for being out through school years end.

The helpers - who care as much about what their patients and families are going through as themselves.

So much fresh air! Neighbors out walking, biking, doing yard work, pulling wagons, sitting on their porches, extending smiles and salutations from a safe distance. Just happy to be out of their 4 walls. 💛

Cleaned out some flower pots and poop pick up - dogs poop a lot ... ALOT! Big dog land mines a plenty!

Neighbors helping neighbors as best we can in our new environment.

Chatting with our friends and neighbors from a distance and William finding it so very hard not to run up and hug his Grammy Barb and mooch his usual snack from her - we huggers are not ok. 💛

It's amazing how much you miss face to face contact until you can't have it.

Seeing the front-line workers first hand is sobering and real. Talking and crying with them. They are human beings who are trying to keep it together for their patients and their families while fearing for the health of themselves and their families - I have the utmost respect. 💛

A good day after a couple of tough ones - fresh air, honest information, human contact and I'm tired. 💛

Sweet dreams to all. zzzzzz

Namaste 💛

4/4/2020

Things I saw today ....

A sleepy puppy. ♡

An anxious young man, lounge chair and BBQ in my raised veggie garden contemplating life. ♡

Legos on the "veranda," cold, but not inside! ♡

Arm wrestling competition - I think William is convinced he needs to start working out with me. ♡

More Dr. Pol and puss oozing wounds!

5 hours of E-Learning email and phone communication, glitch ironing and prep for Monday - respect your teachers; if they're as great as ours, they're working their butts off to keep our kids going and not falling back. ♡

Building and rebuilding Legos, the same project, over and over and over - for hours - focus was rough today, pieces were finding their way into other pieces places but now we have a red Ferrari! ♡

A gift to myself - Hyacinths - my favorite Spring perennial, the fragrance makes me smile and will be transplanted to my garden. I wish they were in bloom all season! ♡

In my own experience with myself and in some around me I'm feeling the strain of isolation peaking faster than the virus itself. Agitation growing and patience waning. It IS hard and it's ok to feel the hard parts. Just don't pack your bags and move in.

Find the joy!

Namaste 🙏

4/5/2020

Things I saw today ....

William, at 1:22am getting water from the fridge ... "oh good morning mom!!"....

um, no, back to bed William ... fell back to sleep at 2:45am after struggling to get to sleep at bedtime for 2hrs - rough night.

Time for baking some GF goodies! Best PB Cookies ever for the boys and Zucchini Brownies for me.

Yard work! Cleaned up the front yard - I love being out in nature and getting my hands dirty - it's good for the soul and my helper is kinda cute - beautiful day. ♡

Easter decorations to brighten up the mood. ♡

A neighbor walked over, as I backed away (way too close) to see if I could cut HIS hair - another who doesn't get what's going on - another who doesn't understand asymptomatic contagions - he was dumbfounded - pay attention people, head out of the sand please!!

I heard of a mobile groomer still out working. It angers those of us following the law, doing our part, without income, to help bring these numbers down, keep our families and others safe and some are out endangering themselves and others. And who wants people at their home right now??? There is no safe way - It's irresponsible and disappointing to my profession.

Boston cleaning out my Jeep for selling, when finances permit others to spend on non-essentials again ... or maybe it would be essential to someone - she was to me. ♡

My supportive hearts finally on display. ♡

Kitchen dance party - anyone who joins me in the kitchen must dance to Jamaican Vibrations with me or at the very least the song of their choice or exit the dance floor.

Planning to make masks from bandanas I had just purchased for my pooches' days before shut down. Just the fold and rubber band ones but if they're needed, I can probably make 100-150 - anyone direct me to the neediest places? I know, they all are, but suggestions? - my doggies will have to do without bandanas when I'm back to work until I can afford more but I think they'll be ok for a while ... priorities

Ending a fulfilling day with some TWD - perfect. ♡

Tomorrow - eLearning begins for the duration - 8am sharp!

Namaste 🙏

4/6/2020

Things I saw today ....

Aunty Lulu and Grammy Barb's smiling annuals after our walk. ♡

First day of E Learning - went well - have been finding that William is so much more advanced academically away from the stressors at school. Teacher noticed and is going to work with him one on one more during E Learning.

A couple of Easter surprises planned for William coming this week shhhh!

3 riveting games of Chutes and Ladders. The final was a tie breaker I won on default ... well because we kept hitting more chutes than ladders so William forfeited and declared me the winner so we could stop. ♡

William somberly watching the neighbor kids jumping on their trampoline. He's been really lonely and a little sad as much time as I try to spend with him it's just hard and it's not the same as seeing someone other than me.

Sooooooo, he asked for a little sister buahahahahahaha NOT HAPPENING! Once I told him he'd have to share his time with me he didn't think it was the best idea! Good cuz it's not possible either! I feel for his loneliness, isolation gets to you after a while. ♡

William was in his lookout tower watching what few cars were driving behind the house. So, I had him tell me every car make and model and color - he's still got it!

This is my favorite time of year. I LOVE hitting my favorite nursery and coloring up my yard, filling my veggie garden to make homemade sauce. Getting my hands in the earth and watching nature create beauty. It truly makes me happy and brings me peace.

It's my only splurge on myself for the year. But, thanks to the Rona finances will not allow for that this year. So, I'm polishing up my green thumb and planted my own seeds for veggies and flowers. There will only be 2 kinds of flowers if they take but it's something.

Funny thing I had only had one kind of flower seed and after planting them I wished I had more flower seeds. Went to the mailbox and in the mail was a free packet of forget me not seeds used as an advertisement from a realtor - wishes do come true.

My Hawk friend flew over today while planting - haven't seen him since I used to drive around more. He came to me. ♡

Most of the time I don't remember what day or time it is anymore. Do you? One day just flows into the next so we make the best of it. Turn on some music, dance a little, laugh a lot, start things that were on the back burner - what do you have to lose?

Keep finding the joy - be grateful for the little things - look for the helpers.

Namaste 🙏

4/7/2020

Things I saw today ....

And early start with the promise of a beautiful day!

A caring, dedicated teacher who cried after teaching then chatting with William today because she saw his tension and texted me privately "Omg I cried big baby tears after our chat. I love him SO MUCH and he seems so tense today" she's a true gem.

Although a great asset, E Learning, Telehealth, Telemed are really hard on special needs kiddos. It's ALL change, sometimes all happens in one day, hard for them to process, causes a great amount of stress. There are many truly struggling in our community right now to an extent that is unexplainable to those who don't live the life. ♡

We didn't finish our academics today and that's ok, our kids are scared too and need grace.

So, we went for a nice warm, sunny, relaxing bike ride keeping our social distancing in our own neighborhood.

We saw a mom and 2 daughters having a McDonalds picnic on a blanket next to the lake in our subdivision. We smiled, waved and exchanged a few kind words.

We saw walkers, bike riders, roller blades, dogs getting their 22nd walk of the day and loving it - even Gypsy for a 2nd walk this afternoon - there were more Pokémon to find of course.

We conquered some Pokémon Go and sat quietly together by the water just talking about the unknown and changes and love.

We found that we had been followed by a drone to our front yard - creepy and yet I feel we made celebrity status! Someone must really be bored to follow "us"!

Another drive by delivery by Paula - the pop of a trunk to reveal a needed can of soup for a recipe ... and wine thank you for your curbside service so I don't have to take William out - you are our angel.

Sharing family holiday recipes with my beautiful niece for their Easter festivities - Easter won't be the same without you - you will all be missed.

A comfort food dinner of Chicken and Rice casserole that mom used to make - must have been good, William had seconds.

A beautiful, long, tiring, warm day in the first part of April.

Namaste 🙏

4/8/2020

Mindful Moments

(New name for my daily prose)

Facetime with my mom! Truly the highlight of my day to see her so happy to see the face behind the voice - a plain phone call isn't the same and an in-person hug will be even better.

The smell of bleach in the air on my morning walk caused me to pause - unusual you'd think, but not for our times.

A child expressing distention in the ranks, in a house, unintelligible, it's quiet in the morning - no traffic or helicopters or airplanes, open windows - frustration creeping in

Buds on the trees.

The grass is getting to be so vibrant with deep greens from spring warmth and rains.

During eLearning my kitchen looks like NASAs command center popping from a laptop zoom to school iPad Epic, Prodigy, Class Kicks to my email for teacher instructions - organized chaos!

A PE class with Miss Emily after morning academics.

2 walks for Miss Gypsy.

Pokémon Go, some walking, fresh air and vitamin D.

I was working out to a Tabata class headed by Becky sweating my ars off and in the middle of jumping jacks with weighted shoulder presses William "judgey McJudgerson" walks in.

"You better be careful you're going to break the floor boards!!!!"

I'm just going to take that as I was working hard and not that I'm too heavy !!

I am never alone, see photo outside my workout room. ♡

Speaking of grass ... the sweet smell of "recreational activities" at 7:30 am - a wake up and a coffee!

Miracle League baseball cancelled for the Spring - disappointing but necessary - hoping for Fall ball.

A surprise visit from Miss Emily (his teacher) and classroom Grandma (her mom) with an Easter gift and smiles! They drove to every child's house as far as DesPlaines to back out here and into Crest Hill (see video) couldn't ask for a better support team.

Leftovers.

I unconsciously stopped my microwave at 2:34 from 5 minutes - if you know me well you know what that means. ♡

The sweet smell of a Spring rain.

Look for the helpers. ♡

Namaste ♡

4/9/2020

Mindful Moments ....

In very few locations can you experience the warm breeze, sunshine and soft rain of Spring on a Wednesday and on Thursday a biting wind and snow.

Shipt....no delivery openings for days. But Instacart did! How great is it to have options?!

Finally certified for UI at 5am!

The eggs are boiled for coloring. Now to get William as excited to decorate them as I am - Easter is arriving with or without our traditions and loved ones so we make the best of it and create a different memory for this year Imagine the stories we'll have to tell years down the road.

A very thoughtful cousin sending an idea for William to help him cope and see the positives Thank you Char they're copied and ready to go.

Homemade creamy tomato soup simmering on the stove while a young cranium is being expanded through E Learning.

Practicing money values in a fun way made learning less mundane - thank you for the share, Paula.

Look at that! A quick check to Shipt and an opening appeared for tomorrow! Put out the positive and you shall receive it in return!

Teachers complete next week's lesson plans with so many additions and options to keep the kiddos engaged - I truly appreciate the work they are putting in.

William says watching Veggie Tales helps him feel calmer about our current uncertainty.

I am grateful for PPE when having to go out.

When your kiddos Dr is out of kid stickers the staff improvises - however you also get a pocketful of suckers.

I'm thankful for Dr Chris and his entire staff at Elemental Care - Health & Wellness Center in Crest Hill for their expertise, compassion and connection. When William is comfortable with someone you know they're good people.

William randomly singing Christmas songs all day, catching himself "whoops there I go again" lol I told him I love hearing him sing no matter what the content.

An urgent butter delivery left on "Gary the Gargoyle" with a ding dong ditch - I shall repay you tomorrow my dear friend Lucy - Thank you!

Another molar yanked before it's prime! - Lordy how does he do that??? So glad I wasn't paying attention.

Keep looking for the helpers.

Can we add more hours to the day??

Sleep well ... stay home.

Namaste 🙏

4/10/2020

Mindful Moments

So many beautiful flowers on my morning walk. 🤍

More purring lessons ... apparently, I wasn't doing it right but I think I've got it now! I'll be tested again in the morning. 🐾

William forgot the tooth fairy visited last night! How does that happen?! Maybe pulling 3 teeth in 4 weeks gets old.

Preparing for Easter Sunday and a sweet treat drop off to mom with Kifle and an ordered Kolache Roll tomorrow. Mom and dad made a dozen of these every Christmas and Easter. Shared with family and friends and served after holiday meals. Tastes almost as good as mom and dad made. 🤍

A bit messy but Unicorn Eggs were fast and easy for a short attention span and described as "fun" I call that a win and they turned out pretty!

My faithful human companion always just "feet" away - man does he look long and lean!

William made his own lunch. Mac n cheese a weekly favorite and comfort food.

A text from a sweet friend out shopping and knew I wanted flower seeds. A thoughtful text and a pickup tomorrow - you're the best Leslie! Thank you for being so thoughtful.

Home Cut Donuts left on Gary the Gargoyle yet another kind gesture from another sweet friend - enjoy your cereal and we will enjoy the donuts! "We" meaning William - Thank you Lucie.

A bit of a challenging day today so we keep looking for the positives, the helpers and a glass of wine never hurts.

"The secret of health for both mind and body is not to mourn the past, not to worry about the future, but to live the present moment wisely and earnestly." - Buddha

Namaste 🙏

4/11/2020

Mindful Moments ...

Today was a special day. A day of learning patience making a surprise even more heartfelt.

Our day started early with William saying "I like how soft your hair is. What kind of shampoo do you use?"

He's going to be a great partner one day. 🤍

Waiting. Waiting in excitement and wonder is even harder. 5 hrs. we waited for the Easter Bunny to cruise by on a motorcycle. It was hard. But we made it.

I'll keep this short tonight.

It was a great day with family. 🤍

While Wiliam played Pokémon Go with Caitlin and Cody, Boston and I had a WHOLE hour Jeep date making a special delivery to mom, had an interesting trip to Binnys and picked up my seeds from my good friend. 🤍

It's a bit surreal when you venture out. Instead of just running to the store and running home. You wait outside a store, in a line, wearing masks, 6 ft apart, waiting for a turn into the doors. So different. 🤍

Good night my friends, sleep well ....

Namaste 🙏

4/12/2020

Mindful moments ....

Our day began at 4:45am with much excitement! It's Easter!!!

The Easter bunny snuck in last night and left William a bunch of goodies! An egg hunt ensued with exhaustion from early rising creeping up quickly.

Upon leaving for a DD drive thru breakfast - a discovery of massive proportions was discovered on the porch and front lawn!

This was not the work of any old Easter Bunny ... ohhhh nooooo! This was the work of an unemployed couple who had offered to leave 25-150 candy filled plastic eggs on your front lawn for a minimal fee.

I chose the 25 and a sneaky bunny drop between 10pm and 1am. What we found was ABOVE AND BEYOND what was offered as you can see! Included were activity books, slime, stuffed bunny, candy, bubbles, snap bracelets, GC to Waxed Hands, ticket to Raging Waves etc. etc. etc. w / a letter from E. Bunny himself!

Calls with our moms, texts to siblings, family and friends.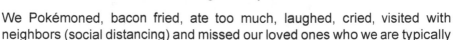

We Pokémoned, bacon fried, ate too much, laughed, cried, visited with neighbors (social distancing) and missed our loved ones who we are typically with today.

The weather was wonderful with sunshine when they had promised rain, cozy around a fire.

With shared hesitation and apprehension, I cut Boston's hair today - I must say it looks damn good!! phew!!

We learn to adjust, be flexible, appreciate the little things and hold memories close to our hearts during times of challenge.

We can learn from times like this if we're truly paying attention to what life is teaching us.

Early morning, fresh air, good food and drink - we are exhausted, every one of us - but with a full heart kind of exhaustion.

And we forgot the Whipped Jello people!!!

Look for the helpers, the kindness, the sharing - whether you spent the day solo, w/ a fur friend or your close family, I hope it was peaceful and most of all safe. ♡

Until we meet again!

Namaste 🙏

4/13/2020

Mindful Moments ....

Another early morning - it's literally for the birds ... and William!

School went well for a Monday!

A surprise was left at the front door last night for Sir William - surprises are so fun! Thank you, Auntie Sarah, the Google globe soccer ball was a hit! Thank you for taking the time to stop!! We'll be out playing soccer this week!

Still amazed at how essential groomers have become and really frustrating that a few are still operating secretly.

I am answering more email daily than a month ago and creating quite a list of new clients for our return. ♡

I also heard through the groomer grapevine there is someone checking to see if we're working and turning us in. I am not. It's illegal and just plain not worth the risk!

I applied for 3 SBA loans -

Unemployment ... glitches, confusion!

Everyone is still trying to figure things out, organize, regroup.

Paper work, paper work, paper work - hurry up and wait.

Stimulus - still waiting, waiting, waiting.

And yet there's a light shining through at the end of the tunnel. A tiny pin hole slowwwlyyyy opening up!

I'm preparing for lots of short pooch cuts! My blades and shears are off for sharpening tomorrow and a spare dryer repaired so we can hit the ground running!

Our new normal is waiting in the wings get ready for it. ♡

Sweet dreams, be safe, stay home or wear a mask!!

Namaste 🙏

I think that when the dust settles, we will realize how very little we need, how very much we actually have and the true value of human connection.

4/14/2020

Mindful moments ....

I never thought that if I were out of work, I would be so much more incredibly busy than when I was working! But it's possible! NO boredom here!

William has more Zoom and FaceTime meetings than a CEO of a Fortune 500 company! FOUR of them today involved with and in between E Learning! Thankfully we have technology for him to continue to receive the education and special services he needs.

I am so grateful for Coops Troops my private Autism / Special Needs FB Group. It's a breath of fresh air and a sigh of relief. No politics, no judgement, no mudslinging - just supportive, validating, real, positive people whose only goals are to lend a shoulder, celebrate an achievement, provide encouragement and positivity, answer questions from experience and empathize with what you're going through as a special needs parent - I've met some really incredible people there.

I cleaned out the pantry at 2 when our meetings ended ... oh wait no, that's not it, I talked to my mom and exfoliated after a shower (It IS Tuesday, the day we get to shower instead of just washing our hands) priorities.

For Eyes mailed Williams new glasses thankfully! No more headaches and straining!

William wishes he could have his old life back. Me too. I told him we'll get a new life back and even better than before.

Struggling today, a little snuggle time with his favorite therapy piggie was welcomed.

"A diamond is a chunk of coal that did well under pressure" - Henry Kissinger

Rest your mind, have faith, look ahead.

Namaste

4/15/2020

Mindful moments ....

I find a fresh untouched blanket of snow beautiful.

Even more beautiful was a mother and 2 yr old son, having a snowball fight and playing in the snow in pajamas at 7:30am. Smiles and laughter filled their front yard.

An informative meeting and much needed FaceTime with mom. 🤍

I'm thankful for the Shipt shoppers so I don't have to take William into the store every week.

I'm thankful for substitutions when the items we order are out of stock.

I'm thankful for healthy food options.

I'm thankful for Chewy.com delivery so our fur babies are fed and cleaned up after on time.

I'm thankful for the continued daily emails requesting grooming appointments from many new clients and existing patiently waiting on a list.

I'm thankful for a client reaching out to assist me in an SBA loan today. ♡

I'm hopeful that UI for the self-employed will be available sooner than later.

We're all learning new skills when our normal isn't available. We're learning to cut our own hair and appreciating our stylists even more. Dog owners are grooming their own dogs and appreciating their groomers even more. We're learning that others' careers that seem quite easy due to a skilled worker require a craft, a technique, a special skill set, education and passion - below is a post from a doodle page.

Out of the dark comes light, appreciation and knowledge - it's what you do with it that matters. ♡

Namaste 🙏

4/16/2020

Mindful moments ....

I'm wondering what else has to be taken off and sprayed down before entering this house.

"I can smell your perfume. It smells pretty" - it was hair spray but this kid is gaining brownie points! ♡

Dr. Robert Murphy states that an asymptomatic person standing near you is much more likely to spread Covid19 to you than someone coughing near you which is why we are in shelter in place - That's important to understand.

William has graduated to quarter pounders with cheese and LOVES them from Happy Meals - it's a good day! I could fill a room with all of those Happy Meals toys that are laying all over the house!

It's amazing how much crap gets "saved for later "in a pantry with 3 different tastes and those expiration dates! - 2 hours and 2 1/2 garbage bags later ...

William struggled to fall asleep tonight so I told him stories of my childhood - no a/c, loud box fans, black and white tv with 6 channels and foil "rabbit ears, making cement with water and gravel from our pre black topped driveway, no electronics - it was hard to continue over his snoring I had so much more to regale him with! 😉 🤭

Someone saved his money, had me order this truck 2 weeks ago and was rewarded with his patience today.

It's the little things.

Namaste 🙏

4/17/2020

Mindful moments ....

Little daffodils wishing they could shed their white wintery coats.

A snowy early morning walk/ride with my 2 favorite 11 yr. olds.

We won our snowman contest with Wills teacher! - his snowman creation was fun and a nice team project - it was great packing snow!!- Keep on Jeepin' on!! - did you build a snowman today ?? let's see it in the comments!

A strawberry phenomenon! Conjoined twins and mega berry all in one container! They were delicious!! it doesn't take a lot to amuse me. 😊

I told William school is closed indefinitely - his reaction is in the video but don't let his enthusiasm fool you. He hasn't been eating or sleeping well, anxiety is high and he misses his routine, friends, teachers, bus drivers and he's terrified of the Rona. 💭

William wanted me to make a burger as big as a 1/4 pounder - I made him a double turkey burger with cheese and steak sauce (his request) He ate the whole darn thing!! Ahmazing!!

I have a couple hundred bandanas that make great face masks. - just pm me - no charge. 💭

As much as closing schools indefinitely was expected its validation hit hard - somehow, we'll get through this and there's vodka.

A couple days ago a long-time client said "his dog" wanted to send me something and asked for my address - I was thinking a cute photo saying he missed me perhaps.

His gift arrived today and Wolfies thoughtfulness and generosity had me bawling - we're all struggling and yet I see such kindness shining through.

Wolf is a GSD who doesn't love my visits, in fact without a muzzle I'd be missing a hand - he is true to his breed, a great protector - but when all is said and done his treat reward is worth the agony of a bath, de shedding and blow dry - getting his nails done is an impossibility he's a stinker but I love him.

I am reminded daily of the good in the world and the smallest of visions are the greatest reminders.

Those little daffodils will shed their white winter coats by tomorrow and be reaching for the sun again.

So should we.

Namaste

4/18/2020

Mindful Moments on Seasonal hiatus until tomorrow due to a much-needed virtual GNO!!

Cheers!!

4/19/2020

Mindful Moments post season hiatus.

First, thank you for indulging me -

I want to share good things, some hope, information, reminders of the importance of the little things, that this isn't forever and we just need to listen to the EXPERTS and do as they recommend and we will get past this sooner than later.

Since my virtual GNO lasted well into early am hours, just like old times lol, it has a place in today's moments! 3 1/2 hrs. of catching up face to face, laughing, a little venting and a couple cocktails was a much-needed uplifting break - apparently, we kept Boston up with our laughing oooops sorry.

Mo you are the best of the best! I look forward to the next!

The day couldn't have begun more pleasant than with William singing while playing in another room - those moments where the stressors of our times are absent for just a little while.

Cloudy morning skies opened up to beautiful blue, sunny skies, warm sun and a cool breeze.

Waiting in hopeful anticipation in a private clubhouse of Pokémon Go and Pokémon cards, walks through the neighborhood and neighborhood park paths getting fresh air, fighting "battles" and capturing animated little friends.

A request for early Switch time was granted after completing 20 jumping jacks and 10 toe touches hehe I'm a stickler for limited tech time, there's life to be lived on other side of a screen.

Bark face, plain and simple - I love this fur baby. 🐾

I've been waiting patiently for better weather to get my hands dirty and clean out my planters, plant the rest of my seeds and prep the veggie box - the herbs are now in the aero garden inside.

A new tattoo for William just as exciting as the first! Now to spend each shower/bath trying not to wash it off.

"Patience is not about doing nothing. Patience is about constantly doing everything you can. But being patient about results."

Listen to the experts, watch statistics, remain steadfast - we've come so far and have so much further to go.

Respect our frontline workers who leave their families every day to try to save ours by staying the frig home!

You want the truth, talk to one of them. Get THEIR viewpoint. A vantage point free of political agendas but stating the facts of the realities of what they experience day in and day out. Protect yourselves and your loved ones, be safe, stay home as long as it takes so we can get on with whatever our new normal will be.

Be well, be safe, be PATIENT!

Namaste 🙏

4/20/2020

Mindful Moments ....

The daffodils are happy now with their heads up to the sun.

Beautiful morning for a walk. Neighbors out on their porches, drinking coffee more than willing to exchange a few words if only for a brief human connection and to warn me of 5 bunnies up ahead who had hopped by just a few moments prior to Gypsy's arrival. 💬

A little E Learning chillin' on the couch.

Look at those adorable puppy paws all twisted and crossed for a nice nap zzzzz

Sir William made his own grilled cheese for lunch today and threw in his laundry - this is a great time to teach important life skills.

He claims to have seen a Pokémon in that cloud mass - I think he just has Pokémon on the brain!

A little king of the hill wishing he could take off running down the street just to get away for a while - I'm right there with him on that running away thing.

Springtime fertilizer is down preparing the lawn for an over seed down the road.

I'm always thankful for leftovers for dinner after an exhausting day.

William still struggles to figure out these interruptions to his life and routine. Trying to make sense of the many emotions he has a hard time processing. Rough day for my little dude - tonight we have a slumber party and tomorrow brings new beginnings.

Namaste 🙏

4/21/2020

Mindful Moments ....

"QUICK OPEN THE BLINDS - I WANNA SEE THE BEAUTIFUL SUNRISE!!"
- William ♡

"When I'm with you I feel calm and chill" - William ... oh my heart!

Thank you signs to healthcare workers, postal workers, UPS, Amazon, FedEx, food deliveries at the end of my street from a family staying the course.

It's FREE taco Tuesday woohoo! Only one taco per person?? Then we need a Crave Case too!

Despite my warnings I caved to insistence when William wanted me to order Dorito Loco Flaming Hot tacos for him.

I'm PROUD to say he ate 4 of them whistling and sniffing all the way! Those suckers have an afterbite that lingers for a while - his great grandfather would be proud. ♡

He has pulled 3 teeth and graduated from Happy Meals to Quarter Pounders with cheese and Dorito Loco Flaming Hot tacos during this pandemic - he's growing up!

Excited to be planning a special birthday drive by celebration for Friday and possibly a Marine send off on Saturday - there are good things to look forward to IF you look for them - paying it forward is a win-win.

Bought gas for $1.55 per gallon - I've never filled a Jeep for $26.00 before!

A welcome fly over my Jeep from my local Hawk friend - thank you for your guidance and vision

My friend Preston never disappoints with his musical grace - thank you for sharing your spirituality, talents, guidance and emotion - never stop inspiring with your music and being you ♡

Stay home, be patient, choose kindness. ☺

Namaste 🙏

4/22/2020

Mindful Moments ....

Today was one of "those" days, as was Monday. Days where it's harder to find the positive so you dig deep and remind yourself that there is good everywhere if you look hard enough.

I struggled to get moving this morning and felt bad we were running late for William's teacher for 8am. Turns out she overslept and was glad she had more time.

Baked some cupcakes for some special friends. ♡

Finished some food prep and laundry.

Talked to one of my 3 favorite brothers, like for real, the old-fashioned way, on the phone it was nice to hear his voice and chat a while. ♡

Already received my blood work results from a draw yesterday, that was fast! Donating blood 2 months ago and refraining from red meat for 2 months brought my iron level from 260 to 109! That's great but I feel like crap again because now I'm moderately anemic - I'll bet I can eat a nice juicy steak now though! And probably get back on iron supplements - our bodies have NO idea how to function after 50!

I put my mechanic hat on today, took Williams peddle kart apart. The chain came off which is on the inside. Not as easy to fix this chain as his bike chain the other day! This one is a beatch! I may have to take the pedals off too but it started raining so tomorrow we'll see.

I can barely keep up with grooming requests, some begging and making deals. It's frustrating because I want to get back to work, I want to take care of them.

Yes, it seems like it should be ok for mobiles because we're at one house at a time, but that's 30-40 DIFFERENT houses in DIFFERENT towns every week. It's illegal for me to do so and first and foremost my health and that of my family remains top priority.

I'm grateful for the loyalty of my clients who have agreed to be put on a waiting list as I've heard there are groomers out breaking the restrictions. Those of us staying home are frustrated but safe and doing our part. We will return when allowed and at the safest time possible with our own restrictions in place. We will wear masks, not enter clients' homes and have payments placed in a large envelope by the client and sanitize, sanitize, sanitize and wash our hands until the skin comes off!

I won't disrespect our front liners by going out before we are cleared to do so - respect- you're saving lives, we're grooming dogs - priorities

I'm happy to loan my nail clippers to anyone local who would like to use them at their home and talk you through the process - long nails seem to be the biggest concern right now understandably. The rest will fall into place in good time 💛

The glass of attitude adjustment was early today, it was 5pm somewhere, just not here 😅

A perfectly timed scheduled Wednesday video call from Williams BCBA (board certified behavioral analyst) from school was a much-needed interruption in what was becoming a very rough afternoon – I'm thankful for continuance of the special needs kiddos services during this time and for Hershey's therapy pig cuddles 💕

Stay home, be safe, find the joy and always, always be kind

Namaste 🙏

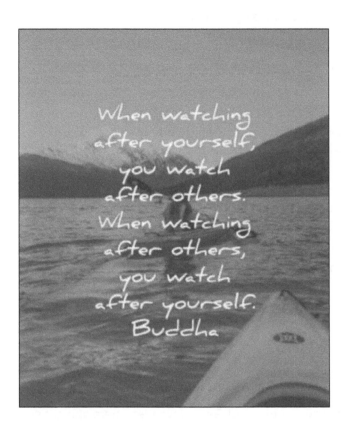

4/23/2020

Mindful Moments ....

I'm starting with the end of the day to move on to and end with more positivity - "we haven't hit our peak", "STAY HOME" is what they say, "shelter in place extended until May 30th because it's a crucial time to keep numbers down " but dog groomers are cleared to return to work May 1st - I'm not happy about it - I feel it's too soon - but with no income , no loans available , there is no choice - because if there was I wouldn't be opening until after May 30th .

I am already making safety precautions, restrictions and handing our health and safety over to a higher power - that's all I'm saying about that. My clients are thrilled.

I'm thankful for Katy helping to protect us.

I'm thankful for google search.

I'm thankful for my analytical abilities and common sense.

I'm thankful for Sarah and her musical performance last night - brought a smile to my face.

I'm an observer. I notice people I pass on my daily walk, while keeping social distance, will look away or at the ground.

Don't be afraid to make eye contact while we social distance, smile and say hello - it does feel awkward to purposefully move away from someone you may normally say hello to as you walk by, but it will bring a smile to someone else's face so make that eye contact, smile and say hello ♡

I'm thankful for my friend and landscaper who cleans up and tidy's the lawn each Spring - this afternoon became too overwhelming to think about photos but I'll grab some tomorrow - he goes above and beyond and does a great job ♡

The buds are opening on the tree I see each morning - I've watched it go from winter to Spring in just a few weeks ♡

Mom and dad duck back for a swim and a visit - and as always, they are socially distanced or having a tiff from being in isolation too long together.

Some guilty paws right there! Gee ...I wonder where she got so muddy?!

A special covert unexpected wine delivery, I swear my neighbors must think I sit here and drink all day ......well, maybe not allll day - thank you for always thinking of me and knowing what's going on without having to say a word Paula ♡

"Embrace uncertainty. Some of the most beautiful chapters in our lives won't have a title until much later." - Bob Goff

Namaste 🙏

4/24/2020

Mindful Moments ....

Suuuuch a busy day!

The daffodils have some tulip friends close by.

I get to bed at midnight and awake at 5-530 trying to keep up with grooming requests - it's insane!

William asked me why I was on my iPad so much. I said if I don't keep up with all of the stuffalupagus I have to do I fall far behind. I make up words a lot, he likes that.

He said "you have stuffalupagatosis - too much to deal with all the time mom" I'm glad I now have a diagnosis for my lack of sleep, lack of free time and lack of sanity. 😌

Another trip to Quest, long line at Starbucks but short lines at McD's and the ATM.

Took some photos of my edged and prettied up landscaping - the front of the house was just arbor vitae and a dying iris.

Jon broke up my day lilies from around the pool and put them in front with some of my landscaping stones - he does things I don't ask - he knows my personality and never disappoints 💙 Hub Landscaping btw.

Highlight of our day was a Jeep drive by 13th birthday celebration for a good friend's daughter - she's such a doll!

William fell in love with Guinness the Great Dane and the twin baby goats with t-shirts and diapers - see the videos - that's love right there 💙 Katy and Caitlin.

On the drive we were singing "I love rock and roll put another dime in the juke box baby ..." but William's version was "I love rock and roll put another straw in the juice box baby" - he really thought those were the words.

William finally got a truck driver to pull his jake brake with the good old elbow pump - icing on the cake for him today.

The pi'ece de resistance was a big bag of goodies left by the front door from William's bus driver and aide - toys, candy, crackers, sensory toys, Pokémon cards and a card telling him to stay strong and hang in there and they miss him, yes, I teared up- heartwarming 💙 I wish I could thank them and tell them how much these gestures mean but I think I know someone who can 💕

Keep looking for the helpers and finding the joy. 💕

Namaste 🙏

4/25/2020

Mindful moments ....

HA I was so tired last night I typed this up and didn't send it 😅 Waaayyyy too much going on right now!

Enjoy!

Coming to you late this evening after a couple of hours of cocktails and goof balls antics with my amazing brothers and sister in-law! Boy did we need to laugh and connect! We'll be zooming again!! Love you all! Rob, Annika, Dave, Boston.

Miss Emily K, William's para, took time out of her busy day to face time with William after work.

We scored some isopropyl alcohol! It's enough to take us through a few weeks and we can procure some in between.

Thank you, Lucie and Barb, for your kind donation.

Boston found some bottles at Shorewood Mariano's but didn't want to be the bad guy and take them all so we have about 10 small bottles.

And he scored a couple packages of plastic gloves!

A client in the financial business walked me through a PPP loan so I'm hoping for the best and all the big businesses don't suck up all the funding again - 3rd loan applied for, third time is a charm ... right??!

Special delivery to mom to brighten her day. ♡

Boston made the top of the super husband list with his relentless supply searching and a couple bonus surprises ... Cashew Milk (discontinued by Meijer), isopropyl alcohol to get us started!! SCORE!!! And the best find, Death Wish Coffee.

The best part of wakin' up is Death Wish in your cup.

Boston made dinner and it was good! Woohoo!! As much as I love to cook, I liked the break.

A heartfelt message outside of Brookdale. ♡

A good day was had by all.

Namaste 🙏

4/26/2020

Mindful Moments ....

I have a short list of moments today ... I know thank goodness!!

Starting at 7am, 9 straight hours of client correspondence! Made a great dent in reschedules - 34 down, 53 more to go and counting.

William was busy with his Pokémon buddy and a new Pokémon tattoo for the books.

Boston's breakfast. A real artery clogger I saw on FB - it sure looked good!

Offers of isopropyl alcohol and rubber gloves for our return-to-work Traci, Paula and if I forgot to thank you yesterday Lucie and Barb, I thank you all from the bottom of my heart! You're helping to reduce the stress of going back out in the germ cesspool a little less concerning. 💙💙

Mr. and Mrs. Duck made up from their tiff and sunned themselves poolside.

I'm grateful for my clients who are being so understanding in the tedious task of so many reschedules in a short period of time and more than willing to participate in our safety procedures moving forward.

Loan #3 applied for with much assistance from a financial client who was at our beck and call for 3 days without a fee - oooooo getting a small business loan under disaster circumstances is like a frat house hazing!!

Thank you for your help, Boston I'm hopeful this one is the charm.

A nice family dinner ended the day with the sandman hitting William hard - head to the pillow.

Now my head needs to hit the pillow - back at it tomorrow.

Namaste 🙏

4/27/2020

Mindful Moments ....

Do you feel like one day just turns into another lately? I do.

Earlier today I knew it was Monday, but by tonight, for just one second, I thought tomorrow was Saturday.

Our neighborhood Seniors being recognized making this difficult time for them a tiny bit brighter. 💍

Some snuggle time with Hershey and Gypsy's weekly washcloth "toss it, roll in it and leave it for mom to pick up" game.

The last 2 days have just melded into each other with many plans being made, accomplishments and planning future goals.

Unsolicited, out of nowhere during eLearning "Mom, I'm sorry you're stressed. When I'm stressed, I think about my family because it makes me happy. You should do that too" this ... this when you know through all the rough days, you're doing a good job.

Today's rescheduling completion of over 75 existing clients. Tomorrow moving onto the list of new clients. It's a time-consuming task that I'm grateful to have to do.

Stepped out of my comfort zone today with a situation that needed to be addressed. It has been lamented over for a year, by me. I now feel confident I'm making the right decision. I just had to decide. 🤚

I have an incredible family and unbelievably wonderful friends - tonight my heart is full.

Namaste

4/28/2020

Mindful moments ....

An early morning walk for Gypsy/bike ride in jammies and slippers for William has become the norm while we're isolated - less people are concerned with what others "dare to wear in public" when thousands are sick and dying - seems as though pj's out in public is pretty ok!

I sat at my kitchen table stressing over work I again started at 6am, for the 3rd day in a row and continue until very late at night.

I looked out the patio doors about noon with a tight chest and angry stomach from not having eaten anything.

I saw blue skies and sunshine. I saw a man jogging shirtless with shorts on. (I specified "man" for my pervy friends who would turn it into a porn post if I said shirtless jogger) And thought "what the heck?!! It must be warm outside!!"

So, I finished a couple more emails, pushed my work aside, had a protein shake, grabbed the 11yr old's and went for a walk!!

A little Pokémon go for William, neighborhood inspection for Gypsy and breathing some fresh air and feeling the warm sun was what was needed if even only for a few minutes!!

We saw blossoming trees, tiny little wild flowers and a few others out getting some fresh air walking, biking, cruising in their convertible.

The ducks are it again - I don't think he put the toilet seat down last night - they're not speaking.

My friend Traci was so thoughtful to offer her remaining isopropyl alcohol and to drop it off for me.

When I went out to the porch to get it I was surprised to see this beautiful bucket of treasures and Pokémon cards for William! He was soooo excited!!

Who would've thought a year ago that a gift of masks, gloves, isopropyl alcohol and essential oils would make you tear up with gratitude - thank you isn't enough Traci - you are a cherished friend. ♡

I am caught up with correspondence! That's a good feeling! Some more planning and paperwork to do, a generator oil change and gas tank fill by Thursday but everything is falling into place. ♡

I've seen some say that isolation has created the most serenity they've had in years and some say it's been the most stressful of times - I am the latter.

I haven't kept up with friends, groups or even had time for exercise recently BUT ...,

This isolation has created a shock to our systems. We were forced to deal with our routine being interrupted. Interruption is what we need in life. Time to either put stress aside and find serenity within ourselves or be forced to face difficult decisions that, in the end, create serenity later.

I believe we are what we create - so create happiness, positivity, appreciation and understanding.

Find the joy and look for the helpers. ♡

Namaste 🙏

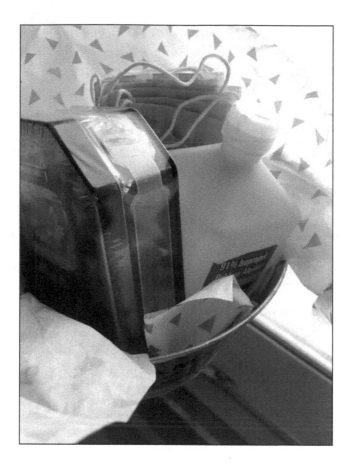

4/29/2020

Mindful Moments ....

It rained today ... ALL day! It's still raining. But the grass is a vivid green and everything is growing.

I like rainy days! I get things done inside and right now that's what I need to do! So, rain is good!!

Listened to the Pokémon theme song ... 13 times in a row ... that was enjoyable.

Piggies had playtime today. They love playtime, running around, squeaking, fresh veggies to snack on and a clean cage - it was a good day for piggies.

We had a little red visitor this afternoon dropped by to say "hey"!

The 20-piece nuggets are down to 8 - not bad Mr. William, not bad at all!

Fielded lots of calls today. Asking questions, educating, researching decision making ....

Clients are booked, safety supplies temporarily stocked, safety procedures in place, a bit more detail tomorrow and we become essential on a Friday.

Kind of a weird day. Planning for things I've never dreamed of and others I had hoped to never plan for - such is life - ever changing, ever evolving, always challenging and educating - take what you need and leave the rest.

Sweet dreams my family and friends

Namaste

4/30/2020

Mindful moments ....

Brought to you by lack of sleep.

Last day to get ready for returning to work.

Generator oil change, done!

Engine oil and air filter change, fluids checked, tires leveled off, done!

Dead engine battery replaced at a THIEVERY price which will be addressed tomorrow. ... however, I'm grateful the Rona got it now so it could replace BEFORE we start working.

Some PPE for our trip to Jiffy Lube and a little head banging fun on the way home ♡ something for you Uncle Tree. ♡

Haircut day for the mini boss before my equipment is cutting dogs instead.

Tooth number 4 pulled while in isolation; I think for him it's like a business transaction - he wants money, he pulls whatever tooth he can wiggle, pull, push and jam loose and the tooth fairy pays off.

A pot of turkey chili for dinner and we're ready to go.

Sleepy time!

Namaste 🙏

5/1/2020

Mindful Moments ....

First day back as essential workers went smoothly. Clients extremely cooperative and grateful using their PPE, had payments in envelopes and zip lock bags and respectful of social distancing - thank you for helping to keep us, our families and yourselves safe while we gussy up your fur babies.

A surprise friend for William today. He loves Cody! They hung out, ran an errand for me, grabbed lunch and played games.

For the first time in months, I was able to sit, yes sit, on the deck and get some fresh air - I almost felt guilty ... almost.

I haven't required wine midday in 2 days to make it through the day without losing my mind - great success!!

I had to putz in the yard of course cuz that's my Zen place. ♡

A busy day for Gypsy sunning, napping and bark face - the life of a dog in isolation ... or is that just every day?!

Transplanted some veggies to their next phase before going into the ground and watching my Larkspur, Four O'clocks, tomatoes, radicchio, chives, banana peppers and Sweet Peas reach for the stars!

The sky was a beautiful blue early this morning - when you look up instead of down you see things you normally miss. ♡

It's funny how when life slows you down from daily routine it gives you the opportunity to tune into what's important - fresh air, blue skies, green grass, everything becoming new again after a long winter.

Nature doesn't stop because we do, it continues to thrive we can learn from that.

Ligia planning a virtual brunch was brilliant! Ligia, Shelia and Denise, laughing with you ladies today made my day! We will be back to the gym and heading to Pho or Crispy Waffle afterward before you know it!! Love you, my friends.

And we make it through another day ... together. ♡

Namaste ♡

5/2/2020

Mindful Moments ....

I saw an airplane today!!! Like a real big one! Haven't seen one fly over here in weeks!! I had to watch it until it flew out of sight as if I'll never see one again.

Apparently even our weather is sick??!!!! see photo.

Legacy Ranch in Lockport had an event today where they brought their horses out street side. You could park across the street and watch them prance around and do tricks - William loves animals, the hard part was not being able to snuggle them - next time.

A little "Jeep hair don't care" after a stop at BK.

Next stop Turtle Lake for Pokémon Go, people and baby geese watching.

He wanted to hold one soooo badly - I warned him that mom and dad goose wouldn't be happy about that! He said he could run.

Social distance fishing and picnicking - A LOT of people out enjoying the beautiful day. ♡

Most were respectful of social distancing on the trail yet some with masks hanging around their neck walking 4 across the trail, not moving - we are quick to jump off the trail and into the trees!

This is the time when you need to keep reminding yourself of the serious situation that we are in. It's very easy to forget how careful you need to be on a beautiful spring day walking through a preserve with many other people. It feels normal and yet it's not - stay on course.

An afternoon of booking appointments, work prep and days end with a sibling Zoom call - I love my siblings and their families - Even though we can't see each other in person we laugh, tease and enjoy each other's company even if miles apart through the airways.

A full day filled with fresh air and adventure. ♡

Namaste 🙏

5/3/2020

Mindful Moments ....

Today was hard. I had to tell someone I love something they didn't want to hear. It made them sad. It made me sad. So, I bought us both flowers - flowers don't fix things but they sure are pretty and hoping it's bringing a little smile.

I think Boston was happy to be with me at the garden center. He saved us a couple hundred dollars in flowers for the yard I admit it, I have very little self-control in the Spring, in a garden center glowing with color - I guess if you have to have an obsession gardening isn't so bad ... right?!

Having to wear masks in public places has gone from uncomfortable to fashionable. There was some mask envy going on while I was wearing my White Sox mask today - mhmm you know it ... jealous??!!

A successful first weekend back on the road and rolling into a week that will prove to be a plethora of hills and valleys. May is coming in like a Lion but it will go out like a lamb. Powering ahead and the sun will rise again every day!

Changes are on the horizon, change can be scary but doesn't have to be bad, it can also be quite good and in the end they will all be what is in life's plan.

Lucie I've been a bit preoccupied lately, my plate overflowing and forgot to thank you for your covert drop off last night - William was in heaven this morning! Thank you for always thinking of us.

Caitlin, you did an incredible job this weekend and even though you moved out 9 years ago you haven't forgotten how to sneak in late at night quietly with tacos.

Time to sign off - be good to each other, give yourself some grace during difficult times and keep looking for the helpers.

Namaste 🙏

5/4/2020

Mindful Moments ....

Katy, thank you for using your gifted talent to help keep us safe while working! Can't thank you enough for making us masks and dropping them off!! We love the reversible paw prints!! Just perfect!!

William folded and put away his own laundry - life skills just as important as academics!

Miss Patricia joined Miss Emily for eLearning today and a fun chat with Miss Kaylie who had some fun ideas for Cinco de Mayo.

Piggies got a clean crib then bellied up to the cocktail and snack bars - they don't understand our problem with isolation.

It was nice to have someone to garden with today! Have half of my gifted perennials planted Annika - he's a good shoveler and wheelbarrow hauler - nice to see him away from technology and enjoying nature.

I'm itching to get in veggies and some flowers - maybe Mother's Day?! The Rona can't take away our enjoyment of nature.

A guitar serenade while cage cleaning.

Ended the day with a glass of "chill the F out".

Thank you, grapes, for being a tasty snack and handy de -stressor - so versatile.

Most people are pretty amazing and some are just asshats - just the way of the world!

Sarah thank you again for another enjoyable musical pick me up! Keep them coming! You can turn a long day into sunshine with a song.

Much to do the next few days so sleepy sleep now.

Namaste 🙏

5/5/2020

Mindful Moments ....

The tulips were smiling at me with hope of better things to come on my walk this morning. 🫶

A special facetime chat with mom - it was nice to see her smiling and laughing - she doesn't understand why we can't come see her - that's hard but with the help of technology it's almost like being there

Checking off and adding many things from a to do list for this week. This weekend will have some things put in the past and new things look forward to.

I'm thankful for my ability to multitask! While chatting with mom fielding client issues, gathering data, making decisions, receiving important calls and texts and holding a bored boy at bay 💗

The last step of my PPP loan completed / now I wait ... again.

My little buddy made herself comfy in my bed until I invaded her solitude, now she's keeping watch over things by my bed. 💗

A couple more perennials in the ground.

Lunch made for tomorrow, William's lesson plan ready for Auntie Paula and it's back to work I go. 💗

One day at a time.

Namaste 🙏

5/8/2020

Mindful Moments ....

I am a recovering people pleaser. If there's one important lesson I've learned the hard way, and isn't that the best way to learn? No matter what you do, or how hard you try, you just can't please everyone.

So, you just keep being you, carry out acts of kindness, do your best, pay it forward and always look for the joy - most times you touch people's lives without even realizing it - you just might be the interruption they need.

I had cause to be in person with my brother Tom, Annika and Todd yesterday - I wanted to hug everybody!!! But we dutifully stood and chatted with masks and gloves and completed our task. sigh - times they have changed.

Would've been nice to stop for dinner or a drink afterward - so strange not to be able to hang out for a bit- so we went our separate ways ....

Thank you so much Todd for helping us out! We'll meet for that drink and perhaps a bacon fry when the world unlocks.

Loving my coffee warmer! I never get to finish a cup of coffee while it's hot - but this sucker keeps it piping hot as long as it takes - it doesn't take much to please me!!

Some before and after grooms - a new StaPoo puppies first grooming and one of my senior girls - makes my heart happy to see all of the animals being adopted during this time.

Doesn't everyone wear their moms flip flops to pump gas when it's 47 degrees??

Leftover Center Pork Roast made nice BBQ Pineapple sliders on Hawaiian rolls.

I was asked in an email from a new client if I'm taking new "patients" right now - if they're patients I'm definitely not making enough.

Apparently, Williams financial advisor was trying to screw him over - as I heard him say on his pretend cell call today.

Tried some Pokémon Go today but apparently my flip flops cause toe crevice pain when walking too far - who knew? Oh wait, I did, when I asked him to put socks and shoes on - but what do I know?!!

It's been a full week to say the least. Too much to even to get into. I'm sure you've missed my posts the past few days.

All kidding aside - I hope to be a positive interruption in someone's day - we're in this together, the good, the bad and the ugly.

One Day at a Time.

Namaste 🙏

5/9/2020

Mindful Moments ....

What started out to be a rainy day turned into a beautiful, blue sky sunny day.

Finally, some outdoor playtime!

Lawn mowing ....

A riveting soccer game facilitated by Grammy Barbs backyard and goal courtesy of Traci thank you very much - much nicer photos covertly taken by Lucie in the social distancing stands of her home.

That was a goal by Mr. William btw SCORE!

A Pokémon Go game ended abruptly by a pee urgency - a 1/2 mile from home "run Forrest run" - I haven't seen him run that fast in years.

I was finally able to do some of my favorite things today. Cooking, baking PB protein cookies and gardening.

My Zen is nature and I was in it today. More perennials joined the team, some digging, planting, watering and I got pooped on by a bird - on the bright side, it wasn't in my hair, it was on my thumb ... nice aim - it's the little things.

Another loose tooth and after a fun day a rouuuugggh night getting to sleep!! He was threatening to stay up all night, um no, we'll just wait this out until you pass out!! Only took 3 hrs.! Must be one of those weeks for many people.

"I want to thank you, thank you for taking my ouchies away, I want to thank you and have a Happy Mother's Day".

William's song to me when his tooth ache and stomach ache went away.

I'll miss our annual Mother's Day gathering at moms tomorrow complete with Browns Chicken and enough shrooms to feed an army, minus the ones that disappear on the way home from pick up.

It's going to be quite different.

Remember to change your underwear in case you're in an accident - you're welcome.

Namaste 🙏

5/10/2020

Mindful Moments ....

Early morning Mother's Day snuggles made a chilly morning nice and warm.

Spending time with my 2 favorite kiddos made the day the best that Rona will allow this year - missed spending the day with mom and the family.

I love when William sings - music soothes the soul and brings smiles no matter what it is.

Caitlin my garden puppy is going to get a special place in the yard and guinea pig socks?? be still my heart.

Boston knows the key to my heart with Volcanica Guatemalan coffee and preparing a delicious dinner of marinated grilled chicken, honey do melon cilantro lime spicy salsa, green beans and rice - be careful or you'll be cooking more often!!There was a lot of chopping and zesting going on!! Thank you for ending the day on a good note.

A bitter sweet visit with mom. An hour chat through a screen is better than nothing at all.

A rainy visit to a greenhouse for a few flowers and veggies I couldn't grow and I'm ready to plant - maybe next week when it's warmer.

Farewell to another Mother's Day - One thing Rona can't take away is love.

Namaste

5/11/2020

Mindful Moments ....

Growing up our back yard was lined with lilac trees. Every shade. I remember the scent in the Spring when the blossoms would open and the breeze would blow toward the house.

Every time I pass a Lilac tree it brings back memories of our yard growing up - this one on my walk today was just opening.

My new groomer went out on her own today. What a breath of fresh air! Very early arrival to get settled in, on schedule all day, back earlier than expected and very pleased clients!! 🐶

I believe she is a great addition to the Miracle Worker family.

William was busy with his chores emptying the dishwasher and folding his laundry - he loves chores.

While I spent 7 hours, yes 7, on the IDES website applying for back unemployment, William was creating a bloody massacre in the living room pulling another tooth not yet ready to come out - on the plus side he was keeping himself quietly entertained all afternoon.

I think those pants need some spray and wash or a forensic investigator!

I scored big time in the dryer "Wheel of Fortune"!! I'm worth much more than that but beggars can't be choosers.

The Pansy flats I bought yesterday were so happy to be inside!! They perked right up this morning but soon they'll be sunning themselves in the yard.

These are interesting days for sure. So much to be grateful for among the challenges.

William has a surprise outdoor activity tomorrow afternoon! Cut wayyy back on tech time and spending more time getting exercise and fresh air - he can't wait to get the pool open - still too chilly for that, but not for long.

Don't let someone else's clouds take away your sunshine.

Namaste 🙏

5/12/2020

Mindful moments ....

William came out of his room singing this morning, just a song he made up made it more special. 🩶

I convinced my boss to take our morning walk / ride with Gypsy and I this morning.

It was a pretty morning. 🌤

Along the way we saw some Spring flowers and a bunny waiting for someone to answer the door, even the wildlife is looking for friends.

The tooth fairy was kind and all evidence of the tooth pulling massacre of yesterday have vanished, thankfully.

I feel it from William, even myself and hearing from other kiddos that they're depressed. William described feeling like a black hole and another little guy said to his mom "do you ever feel like things just aren't exciting anymore? You know like the things that used to be fun but they're just not fun anymore?" I feel this.

We need to remember that the kiddos are having a rough go of this isolation, much worse than we as adults - they don't know why they're feeling this way or how to manage it.

I mean kids are supposed to be happy, carefree, hanging out and having fun, right?! But not now they're not. Nothing is the normal they crave.

Be kind, give them your time and understanding and give yourself grace.

So, we had some fun today! Two walks one with a ride and one with Pokémon Go!

We surprised William with an archery set for the yard. He was doing so well at the Archery Place before this all went down, I thought it might perk him up, and it did! He's pretty good! A better set for him as he improves; he asked if Uncle Tree would shoot with him sometime - I said I was pretty sure he'd love to.

Even gypsy and the piggies had playtime with social and safety distancing today lol.

One of my newly planted perennials is already sprouting some flowers Annika - I can't wait to plant the rest of my veggies and flowers this weekend.

"Someone" put a fake cockroach under dads pillow last night (thank you Sarah Putts lol); It's missing so I'm thinking it was found but not sure where it is now!

We're sad that Miracle League baseball was cancelled for Spring but it was so nice of the coaches to make a YouTube video for all the kids they coach from the heart every year!

I have to say today has been the most relaxed day in months - I even had time to sit down for a few minutes without working on something and shower.

Back on the road tomorrow to spruce up some more covid tattered pups!!

Sleep well my friends and stay home.

Namaste

5/13/2020

Mindful Moments ....

I always see some interesting things being out on the road working. Especially now. Makes my travels interesting most days.

Some photos of a few of my "patients" today.

Riley the 4-month-old Aussie did an amazing job at her fist grooming. I love puppies! They're full of energy, playfulness, unconditional love and curiosity ... all of the things we forget to be as we get older.

Then we have Wolfie - he doesn't like the blow dryer or having his nails cut / he bites the dryer and my hand is dangerously close to those sharp determined teeth - so a safety muzzle it is!! He didn't keep the headphones on they were just cute.

Bohde my love bug. Takes 2 of us to get him in the van but he's a good boy Terre and so obedient for his treats. Somehow, he is so much more cooperative going back into the house.

I saw Mayor Lightfoot today, had to do a double take but sorry Mayor, no staying home for me!! You said it was ok??!!

An old pickup just happened to be parked next-door to Wolfies house. I grabbed a quick photo for William.

I saw not one but 3 social distancing birthday celebrations on front lawns. Complete with balloon sculptures, signs and lots of friends/families, at safe distances, chatting and laughing - amazing how well we can adapt to new environments when we are placed in them. We are a hearty, tough bunch!

William pulled another tooth today and this one I'll give him - I think it loosened with the work he did on the other on Monday - it came right out, no massacre this time and I think it's the last one! Puberty is hittin' hard lately!

Hershey's kisses- pun intended - and snuggles are great pet therapy for William. She was truly meant for him.

I've been thanked for working several times this week - it's nice to be appreciated.

5:30 comes quickly - I'm off to sleepy land - hoping you all enjoyed the beautiful day.

Namaste 🙏

5/14/2020

Mindful moments ....

Does anyone hear rain?? I'm thinking flooding tonight! Gypsy has already settled into the bedroom for safety purposes of course (she's scared.... shhhhh)!

Allow me to introduce you to my fur babies today.

On your left is Henry. He's a little dude with loads of personality and my good friend's little man! She's said he was running around the house like a nut after his grooming. They take off his bandana, fill it with his food and let him play with it until he gets the food out.

On the right Gibbs. He claims to have "put on a pound or five during isolation" and blames his owner - it's probably the Reddi Whip snacks.

Next you see before and after of my favorite Tom boy girls! Teddy and Beasley. These girls live the best life with the best humans!

They live on a self-sustaining farm with vegetables, honey bees, chickens, goats, horse, Llama and a lake ... the lake, my nemesis! I made human mama promise not to let them swim until I pull away. But before I left, I visited Rosie the Llama and several other curious fur babies. The sheep had sheerings and Rosie had a new do too.

Thank you for the extra's Cindy- and medical grade alcohol is amazing!!

Miss Emily stopped by with a movie goodie bag. Williams class is watching Sonic the Hedgehog movie at noon as a class tomorrow so they now have their ticket and movie snacks! So excited!!

And William gave her some pansies for her Yard.

Thank you for the great pics, Auntie Paula and for taking such good care of him while I'm at work.

I see this post going around demeaning the purpose of our isolation.

Wise up people ... go talk to a front liner in the hot areas - that's where your truths are - I had talked to nurse and Dr. friends for advice when I reopened my business - their advice for protection is that of a front-line medical staffer and is above and beyond what I can provide for myself, groomers and clients but we're doing our best with what we have to work with and hoping we stay healthy and keep our families healthy.

Don't judge unless you intend to make their sacrifices for yourself.

Thank you to our front-line workers and all essential workers for their sacrifices and that of their families.

Good night and good news.

Namaste 🙏

5/15/2020

Mindful moments ....

Did we get some rain last night or what??? Holy smokes it poured and I hear more to come! We had to have gotten 4 or 5 inches.

Working from home today. I roasted some butternut squash, steamed some broccoli and asparagus and made a pot of Albondigas (Al Bundy Gas) Soup - cooking ... my other favorite pastime when time allows.

Some sunny side up eggs with roasted squash for lunch was delicious!!

Miss Emily's grand production of Sonic the Hedgehog via Zoom didn't go well sadly 🙁 some tech and sound issues ended it early. We'll try again next Friday.

But we're going to watch it tomorrow at home another way.

So, we went outside for an ATV ride. William has this spot around the corner from our house, under a tree, where he goes to contemplate life and clear his mind.

He finds peace there, as he told me today. So, we hung out on the sidewalk under a breezy tree for a while - it's was very relaxing, you could see the serenity in his eyes.

Waiting for us on the porch when we arrived home was a much-anticipated delivery!

A Marvel Lego set ordered beginning of the week - a nice distraction from the day's excitement.

As much as I love cooking, I'm tired of it - there I said it! Tired of meal planning, coming up with something everyone will eat, grocery orders, putting groceries away, cooking dinner - I just want someone to wait on me every-day, set a plate in front of me and then clean up - is that too much to ask - oh wait I just woke up from a dream - burgers on the grill tomorrow and mahi mahi Sunday.

Cody dinner was fantastic tonight GF pasta, homemade alfredo sauce with shrimp and garlic bread twists - thanks for giving me a break with your incredible professional cooking!

Hoping to get in all of my plants tomorrow before more rain. Would be nice to sit back and look at a flourishing, tidy yard!

"Life is really simple but we insist on making it complicated." Confucius

Namaste 🙏

5/16/2020

Mindful Moments ....

Planting day/rain tomorrow!!!!! Veggies and flowers are ready to flourish.

Every year I walk through a garden center and let the flowers pick me. This year they were yellow and purple combos and the pool is always decorated with geraniums and day lilies - I like to sit on the deck and admire mother nature's miracles.

There was a busy bee very interested in my pansy's pre-planting - he was kind enough to strike a pose for a photo.

Pool cover is draining - almost time for a dip!!

My favorite time of year. Low humidity, cool breeze, no bugs, fresh air ... nature.

3 times today I heard honking in the distance.

4 months ago, I'd think there was some road rage going on. Now I smile because I know someone's special occasion is being celebrated.

Again, we adapt - we turn disappointment to gratitude.

William and Cody had a busy day. Lego building, archery, bike ride, Pokémon Go and Pokémon cards. After rising at 5am William crashed into a peaceful, exhausted slumber - thankfully.

William is becoming quite good at archery. Cody filled solo cups with sand and William nailed them 3 times! Some photo and video ops courtesy of Cody check them out.

A BBQ of foil packet potatoes and onions, burgers and chicken breasts.

Working outside, for me, is peaceful - better than any gym any day.

Mind - Body - Soul.

Namaste 🙏

5/17/2020

Mindful Moments ....

Someone sat next to Gypsy ... she's horrified that her personal space has been invaded and don't even THINK about touching me!!

Our pictured models pretty much sum up the day ... a walk with no umbrella.

Dropped off some things for mom and was able to window chat for a few minutes. ♡

She was so happy to see a familiar face I just wanted to hug her and she wanted me to sneak her out the window and put her in my Jeep.

I watched some of my freshly planted flower's float to the top of their new homes.

Dumped off some water put some undercover and wait for them to dry out.

Some incredible flooding in local neighborhoods. I feel for some of these residents, their homes and businesses with flooding. An additional hardship they didn't need during the rona shut down.

The sun will shine and dry up all the rain and the itsy-bitsy spider will climb up the spout again.

I believe we all know our kids best. William was definitely off today. I believe it's the weather.

Being exceptionally sensitive to emotion and energy, days with storms and heavy rains cause anxiety for him. Especially since having a tornado come through our neighborhood in the middle of the night years back.

This evening was rough for him. He doesn't always know how to express his emotions through words - this I know.

We talked and hugged at bedtime, he expressed some things more easily discussed alone and he fell asleep soundly - sweet dreams sweet young man. 😌

William earned the Six Flags Great America Read to Succeed contest with a free admission this year - he's gone up 5 reading levels just since he's been out of school - so very proud of his hard work!! Now I hope we can get into Six Flags maybe by Fall. 🙏

This week is our last week of eLearning until ESY begins June 10th. Creativity will need to kick in to keep those days off busy!

Little sleep and full days have me exhausted - sleepy time.

Namaste 🙏

5/18/2020

Mindful moments ....

Well, it finally happened. There have been many dogs adopted during this pandemic, one of the beautiful things about it really.

I've been waiting for an appointment request from a new client with a dog named "Rona" and today was the day! The Humane Society named her so the new pet parents kept it!

She was adopted a month and a half ago, she's a German Shepherd and has her forever family and now it's our pleasure to keep her groomed and feeling special. Welcome Rona!

Williams first time walking Gypsy. Not that he's not capable but she's a maniac if she sees another dog, rabbit, cat, bird, chipmunk ... you get the picture! She would pull him down the street or he'd let go of the leash - They both did great!

There's that Lilac bush in its final bloom of Spring - My goal is to have one in the yard.

Hershey helped with some anxiety today – she's such a great support piggie! Then we cut her nails, they were loooong - she didn't like that so much.

My first workout in 3 weeks today. Self-care went by the wayside on April 24th when we went from non-essential to essential, non-essential. My phone and email exploded.

While home schooling, managing therapies, helping to advocate for mom, hiring a new groomer, clients were contacted, booked and consistent incoming requests attended to daily. Most important - safety procedures put into place for our safety and that of our clients. Little sleep, lots of work, lots of stress and lots of wine! Thank you, Paula for door for door trunk deliveries.

Time for a little me time now whenever I can get it!

I was gifted a fire truck made with miscellaneous Legos, a great creative mind and love ♡

LOVE my Mother's Day gift Jeep hat that arrived today, it's perfect - the Rona has slowed deliveries of all non-essential items. I'm happy to wait for surprises. ♡

I was grateful for Albondigas Soup for dinner made over the weekend - gave me a little time to sit and watch part of a movie with William (William likes it and ate it but I won't tell him there was zucchini in it, it's green, he doesn't eat green lol).

I'm glad I stopped watching Rona briefings every day. Once we returned to work it didn't matter how many were testing positive or dying or when we we'd be released safely to work, ready or not we just protect ourselves.

I've grown tired of everything becoming political. This side hates that side. If you don't believe the way that person does then you're wrong, stupid, snowflake, libtard, righty, lefty whatever the name calling is now. So, I choose to refrain from sharing opinions or comments in those posts seems that rarely an intelligent, respectful meeting of the minds can happen. I don't have room for that in my life.

Enjoy each day as a gift as there are many who didn't expect their last day to be so soon.

Don't let anyone take your joy. ♡

Namaste 🙏

5/19/2020

Mindful Moments ....

Do you ever have one of those days that you feel like you're non-stop all day but have accomplished nothing? Yea, that was today.

William, CEO had his full video conference agenda. Our attempts at connection were thwarted by low battery computers and hurried attempts to plug in with cords too short to meet his needs and connect on time.

But we made every one of them! It was a good day for making progress with therapies.

We had some anxiety to work through - he's much better at expressing his feelings and knowing he needs help and asking for it - huge progress!

We played meditation music to chill and he found it to be sad so we switched to reggae, his request, that made him happy but at low volume.

Music is personal interpretation - how it makes you feel is something to look at, no matter what feeling it gives you.

Top priority of the day was making all of his goals so he could build his latest Lego project, which he proudly showed to each video observer.

I'm proud of his self-awareness of noise discomfort, focus on projects and all-around relaxed demeanor today. It was a tough few days for him.

He asked for a "sleep over" last night. He needed the comfort of his person, I complied and it worked. He woke up calm and ready for the day.

We all know what we need deep down and at 11 he's more aware of himself and willing to ask for help than most adults - I'm glad he's learning self-care now rather than turning to outside substances to mask and numb himself, then burying feelings that will inevitably arise in an unhealthy way later. ♡

He made our lunch, turkey burgers.

Emptied the dishwasher, fed the dog, helped put piggies out for playtime, replenished food and water, helped clean their cage and took out the garbage!

Marshmallow and Hershey shamelessly gorged themselves on fresh veggies and a few strawberries for a special treat.

Williams latest Lego creation took 2 hrs. 20 minutes - not bad for 478 pieces, one small glitch quickly and calmly fixed. Entire project completed without help! Bam!

While he created cool toys I attended to work - win win

He's proud of his creations this past week and loves to show them off.

We're hoping for a dry day tomorrow to get out for a bike ride, maybe some archery and get some fresh air. These 4 walls can really close in sometimes.

I'm so very proud of this young man. Despite his lifelong challenges and painful events, he's strong, resilient, loving and determined - he'll go far in life and I can't wait to see him spread his wings and fly.

You can't help everyone but everyone can help someone. ♡

Namaste 🙏

5/20/2020

Mindful Moments ....

I had a decision to make this afternoon. Do I eat a handful of grapes or do I drink a glass of repurposed grapes? Guess what I chose!

I'm excited to say that after several years with no flowers, my climbing rose bush has buds! I can't wait to see them bloom!

Annika the Columbines you sent are starting to bloom! I didn't expect them to this year but they're looking good and were just planted a couple of weeks ago!

Nice to dance with Jennifer and the girls this morning at least for a while - had to cut out with too many interruptions but had a good time Jenn! Thank you and the other instructors for continuing to give of your time so selflessly.

We went on an afternoon walk to get some fresh air and catch some Pokémon. Our plans were to go for a bike ride this afternoon. My Shipt order was 3 hours late, with no reason to be, so it blew the afternoon. But a 10-minute walk is better than nothing!

We needed to get out of the house today after eLearning. So, our field trip was a trip to the ATM and lunch pickup at Culver's with a double scoop of the day of course - I consider it lessons in finance and culinary arts.

The two most common alcohols in people's houses these days, the drinking kind and the disinfecting kind! I traded them for milk - good deal I'd say ♡ PK.

Regarding the photo of the pooch at the end ... this photo was taken right after a grooming, from a different groomer. A new client sent it to show me how she typically looks after being groomed so we'd know what she likes cuz "she's a wooly girl right now".

PSA If your dog comes home looking like this after a grooming it's time to find a new groomer!! Not everyone is cut out to groom dogs! Pun intended!! Maybe this is why her shop is closed?! She will be pleasantly surprised after she sees Shannon next week.

Need to tie up some lose work ends before I hit the hay!

Sweet dreams of puppy dogs, kittens and unicorns

Namaste 🙏

5/21/2020

Mindful Moments ....

Meet Bentley and Beckett. These boys are brothers with different human mothers, from the same family. ♡

They are both sweet big boys from even sweeter families who went from Shut Down shaggy to Covid coiffed. ♡

A lot to reflect upon today ....

I continue to experience random acts of kindness that take my breath away and bring a tear to my eyes. I received two heartfelt notes with enclosed gifts today. The most beautiful heartfelt words and kindness. I have to remind myself that I'm deserving of such kindness. Thank you to an unnamed client for your completely unexpected kindness and generosity. ♡

When you travel from day to day and moment to moment just doing what you do and being who you are you don't think about it being noticed because you aren't who you are for recognition. I suppose that's why I'm taken aback at being the receiver of kindness ... if that makes sense.

Sarah, from the bottom of my heart - thank you for your kind words and surprises. You are so very thoughtful and make William's day whenever something arrives in the mail box for him.

It reminds me that without knowing it. With just being your authentic self. You can really touch someone and isn't that what it's all about?

As I'm seeing some becoming relaxed, too relaxed in my opinion, with the seriousness of this virus, I'm seeing some others just the opposite.

My clients today amazing with PPE, masks, gloves, payments enclosed in envelopes and baggies. But there was one that sticks in my mind the most.

A house I service twice per month. I usually go in, as they are not typically home, and get my friend Cash. I'm not going into homes for the foreseeable future so mom wasn't home but the kiddos were.

I texted the oldest. Our new procedure is to have clients come to the van masked whenever possible, as we are masked as well. A boy 15ish came out with mask and gloves on. He looked scared. He was afraid to come too close, kind of reached the leash around the front of the van.

I get him and felt for him and it made me sad. I'm one of "those" still taking this quite seriously - I have a family to keep safe and maybe someone who relies on me solely. It's a heavy weight to carry. You know, the responsibility of having to live forever.

This same boy I used to see happily playing basketball while waiting for his bus when I'd arrive early in the morning. Constant reminders of how things have changed just in case you're forgetting, and some are forgetting.

Mask or not, put a smile on your face. Your eyes can smile. They are welcoming and calming. It doesn't cost anything to soothe someone's concerns with a simple smile.

Ended my day with sweet sounds from Preston - you and Ari never disappoint my friend. ♡

If you made it this far ....

Side note, what's with the green bananas from Meijer?? Two weeks in a row. Last weeks never ripened, threw them away. Waiting to see what happens with these. Aren't there any other options??

Wear a mask, stay 6' away and wash your hands - it's pretty simple.

Namaste 🙏

5/24/2020

Mindful Moments ....

This! 🫳

Namaste 🙏

5/25/2020

Mindful Moments of the weekend ....

Friday, we joined "Illinois Jeephers" among many others in a birthday parade for a little girl fighting her way back from a near drowning a year ago. An amazing turnout for a sweet girl with a long road ahead.

It's heartwarming to continue to see physical distancing celebrations joined by families, friends and strangers! There's something magical and exciting driving by someone's house during difficult times and seeing a smile on their face. Anything to spread the joy.

The boys spent Friday afternoon playing Minecraft and going for a bike ride - a little break for me.

I enjoyed sushi from Caitlin and Cody from their visit to B.A.S.H Burger and Sushi House in Oswego - I've missed it!! My girls and I went out occasionally after the gym for sushi - it's been a while.

My friend Barb sent me a bottle of "alcohol" and said I could either drink it, or clean with it - I did both jk I drank it.

Sharon so great to see you and Kelly and thank you soooo much for your isopropyl alcohol donation we are certainly going through it - love and miss you all tons!!

Stopped by Lesa's for a kolache pickup and picked some of her Lily of the Valley. The perfume from those flowers brings back childhood memories from moms Lily bed behind the garage.

Cookies were delicious Lesa, mom loved them too.

Opened the pool Sunday - hot and exhausting but soooo happy to have something else to do now while we stay home and stay safe - William has always been a fish and the play/exercise wears him out.

Today was the pools first inhabitant of the year - William of course! Only an 11yr old can stand that water temperature!! We feet dipped until maybe tomorrow, perhaps a bit too much sun but what a nice change of pace and fresh air.

Couldn't understand why this goofy blackbird brought poop in his beak and tried to drop it in the pool and put it on our patio table, repeatedly!

We learned, thanks to google, that they want to hide their nesting sites from predators so they would drop fecal sacs in the nearby water.

There's a lake down the street, how about that instead bird??! This may explain why people have issues with grackles around their pools and birdfeeders. You learn something new every day.

William loves his squirt gun floatie so Boston paid him .50 for every bird poop pile he could shoot off the edge of the pool - he made $4 - young entrepreneur.

We were very fortunate to have missed Saturday's tornado. A few miles away roofs were blown off and trees uprooted. I'm grateful it wasn't worse.

Haircut day for William but ran out of time for Boston - next weekend?

I finally hit the "my hair needs help" stage but I can't cut my own hair so ... hats.

Generator oil changed; engine oil added - the old girl has worked 24 days straight 8-10hrs per day - oil was dirty!

Of course, the highlight of a busy weekend was to see mom, and not through a window.

I'm pleasantly pooped, feel accomplished and ready to tackle another week.

Just because the weather is nice and we're bored and missing friends and family doesn't remove a pandemic - follow guidelines - let's save lives and avoid another shut down.

Namaste 🙏

5/26/2020

Mindful Moments ....

Where some are excited with the sudden upper 80 temps, Gypsy seeks out the most exposed a/c vent to lay on after her walk, smart girl. ♡

Even Gypsy is a bit stir crazy - I think because we're home all the time - she tore around the backyard, dug up some landscaping and wanted in the house with muddy paws - nope!

Day 2 Cannon ball brought to you with smooth Jazz-William's choice ... I love William's appreciation for ALL music - Jazz, Reggae, Rock, classic rock, country, metal, Blues you name it he gets into it. Although I do believe he'll find a favorite one day.

Thank you Auntie Lulu for fence popsicle drop off - there's nothing like enjoying a popsicle in the pool on a hot day.

Watched that same black bird plant his fecal sacs on the pool edge and in my planters - I showed him - I splashed him, he flew away - he'll be back - it's on bird!

My bike gets fixed tomorrow! Front porch service from an old friend with a bike business. Very happy to get back in the saddle and get away from the house. 🐢

William and I hung out in the pool this afternoon - he won extra dessert by making 10 midair catches while jumping off the ladder into the pool -

Then me on my pizza slice floatie and William in his UFO - we closed our eyes and pretended to be on vacation in a luxury resort, pool side, gentle breeze, blue sky, bright sun, good food, no worries, reggae music and no responsibilities - we can dream. 💭

Namaste 🙏

5/27/2020

Mindful Moments ....

I learned today that you can call poison control at 6:15am and sit on hold for 15 minutes ... what???

Everyone is fine - no ER trips - a mix up of meds but yeesh how many people are getting poisoned that early in the morning??

Robin thank you for your post regarding China Gel - my knee has been in the worst shape this week and it's been amazing! I smell like my grandfather, but it's amazing.

My musically diverse boy was singing Space Oddity while playing Lego World - yesterday Jazz ... today, Bowie, what will tomorrow bring.

These past months have been a time of reflection for many, myself included.

Over the past year due to unrelenting circumstances, I've considered, more like lamented over, shutting down my business.

Being home and unable to work allowed me to step away from the stress, calm my mind and regroup as I've mentioned in days past.

But 22 years ago, when I went mobile with my business I never thought of how essential and appreciated our personal service would become - especially for those at high risk of this virus who are self-quarantining. ♡

I'm glad I stayed the course, trudged through the muck and am honored to provide a service for many seeking out to protect themselves and their families. That services like mine can make that happen for them.

I'd like to thank Boston for introducing William to "Jay Leno's Garage" we have now watched 432 episodes since Monday, twice.

He may find interest in new things here and there but his love for classic cars (and furry animals ♡) will always be at the forefront. ♡

And to all a good night.

Namaste 🙏

5/29/2020

Mindful Moments ... yesterday dedicated to George Floyd.

Today a bit of a break from the events of the week ....

In Dec 2018 my amazing neighbor Pam moved away and the home next door was rented out.

The renters moved in and never mowed all last year. They were kicked out in February and the homeowner didn't show up to check on the place until a week ago.

He hired this poor guy out there mowing who busted his rear end for hours to clean up the mess left - nice to have that eye sore gone. ♡

There's been an abandoned house on 135th and Archer near Lemont for so many years I can't even count. This house has always intrigued me. Its design is either old west or Native American it seems. Anyone know the history of this house?

Yesterday's shut down shaggy to covid coiffed was Gio.

Last grooming Feb 9 looking particularly adorable with the help of my assistant, William the dog whisperer who lent a hand and a heartfelt talk with the nervous Gio making his grooming calm and peaceful.

While Cody taught William Frisbee Golf today, which he loved and played all the holes, I had kitchen time!

An eggplant lasagna, regular lasagna and peach cobbler for dinner and some prepped veggies for the week.

I've learned a couple things about face masks. The thick ones are great until you start feeling claustrophobic in them from wearing them a lot. And they highlight your eyes. Brings to light how long it's been since you plucked your eyebrows.

I'm impressed with the young guy working cashier at Target with a difficult lady checking out.

He was patient, polite and helpful despite her demands and a long line behind her. I pointed out his patience and helpfulness to him. That this type of great customer care under difficult times does not go unnoticed and thanked him for working.

Ended our day with the first bon fire and s'mores of the year - perfect night for a fire. The smore queen is back.

The country was tarnished by yet another heinous, preventable act this week. So much anger and violent escalation.

It's time to stop ignoring these situations and start acting on them. We don't need any more hatred, division and death - we do need to band together for change. What can we each do to better ourselves as a people? What part can we each play in moving forward?

Peace to George Floyd and the people of Minneapolis/St. Paul. ♡

Namaste

6/1/2020

Mindful Moments ....

Boy this is getting harder for me by the day.

I couldn't post anything the past few days. My heart hasn't been in it.

If 2020 hasn't slapped us in the face enough Hershey passed away during the night.

Williams comfort piggie, like some who have therapy dogs, who has helped him through so many difficult times. Always kind, still, patient and snuggling his neck when he'd need it the most.

This child has been through hell since Dec 31st, some things that haven't been mentioned on FB that are beyond unreal - this has broken his heart.

He is devastated. My heart hurts for him.

We are barely recovering from pandemic shut down and now our businesses are being destroyed, more aftermath jobs are being lost and I may need to shut the van back down because of the rioters. Just defeating and disheartening.

I am the ultimate optimist but today I am digging deep, very deep for gratitude.

I'm thankful for my family.

I'm thankful for my friends.

I'm thankful for food on my table.

I'm thankful for a roof over our heads.

I'm thankful to have a business I may need to shut down.

I'm thankful for my loyal clients.

I'm thankful for the time William had loving Hershey and she him. ♡

I'm thankful for waking up each day.

I'm thankful for strength.

I'm thankful for resilience.

I'm thankful for the sun rising tirelessly each day.

I'm thankful for all of our emergency responders, our Drs, nurses etc.

I'm thankful for the helpers.

I'm thankful for hope because without hope we have nothing.

Please keep William in your prayers.

Be kind, be safe, find the joy in all of this devastation

Namaste 🙏

6/2/2020

Mindful Moments ....

The sun shined a little brighter today ... because it had to.

I'm a survivor, a fighter, a fixer, a motivator, an advocate - I don't allow tragedy to hold me back for long. I can't emotionally live like that.

On our walk today I noticed things I've seen before but are brought more to the surface now.

We live in a very diverse neighborhood, which I love.

Every Asian, black and Hispanic neighbor we walked by William gave a huge hello and good morning!

Each neighbor looked up, smiled and returned his salutation.

Kindness comes naturally.

I noticed that he doesn't see color of skin, he sees people and shows kindness even when his world is sad, scary and confusing. That's because that's how he lives and we learn what we live.

It made me wonder.

How do these people live who are so hateful, angry and destructive? How sad for them when life has so much good to offer.

But how long do you blame your present on your past? When do you open your eyes to what's in front of you and take responsibility for the decisions you make that can hurt other people?

I took a walk through my yard today. The colors were brighter. The sky was bluer and the grass greener. Perspective.

We had 6 turkey vultures soaring near the yard - must've been something good down there.

Over the weekend the boys went frisbee golfing - Williams first time and he finished the whole course and did well.

Friday night we had the first bonfire we've had in a couple of summers - last summer was ... well ... rain and heat!

Some laughs, a couple cocktails and the smore queen at her post (me) I make a good smore.

As we've seen the unrest of this past week and the continued concerns of a pandemic some are forgetting still exists, we've also seen the helpers. ♡

We've seen police reaching out to protesters to find common ground. We've seen volunteers cleaning up the devastation that looters leave behind. We've seen food and supplies offered to those in need.

We've seen neighbors and strangers join hands in solidarity.

Out of the broken glass, fires and anger we see others joining together for the common good of all backgrounds. ♡

You can choose what you see in any situation.

Good will prevail.

Because it has to ....

Namaste 🙏

6/3/2020

Mindful Moments ....

I saw so many things today being out and about.

It's easy to sit at home and hear what's going on out in the world and then turn the channel and move on with our lives. It's different to leave your home and "see" what's going on.

To see the barricaded shopping malls with police prescience, paddy wagons and check points. Oak Brook and Chicago Premium Outlets.

Tonight, I88 and Eola Rd exit closed with a flashing police car keeping everyone away from Aurora and Naperville.

Naperville, a war zone. Explosives being thrown at officers.

Snow plow trucks poised at the ready roadside for crowd control.

I come home turn on the tv and watch a police chase in the city reminiscent of OJ.

And did you know there's still a virus??

What has happened to everyone?? It's surreal!

The divide that has been created needs to be repaired. That comes from every one of us being accountable for our actions to create peace and unity. Actions speak louder than words. What can YOU personally do to end the divide that has been created and is being fueled by so many?

BUT above it all was this beautiful sunset I could only capture quickly as a passenger in a car. Thank you, Paula, for your personal Uber service to Batavia.

That's all I needed to see to remind me that we weren't created this way. This behavior was learned. Behaviors can change when we take personal responsibility to make those changes happen.

Sit back, take some deep breathes and enjoy a sunset.

Namaste 🙏

6/4/2020

Mindful Moments ....

William - the child with the heart of gold.

The young man who's "the dog whisperer".

The young man missing his piggie terribly.

He soothed Tito (yes, I love his name!!) and his owner through their first grooming today. He talked him through breathing exercises (adorable) and gently stroked his soft head.

Very proud of his compassion and empathy and a happy fur dad worried about his epileptic pup in a new environment.

No worries with this team.

My roses bloomed for the first time in years bringing hope.

It was certainly a first having a tire delivered by UPS and then the driver asked if I'd engage in Jeep talk before, he took off - of course I will!! He has 2 of his own and Jeep geek conversation ensued.

Tree and Alex I have a new rear bumper with bracket on the way - we might have to put that on and remove some fenders soon ... yes?!!

William went out to the backyard after dinner to play. Upon checking on him several times I couldn't find him so I went outside to see him floating on the pool lounger, with his clothes on, and a squirt gun in each cupholder love this kid!

He's still very sad and lost without Hershey. He was looking for something to help him find peace.

Hershey is back home now and in waiting for the right time to show him I realized it was time - although afraid it could go either way.

I am grateful for these services for our beloved pets /friends. He cried when he saw her tiny paw prints but suddenly looked relieved and relaxed that she was near him again.

We picked out a nice urn with photo compartment and a shadow box for her paw prints with photos for his wall next to the bed.

Tonight, he went to sleep feeling a little less lost and a heart a little more repaired. ♡

Thank you, Preston, for your magical Rainbow Bridge meditation tonight - a needed musical experience in a turbulent time for everyone - I always look forward to your next work of art.

Namaste 🙏

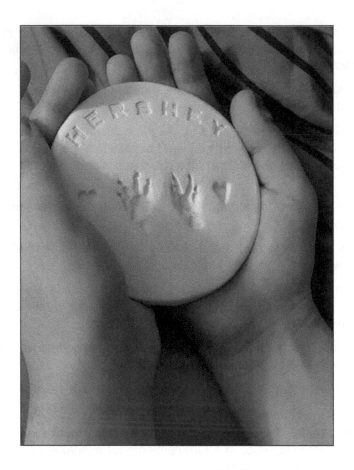

6/5/2020

Mindful moments brought to you by Caitlins 30th Birthday Celebration!

There may not have been a big party with bacon fry and bon fire but we had the best day with so much fun and such thoughtful gifts, videos and texts.

Our topless cruise with some old favorite tunes played mayyybe a little too loud and a visit to Nana. ♡

A little looting at Iron and Glass!

A dip in the pool.

Friends and family birthday parade.

A requested build your own chili dinner with homemade Key Lime Pie, presents and love.

Aside from birthday fun it was just great to see so many familiar faces in person - it's good for the soul.

Happy birthday my beautiful daughter!! My heart is full tonight.

Namaste

6/6/2020

Mindful Moments ....

Today was an amazing day with so many fun events BUT.

This photo, this meeting brought a few of us to tears today.

William knew he was meeting a new friend today who has alopecia and doesn't have many friends, like William.

He knew he likes Pokémon cards and Avengers, two things aside from age they have in common.

I asked him to get dressed so we could get on the road.

He came down dressed and said: "I'm wearing my Autism shirt so he doesn't feel alone." ♡

THATS what this world should be about people - a lot of adults should take the lead from a compassionate child and maybe change can happen.

BAM! ※

NAMASTE 🙏

6/9/2020

Mindful Moments ....

Feeling a bit down the past few days (no sympathy please that's not my purpose) so doing some reflecting is needed.

We all have "those" days, we feel let down sometimes - shit happens in life when you're not expecting it.

Summer school eLearning started today - he needs the routine but I didn't miss the battles through academics and one zoom after another to get to.

I AM grateful for the amount of work these teachers put into trying to help these kiddos learn at home - it's just as hard on them as it is on the kids and parents - we're all doing our best to get through these changes.

They're planning to start back in August but they'll be wearing masks all day and have guidelines to follow - should be interesting for special needs kiddos with textile sensory challenges - thankfully William has been wearing his without issue but some kiddos won't tolerate it.

So, water gun battles in the pool will open your eyes ... literally! This child has great aim, or maybe poor aim, but right in the eye every damn time!! The chlorine has cleaned out any crap in my eyes along with my sight.

We don't have much shade in the yard anymore so when William wants some quiet time he heads to the back corner of the yard, under the part of Grammy Barbs tree that reaches over our fence for some solace, smart boy.

While playing a riveting game of Pokémon cards on the deck before lunch yesterday, William announced that the birds were "fighting "- see photo.

We had a nighttime trip out to Batavia to pick up my van last night - William was excited to go until tired kicked in. A towel for a pillow and a reclined seat provided a 40-minute nap before bed.

There sure has been a lot of heartache here. Hershey's passing has really upended an animal loving child and her sister Marshmallow.

Marshmallow is really showing her loss. She seems scared, hides a lot.

So, I decided it was time to bring these 2 together.

Each day we've spent snuggle time and time in the room with Marshmallow - she comes out more when we're there and she's getting more socialized and they are forming a bond.

William avoided her for over a week - he had feelings he didn't know what to do with so he stayed away - she just wasn't Hershey.

I felt bad for both of them / they're both feeling a loss.

I still think she needs a cage mate - they are social animals and can die from loneliness - we'll look into that.

We need something to turn these frowns upside down.

Life has a way of showing you things that you need to see - sometimes they're good and sometimes not, sometimes they steal your joy - it's what you do with what life serves you that matters.

You embrace the good and don't let anyone take your joy with the rest.

Namaste

6/10/2020

Mindful Moments ....

William woke up happy and singing today! His bonding training with Marshmallow seems to be lightening his heart. ♡

Is there a full moon today? Cuz I feel like there should be a full moon today!

What a crazy, bazaar, eclectic, emotional day! Phew my emotional energy is spent!

Had a new client tell me "I don't wear a mask on my own property." really?? Do you have a Rona fence that zaps the germ before it reaches your grass?? Well sir, WE are wearing one to protect YOU because we could be bringing the Rona past your Rona line, thanks for thinking of us and our families!

Getting very laxed out there with the mask wearing!

Keep in mind that just because some restrictions are lightening up doesn't mean the rona is gone and the fallout is over.

I call it the next wave of the pandemic.

A lot of jobs being lost due to of the lack of income to companies during shut down. Some are returning to work and some are losing their jobs - we are closer but nowhere near an end to the ramifications of this.

With so many large events being cancelled this summer, my June 20th Elton John concert is now rescheduled to June 7th 2022 ... on a Tuesday ... yes, it's been rescheduled in 2 years! So, I've got that to look forward to.

In EJ's defense he didn't want to reschedule to next year only to have to reschedule again. He wants there to be a vaccine before he tours again so as not to put himself, his crew and his fans at risk - common sense, I think.

We're all feeling frustrated with so many limitations.

Life is about perspective as I've said. The more we're restricted the more we appreciate the freedom we had. If we're smart, IF, we won't take those freedoms for granted when this is over.

"Remember that not getting what you want is sometimes a wonderful stroke of luck." - Tenzin Gyatso, Fourteenth Dalai Lama.

Namaste 🙏

6/11/2020

Mindful Moments ....

I was happy to be working at one of my favorite places today ... Honey Bee Family Farm in Downers Grove.

Rosie is always up for a photo op and the goats, well, I was just an interruption to their sunning and living the good life.

A peaceful serene sanctuary that was an asset to my week and a loving sanctuary for these fur babies.

The situation at the Congressman Rush campaign office was disgraceful. BUT let's remember the thousands of officers who were actually out doing their jobs during those 5 hours of self-imposed R and R protecting our city. Those 13 officers don't define an entire force. I'm hoping the punishment more than fits the crime!

I've been watching William go through the 5 stages of grief, we talked about them tonight so he knows it's ok to have these feelings and not fight them.

It's awful to see him so sad. We've been in depression and confusion and today we hit anxiety, anger and bargaining. My heart hurts for him but he needs to feel the feels to get to acceptance - the hardest part of loving someone / something is losing them - sigh - he's getting there.

I think he needs a visit to Honey Bee Farm and do some fur baby snuggling I think Rosie wants a hug, or not.

Time seems to be slowly flying by if that makes sense.

There's the anticipation of wanting to get back to whatever our new normal will be and the realization that patience is a virtue.

I empathize with everyone who continues to suffer the ramifications of this pandemic with job losses, business uncertainty and financial hardship. I feel you.

All I can say is it's going to be ok. One day at a time, one minute at a time. Good things happen to good people and lean on family and friends for support.

We continue to be in this together.

Busy day tomorrow with some fun surprises.

"You're braver than you believe, and stronger than you think, and smarter than you think." - A.A. Miline

Namaste 🙏

6/12/2020

Mindful Moments ....

By 10am I had gotten some work done, walked Gypsy, baked and frosted cupcakes.

Off we went to Guiding Light Academy to pick up some summer school work. What a refreshing visit! Seeing some familiar faces of Miss Patty, Miss Tabria and Mrs. Deven brought back some "normal".

William adores Mrs. Deven and tried to break free to hug her.

She put on her mask, wrote him a special note on a post it and brought it the window for him.

Then she went to locked glass doors and they air hugged - that is one happy boy.

What an amazing team at GLA!

Off to do some banking then a care package drop and window visit with mom.

We talked for an hour by that window, cicadas screaming, lawn team swiftly fertilizing, so frustrating, so close and yet so far. Growing Covid cases at this facility keep us from having outdoor sidewalk chats. Sometimes it feels like it's just not going to end.

She's another special lady in William's life. He misses her - so they touched hands against the window - be still my heart.

Our afternoon was a Jeep top drop, balloon and sign toting parade to the home of a special friend for her daughter's 18th birthday and HS Graduation. Great turn out!

We've come to love these parades. It's something to look forward to, to plan for, to see familiar faces, watching smiles for miles after being in isolation for so long.

I feel for these high schoolers. I remember my prom and graduation. Their memories of their senior year will be quite different.

They are our future and have endured events in history we had never dreamed of when we were young.

Life was simpler for us but their history makes them survivors. Makes them strong, resilient, proud and capable of turning this devastated country around - I look forward to the goals they will reach. ♡

Back home for a quick dip in the pool before the cool weather this weekend, dinner and bedtime.

Now tonight I patiently wait for Caitlin's arrival so she can get on the road for both of us tomorrow and bring in some bread and butter.

It's been a week, that about rounds it up.

Today was filled with excitement, happiness, some frustration, seeing so many faces we're missing so very much and hope that we will all be together again soon.

Namaste 🙏

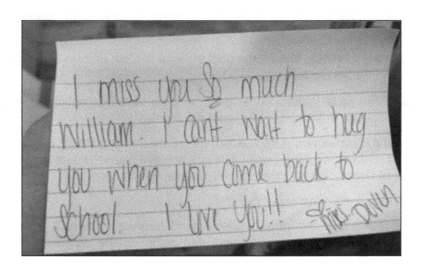

6/13/2020

Mindful Moments ....

Was this an absolutely gorgeous day or what?!! 70's, no humidity, sunny, blue skies and no bugs Loved it!

A very productive day here at the Mateblatts!

While Boston ran some errands and painstakingly tried to tackle a corroded bathtub spout and cartridge - to be continued - I tackled outdoor stuff!

But first William took me on a bike ride. I asked where we were going and he said "just follow me I'm taking you on an adventure!" I love surprises and adventures!

We rode through our neighborhood section, past a neighborhood grammar school where we saw a kickboxing class being taught in the parking lot - I need to get info on that!!

He continued past wagging dogs excitedly watching us ride by and other riders, walkers and joggers out enjoying the fresh air, wearing masks.

We headed home and hit the yard.

William put his Jeep up on "a lift" and "inspected" every "belt, piston and plug".

Gypsy chased rabbits, laid on the cool bricks and deck and barked, well, at everything! Living her best life. 🐾

Auntie Sarah gave William some geodes to explore. Our patio and a firm hammer opened them up to some cool discoveries!

I decided to rearrange our deck which then turned into cleaning out coolers from last summer, sweeping and OH! Look at these 2 bench seats I can clean and paint! Don't all small projects turn into many projects?!

They are cleaned, tomorrow I paint!

I'm excited to use my new cordless hand trimmer to spruce up some evergreens around our a/c unit and start sculpting the arborvitae into a privacy hedge. Pics tomorrow.

Ended our day with a grilled steak and sweet potato dinner with my favorite girl Caitlin. 💗

Fresh air, exercise and hard work will bring a peaceful rest.

The outdoors is my Zen, my happy place and tomorrow will be just as beautiful. 💗

Namaste 🙏

6/14/2020

Mindful Moments ....

Again ... BEAUTIFUL day! Warm in the sun, cool in the shade.

Mr. William came downstairs this morning with some interesting bedhead.

I showed him this photo. His response, "YEESH"!

William was on the struggle bus today so a break for a little Prime Video on the deck wrapped in a blanket, bedhead included.

At 6:10am - *grouchy* "Mooooooom! I'm so freaking tired!!"

Maybe you should sleep later? Just a thought!

Finally trimmed the evergreens around the a/c today with my new cordless trimmers ....

William "that's an awesome bush cutter."

I've learned to keep my snickering inside.

I'm sorry there are parts of my personality that will be 12 forever.

It's nice to have those unruly suckers tamed!

The bird bath is open, no social distancing for the birds - diving board goes in next week.

Took a little stroll through the yard to see my blooming flowers and found this little lady - my phone takes some darn good photos and the new perennials are coming along quite well Annika! I had enough to share with Lucie and here are doing great as well!

Mr. Turbo Powered pedal kart Jeep sprung a chain. I removed the screws and William insisted he was going to get the chain back on.

With fingers covered in oil he decided dad should do it and went in to wash his hands. He came back out and said "I can't get all the grease off" which we replied that was fine we'd get it off later.

Forgetting about that I later went in to use the bathroom and the last photo will show what I found ... BOYS!

The beautiful weather drew us outside, away from news, viruses, unrest and social media ... a beautiful weekend break from a turbulent world.

Namaste my friends 🙏

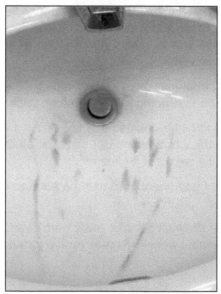

6/15/2020

Mindful Moments ....

Dare I say another gorgeous day?! Loving it!

There was a donation of books available on our neighborhood FB page. When I reached out for some for William and for his teacher, I had no idea the huge bin she had for us! Thank you, Paula for the pickup, just no extra time for me right now and I need to reach out to this wonderful lady for her kindness.

Miss Emily is very excited to have them!

From those books we kept, I saw William out on the deck reading them. That's a rarity! ♡

Since the gazebo was put up and the "redecorating" of the deck he wants to spend all of his time out there. It's peaceful and relaxing and a place to escape the isolation and emotions inside. ♡

Upon arriving home from some banking biz William grabbed the mail. Inside was a huge envelope from The Miracle League of Joliet- his baseball club that had to be cancelled for Spring ... Rona.

They sent the kiddos a care package of things to do, stickers, an inflatable baseball bat and a letter of encouragement. So very thoughtful!

What a great organization who knows how important inclusion is for these kiddos. Were really hoping to play ball in the fall!

All of my Clematis are doing great this year! One of the reasons I wanted to move the grill off the deck. The heat was killing them!

I have yet to paint my benches. Hoping life slows down a little by end of the week before weekend rain to get that done!

This new ESY schedule is really crazy! 3 Zooms per morning with the same amount of work to get done as 4th quarter.

ESY is important to Autistic kiddos. They need the structure, routine and change is difficult so having an entire summer with no academics or supports sends them backwards way too far.

William is doing well but it's ALOT on our plates when you work also - so I'm picking and choosing certain things each day to keep him doing well but not to frustrate him ... and me.

I was told last Friday he was one of their top students for attendance so I'm thinking some parents aren't pushing too hard or have kids who just can't deal with this - I understand that -

At least 2 more months of this feels like forever some days but going back to school with masks all day will be hard enough - I don't want him struggling academically also! Life is hard so suck it up buttercup!

His class zoom today had only 2 of the 10 kids on it. Probably the other parents throwing in towel feeling the additional stress also.

Oh, and every household should have a food service quality control officer on staff - ours is Gypsy - always so kind to check out the dinner plates and make sure everyone enjoyed their meal ... or maybe if they left anything easily snatched?!!

Tomorrow is another busy day so off to sleepy land.

Namaste 🙏

6/16/2020

Mindful Moments ....

Let's just say two main events highlight the day and the rest is gravy.

The first, and in William's opinion, most important, a drive by Plainfield classic car show!

Every Tuesday in the summer downtown Plainfield has cruise night. William lives for those nights but of course they've been canceled this year.

This classic car parade was supposed to take place two weeks ago but due to protesting it was postponed until today.

We found a spot on the route, put out a blanket and enjoyed the show.

It was brief but so exciting and made his week.

The most important, in my opinion, I GOT MY HAIR DONE!! Woohoo 5 months people!! Man did it get long but I like it so I'm keeping it for a while.

This ESY schedule is CRAZY!! I think every teacher and every parent who had to become a teacher, especially for special needs kiddos, when this is over should be honored, adored, worshiped, massaged and sent away on a month-long tropical vacation!!

Who am I kidding - I can dream!

Our neighborhood is at it with fireworks .... every night. Already tired of it.

Gypsy hit my "list" today. Looks like she was digging to another neighborhood!! Naughty girl!!

The day ended in Hershey tears SOOO Marshmallow to the rescue - her cuddles are different but have a similar affect. ♡

Off to work tomorrow! Sleepy time.

Namaste 🙏

6/17/2020

Mindful Moments ....

I arrived at my first appointment today. I set up Mr. Poop emoji Bluetooth speaker to listen to my favorite radio station when I realized his left eye had fallen out!

When questioned he swore to me that no unauthorized partying was done in my van overnight because social distancing was to be strictly adhered to.

I THINK NOT POOP, I THINK NOT! I hope it was worth it now that you've taken an eye out!!

Sooooo I haven't had time to paint my benches yet BUT the grill is moved off the deck which really opened it up! I like it!!

Maybe, just maybe I'll get those benches painted over the weekend!

After work and putting groceries away Sir W was looking for some attention and asked me to go out front with him ....

He's quite the entrepreneur and decided to start his own mobile restaurant on the sidewalk.

Although the menu was vast, I had the steak, baked fries and refreshing strawberry lemonade - which was quite the culinary artistry!

However, ... the health inspector arrived and shut the place down for unclean conditions and possible spider and mouse infestation.

Mr. W carefully cleaned all surfaces and crevasses, with the hose, and I'm happy to say, was given the green light to reopen immediately!

You missed out Auntie Lulu - he was waiting out front for you to come out for a walk and a hot dog!

Love his imagination! - he'll do great things in his life and I can't wait to see him reach for the stars.

I have much paperwork to do and another full day tomorrow so I bid you all adieu, wish you a restful slumber and a strong cup of coffee in the morning.

Namaste 🙏

6/19/2020

Mindful Moments x 2 days...

Yesterday my dog whisperer came to work with me to groom this adorable pooch.

Chewy is a doll, smothered William with kisses and love - the feeling was mutual.

I've heard some great dog names over the past 30 years but the most recent pup I booked takes first place.

The clients adopted a dog whose name is Alfred. They knew it was meant to be since their last name is Hitchcock.

That brought back memories of watching Alfred Hitchcock movies with my dad and always watching for his infamous cameo.

Speaking of watching things - have you ever watched tv upside down? Apparently, William finds the view appealing.

Today we had lunch on the "veranda" and a dip in the pool while dancing and singing to some classics on this beautiful warm summer day!

Gypsy has a few little habits she's created over her 11 1/2 yrs. Snatching Williams socks and hiding them is one and the other is snatching a washcloth off of our tub, tossing it in the air, playing with it then wipes her face on it - caught her in the act today - at least she uses it appropriately.

It's been a hot couple of days! Quite a switch from the cool breezes of last week but great pool weather!

William had a visit from a special friend yesterday and they rough housed in the pool and had lunch together - although I think he swallowed more water than lunch - she's an amazing person and really made William's day - the world needs more people like this woman.

We had a visit from Mr. Cardinal today - it's been a while. ♡

Although the pandemic has come with its challenges. It's also come with realizations and accomplishments.

I'm so proud of Williams accomplishments, his intelligence and his ability to persevere through some pretty challenging life events.

Due to circumstances beyond his control, William's anxiety has been an incredible challenge for him these past years and especially these past 8 months. He was testing at a 2nd-3rd grade level in academics when a few years ago he was ahead of the game.

In working with distance learning these past 3 months, without distraction and disturbing circumstances he is at and above his soon to be 6th grade level!

This shut down has given time to see how best children learn and with what circumstances they can fall between the cracks at no fault to their own. Now his teacher knows what he is capable of and she can help him reach his goals!

Hearing him say he's proud of himself yesterday was music to my ears! His self-esteem has not always been what it should be.

For this I am grateful! He is one of 2 maybe 3 students in class who continue to work hard through ESY. He has amazing courage and drive.

This weekend is set to be eventful so I'm off to watch another Friends rerun to fall asleep to.

"Never regret a day in your life. Good days bring you happiness and bad days bring you experience."

Namaste 🙏

6/20/2020

Mindful Moments ....

Today was to be the Elton John concert which has now been rescheduled to 2022. Only 717 days to go.

I watched Mr. Baby Squirrel run the fence top like an experienced tight rope walker chasing after a robin - robin got away, go figure.

We had a covert operation today and discovered that William is as tall or slightly taller than Annika- does that make him tall or her height challenged.

Annika and Tom thank you for your kindness in sending dinner home for us. 🤍

I had a ton of work to do when we got home and not having to think about dinner was fantastic! Every bite was delicious and Boston has a food baby kicking from the pasta! Gender reveal ... ohhh probably tomorrow morning.

While watching Mr. Squirrel I noticed a father and son playing tether ball in their backyard.

I had completely forgotten about the tether ball dad had expertly put up in our backyard as kids, cement base and all - dad did everything with purpose and perfection in mind - I didn't think they were a thing anymore.

Loving the storms rolling through!! We really needed the rain; the grass was turning to straw!

Happy Summer Solstice and Mercury needs to be evicted from friggin' retrograde!

Namaste 🙏

(This photograph explains why I end my prose as such for those who may wonder what it means 💭)

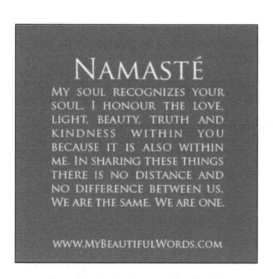

NAMASTÉ

MY SOUL RECOGNIZES YOUR SOUL. I HONOUR THE LOVE, LIGHT, BEAUTY, TRUTH AND KINDNESS WITHIN YOU BECAUSE IT IS ALSO WITHIN ME. IN SHARING THESE THINGS THERE IS NO DISTANCE AND NO DIFFERENCE BETWEEN US. WE ARE THE SAME. WE ARE ONE.

WWW.MYBEAUTIFULWORDS.COM

6/21/2020

Mindful Moments ....

A wonderful Father's Day was had by all!

After a morning of gifts and adoration we headed out to Rochelle.

I may have been slightly annoying to my Jeep mates as I like to crank up some Zepplin and Hendrix and sing, loudly lol Sorry guys you're stuck with me and that's how I roll!

Salt had a bottomless bone in wing, fries and a 16oz beer Father's Day special which was so generously provided to us by Caitlin and Cody - Thank you.

The weather was perfect, food delicious, company fun and entertaining, ran into Williams new friend and dined at a restaurant, outside, for the first time since February 2nd! Good for the soul.

Our day included a visit with our newest grand kitten Harvey who was too scared to hang around long. Mew, Lewis, Clark and Midas all made a brief appearance - well Midas was more of an "in your face pay attention to me" appearance.

I'm grateful for a wonderful family, a dedicated loving husband and a beautiful day to celebrate it all!

Wishing all dads, step dads, step -up dads, moms who double as dads, fur baby dads and dads in heaven a special, peaceful day doing what you enjoy.

Missing my dad today and every day. 💭

Namaste 🙏

6/24/2020

Mindful Moments ....

On top of eLearning and aside from a lovely visit to moms, the first 3 photos pretty much sum up Monday!

The hole in the pool foot bath was "an accident" however, he's a good shot and the target is a bit higher and to the right!!

The egg "jumped off the counter" or apparently didn't want to be a part of the coating for the fish for dinner, none the less all present scattered to avoid gooey clean up.

I was happy to see that my neighbors Christmas tree made it out for recycling or at this point would've made great kindling with a lovely aroma!

We also ran across a "really cool car" on our morning walk.

William enjoyed a McDonalds picnic under a tree and chatted with an elderly resident at Brookdale. They covered lunch, Minecraft and politics while I chatted with mom.

A beautiful day for a window chat. ♡

Mom was having a sad day Monday. Isolation is understandably frustrating. The walls start to close in and lack of family hugs is hard - I think our visit perked her up a bit and that's what matters. ♡

I don't know where the days are going - we're nearly in July and talk of back to school is on the table and waiting to see what that will look like. It will certainly be different.

Today was insanely full with managing a haircut for Gypsy - she's lucky I love her cuz man is she a pistol on the grooming table and tub!!

One day we'll look back at all of this laugh ...??

Tomorrow is a new day and the sun will rise again, make the best of it.

Namaste 🙏

6/25/2020

Mindful Moments ....

Look at this beautiful fence! Michael thank you for bringing this stain to my attention and for doing another fantastic job! I highly recommend my friend for your deck, fence etc. needs!

My yard is my Zen. My happy place. It's full of life and color and makes me smile! Everyone has their place of peacefulness and this is mine.

While the fence was being spruced up I and my intern were at work.

I gave Siri an address with the street of Falkner Dr.

William "FALKNER hehe that's funny FALKNER FALKNER FALKNER HAHAHA FALKNER FALKNER FALKNER THATS FUNNY" 😂

boys. 🙄

While brushing out a friendly golden retriever William asked,

"Am I getting paid overtime for this?"

Me "um no, it's 10am and you just started a half hour ago - do you think you're special or something??"

W "YES.I.DO."

Well, you are, but no OT!

He is quite the dog whisperer I will give him that.

As our day was ending, he pointed out a bump on his knee the size of a golf ball - Yesterday it was itchy, thought it was a mosquito bite. Today, it's itchy, hurts, is hot and swollen.

Off to urgent care - it was diagnosed as an infection from an insect bite for lack of different options as of now. He's taking antibiotics so we're hoping we caught it before it abscesses - that won't be pleasant!

He was great at the Drs. office especially with having to keep a mask on for a while.

When we walked out, he looked at the PA and said "thank you for taking care of me" she looked surprised; I'm sure they don't hear that much from anyone especially kids, he's a sweetheart!

We got home around 330, he was resting, so I went outside to check out the fence and water. Everything was thirsty after a dry week.

The flowers are all so vibrant and full of life after last weekend's rains and the warm weather and the perennials are filling in so nicely.

I need to get out and weed and straighten things up, haven't had time this week ... tomorrow ... maybe!

It's been a crazy week - one thing piled onto another but I'm grateful for being an accomplished multitasker - it gets me by.

I have a bunk mate tonight who's not feeling great so maybe I'll get to sleep early myself Bahahaha who am I kidding?!

"Great things never come from comfort zones."

So ... step into your courage zone and make great things happen!!

Namaste 🙏

6/26/2020

Mindful Moments (from yesterday) ....

While I had busy day of domestic goddess duties, William found some things to do, that of course involved me at times.

In preparation for a potential opportunity to play Pokémon tomorrow he made a new Pokémon deck planning to wipe his competitors off the board.

Harry Potter made an appearance. I'm grateful for past Halloween costumes for play later. Money well spent.

CHOICE PLUMBING came out to repair one of our bathroom tub faucets. I highly recommend them! They quoted us a fee before coming out and although there was one additional part needing to be replaced, only charged for extra for the part. Very reasonably priced.

You know how you get that anxious feeling in the pit of your stomach when the thought of the fees of a plumber come into play?! This is one plumber that debunked that concern.

We called several before one responded day's a later. They arrived timely, professional, masked, gloved, shoe coverings.

They explained everything as they went along, showed me the broken parts and were very understanding asking if I wanted a receipt sent to me instead of touching the paper one. He had mentioned whatever they touched in the bathroom and offered hand sanitizer after I signed the paperwork. Choice Plumbing - Mark, owner came out with an assistant 630---------.

While they were at work, I was fielding some phone calls, paperwork and food prepping for the week.

18 cups of spaghetti sauce with homegrown basil. Soon I can use tomatoes from my garden!!

Mom used to cut the acidity with sugar. Keeping it healthy I put in carrots. It does the same thing with their natural sweetness and you can't taste them once I emulsify all the cooked ingredients together and add some meat. It's frozen in freezer bags, 6 cups each, for future use.

A pot of chicken soup with tons of vitamin filled, tasty veggies, chicken salad with avocado mayo for lunches and Rhubarb Kuchen.

When Boston got home from work, he was telling me about a Dr. appt. he had. He was due to have his neck pain treated as shut down hit and they cancelled his procedure.

When asked the other day when he could move forward with the procedure the Dr. suggested massages. She said she'd write a prescription for that. Then she said "just have your wife give you a daily neck massage" - he said "can you write me a prescription for that?" Lol So she did. Well, I'm happy to do that in my spare time and want to know who's going to cover my fee?

So, I've added massage therapist to my list of human hair stylist, cook, business owner, teacher, POA for mom, video conference organizer, child activity chairman, therapist, gardener, dog walker shall I go on? - Im putting in for a raise with HR I'm wayyyy past due!

Today is another busy day - housework woohoo so we can enjoy the day tomorrow. As a kid, if we did our chores and helped out early, the rest of the day was ours, I go by the same rules. Work first, play later. ♡

Enjoy your day!

Namaste 🙏

7/1/2020

Mindful moments ....

I'm one who believes in signs, premonitions, spiritual connection.

Friday night I took out Mr. chicken here to make upside down beer can chicken for dinner Saturday night.

Saturday morning, I randomly grabbed this coffee cup.

On Saturday evening my BFF passed away, which I was unaware was coming up until 2 hrs. before.

What's the significance you ask?

I had said that literally everything reminds me of our friendship.

Many years ago, Tom told me that after stopping at Cabella's, on his many road trips north, he found this "really cool" beer can chicken roaster I just had to try so I bought one!

I haven't made beer can chicken for a long time but it was on the menu for Saturday night. It wasn't made until Monday. I didn't feel like cooking Saturday night.

The coffee mug I grabbed, Saturday morning, was given to me by Tom and Jim when they surprised me in Vegas some 14 years ago in a stretch limo when I was taken there for my birthday.

We had the most incredible night on the strip hitting roof top parties and Fremont Street ending back at their hotel for Whataburger then back to our hotel as the sun rose.

Monday William said "me no likey ..." something Tom said all the time that William never heard him say and I've never heard William say - he doesn't remember saying it or why.

One of Toms last post memes:

"In lieu of flowers throw a cup of hot coffee in the face of someone not wearing a mask" lol that would be Tom.

I could go on forever.

These 2 particular items came to the forefront on Saturday.

The most important take away from our friendship aside from the 40 years of amazing great times are the friends I've made as a result. Jim, Greg, Laura, Nick, Karen, Steve and Tom's family to just mention a few - Thank you Tom T.

My hubby surprised me with this Tito's sweatshirt and now I want it to be cold so I can wear it!!

We all need interruptions in our lives to be able to stop and reflect - these geese gave me a few more moments to contemplate my late appt arrival! I thought it was very sweet that the one at the back of the pack turned to the two who had stopped on the other shoulder and held traffic for them to catch up.

My pooches today - Mr. Coconut with the bumble on his snoot I won't be seeing anymore after over 10 years of service - he's moving away to Fla next week. Great family and pup - more goodbyes this week.

Henry and Bijou always make my day. Such good boys.

"The sorrow we feel when we lose a loved one is the price we pay to have had them in our lives" so we love on. ♡

Namaste 🙏

7/2/2020

Mindful moments ....

Went out to water my yard of life today and am happy to see a harvest on the horizon! The banana peppers and green peppers I grew from seeds in my aero garden and tomato plants were purchased.

I've had some trouble with my raised garden the last few years. One-year aphids enjoyed my spinach and snacked on tomato and pepper leaves until I brought out the Dawn and water so I'm happy to see growth.

William and I went to run a couple of errands today.

I was nearly out of coffee!!!

I set up Spotify on the stereo on random cruise songs that I enjoy.

The first song that came on was "Brown Eyed Girl". It has a very special meaning to me. As I was reflecting on a particular memory of that song a cardinal flew within inches of my windshield. Those who get this, will get it.

For some odd reason hardly any authorized service is notarizing right now - why?? Not some banks, currency exchanges ... why? I finally found someone to notarize what I needed but yikes the hoops I had to jump through!

I heard that Coca Cola sales are sliding Lesa! Where are you when they need you????

Shout out to Jiffy Lube in Bolingbrook for a speedy oil change and fluid check today as always. professional, polite and efficient! The old van has worked hard these past 2 months and put a lot of miles on!

Marshmallow obliged in snuggle time at bedtime tonight.

She may have a friend soon - it's time for something happy in our house and what's happier than a new fur baby??!

"Breathe, darling. This is just a chapter not your whole story." – S. C Lourie

Namaste 🙏

7/3/2020

Mindful Moments ....

Fireworks suck ... William can't get to sleep and Gypsy is in the bathroom to keep her from the noise and barking and it's only the 3rd ... that is all!

Sooooo I had an unexpected work day today - my groomers daughter is sick so she called off at 4:30am.

So, off my apprentice and I went.

He had the most awesomeist of days!

We saw a Lamborghini followed by a Farrari around the corner from a Chevelle SS - heaven!

My second client was in his driveway tinkering with one of his 3 custom built motorcycles while I groomed Mel - he's done 17 in all - William watched while the man revved the engine for him repeatedly and offered him a Pepsi - talk about a lucky day for William!! He also got a $5 tip for helping groom Mel - score!!!

Allene remember when we discussed turning down the radio to find an address?? Yep, did that today! Seems to help though!

In between work we managed to get in some school work due next Tuesday.

He watched one of those unboxing videos on YouTube - I don't get the fascination of someone else opening and playing with a toy but then I watched Otis, Mayberry's overserved citizen, lock himself in a cell to sleep off a bender every week.

William did a good job - he's learning well and yes; he is paid $5 for every dog he helps groom including cleanup and other chores. $25 today with his tip - not bad for 5 hrs. "work"!

We both needed a quick dip in the pool to relax after work.

Then s'mores after dinner - on the stove Laura and Lucie.

Hoping we get some sleep this weekend - fireworks going on 3 hrs. now and it's only 9pm.

Sunday can't come soon enough - 4th of July stopped being fun years ago.

Sweet dreams y'all!

Namaste 🙏

7/5/2020

Mindful Moments ....

I'm so grateful my neighbors had fireworks leftover today so that we could hear more tonight because 12hrs of them yesterday definitely weren't enough.

We spent our weekend reflecting, getting some projects started and spending time together. We've had a lot to manage this year. This past month has been a true test of resilience and perseverance and it was time to step away from phones and social media for a bit and just be.

Thank you, Karen, for filling in some blanks and helping to heal a broken heart. I am forever grateful for your friendship and we will always share a special bond. ♡

William and I worked on his memory box for Hershey. He picked out some great photos and was very happy with the outcome. It will have to be hung next weekend, for now it sits next to his bed.

It was haircut weekend at the Mateblatts! So happy William was ready to cut his hair! I waited it out knowing that hair hanging in his eyes wasn't going to cut it (no pun intended) - he's very happy it's shorter. Boston loves his peewee Herman look - I think it makes him look debonair, don't you?!

However, I left the 2 of them alone for 20 minutes to shower and came down to blue hair and silly string everywhere - time well spent boys.

Thanks to Auntie Lulu we had s'mores .... on the stove!

Two cardinal fly overs while in the pool this weekend, a brief landing on a fence post, momentary eye contact and flew off to do their thang - if they were any closer, they could've landed on our heads.

We have a project going on in the backyard corner. Today we hacked down and cleaned out the brush and put down weed killer. Project to be continued ....

I'm grateful for a home to improve upon, a pool to cool off in after a hard day's work, family time, hope, happy memories and the opportunity to wake up to a fresh start each day, not everyone has that opportunity.

Hope you all had a safe, pleasant weekend.

Namaste 🙏

7/7/2020

Mindful moments ....

This pretty much sums up our day. ♡

Aside from the usual busy work, errands and a window visit with mom of course.

She's soooo tiny, only about 2 months old, scared of the giant humans and in her forever home.

She looks like a raccoon so her name took a while to come up with. Bandit was an early suggestion but William's face lit up with Rocket.

Rocket is the raccoon from Guardians of the Galaxy, a favorite show of Williams, for those who may not know.

I'm not sure how fond of her Marshmallow is since she sniffed her and then nipped her ear but it will take some time to slowly introduce them - I think they will become fast friends.

New day, new life, new love.

Namaste 🙏

7/8/2020

Mindful Moments ....

Today was Rocket and Marshmallows mini-introduction play date.

How nice it is to pause from our troubles and enjoy a new little life exploring her new world.

And an older fur ball trying hard to accept an annoying little ball of energetic disturbance.

They did well for a good 20 minutes, Marshmallow's tolerance was surprising, then back to their separate homes they went - a good first experience.

A little dehydration issue for William kept us inside today with lots of hydration - don't think his symptoms didn't have Rona crossing my mind!! He's fine now!

The rain has been nice! Lucie and I had dueling sprinklers the past few days - crunchy grass and dead flowers aren't pleasant!

We didn't use it today but I'm soooo grateful for our pool. Especially with this heat and being limited on things to do and places go.

Hoping for the heat to break so we can get in some batting practice! Looks like Miracle League will be starting in the fall with a lot of guidelines and safety precautions but I think it's great - something to look forward to!

Congrats to Boston's kids' team at school who again won the Diamond Challenge in Shark Tank in a nationwide competition!! A shining star in a stressful month.

"What lies behind us and

what lies before us are

tiny matters compared to

what lies within us."

- Ralph Wado Emerson

Namaste 🙏

7/9/2020

Mindful Moments ....

I just spent some time outside watering my happy flowers and having porch talk with my lovely friends and neighbors!

With the heat it's rare to see anyone outside but timing was perfect at sunset, little breeze and mosquitos ... they tend to crash and ruin parties!

2020 I have dubbed the year that keeps on giving. Our a/c went out this afternoon so we've got that going for us.

Illinois Climate Control will be out tomorrow morning to either fix or bid adieu to our 25 yo unit - hoping for a fix !

We're fine - furnace fan circulating whatever cool air was left in here at 3pm and fans - Gypsy is not a fan since it's 78 in here at the moment and rising but then she's spoiled.

William suffered through the evening with a 1/4 of this Caramel Apple Pie - it was quite a sacrifice but he's a trooper!

While chatting with Lucie our evening ended with an adorable Frenchie out for a walk who could NOT resist dragging her human over to us allowing Lucie and I to scratch her happy, wiggly belly. Ended our crazy day with a smile 😊

"You don't always

need a plan.

Sometimes you just

need to breathe,

Trust, let go and see

What happens."

Mandy Hale

Namaste 🙏

7/10/2020

Mindful Moments ....

We now have air conditioning and with a quick fix! It was the flux capacitor OK maybe it was just the capacitor it's just more fun to say it the other way.

One of those many modern conveniences you take for granted until you don't have it!

Cody my living room meat is now preserved and frozen.

It was cooler outside this morning so pooch and I hit the deck with breakfast and work - nice breeze and clouds kept it pleasant.

Sleeping was ok - fans and the house closed up helped - just don't ask Gypsy what she thought of sleeping on a leather couch in what she viewed as "The Sahara Desert". - it didn't get higher than 78 - spoiled.

Gypsy was also not impressed with the storm last night - she brought her overheated, scared, furry butt up to the bedroom and slept next to me, on the floor ... by the fan ... or was it her master plan??

We apparently got a lot of rain - that makes me happy, saves on the water bill.

It takes a savvy parent to turn pool time into a lesson of money counting, exercise and teaching goals! $4 in quarters, tossed in the pool, .50 cents at a time, had to be found and added up then he could keep it - cha ching!

The trick is to find out what motivates your kids and give them something to work for.

Of course, Boston uses this tactic as well to pay William a dollar for every beer he fetches on the weekend while Boston relaxes in the pool - William reminded me, several times, you still owe him $3.50 for last weekend!

We had an anatomy lesson while swimming today. With boys it's either farting, burping or laughing at body part names.

I think I've finally made it clear that boys don't have "peniles" as he likes to call them, they have ... well you know and girls don't have "peniles" they have .... again, you know.

My son walked up to me with his hands dangling under his chin, fingers spread out and wiggling around.

Son: "Mom, you like my beard of testicles?"

Me: "... what? ... beard of ... what??"

Son: "My beard of testicles ... I'm an octopus!"

Me: "TENTACLES kiddo, they're called tentacles!"

Son: "Yeah, that's what I meant."

Namaste 🙏

7/11/2020

Mindful Moments ....

This first photo is pretty amazing for me. William is a very smart young man but struggles with fine motor. He despises hand writing and coloring because it's difficult for him. Uses AT device for school work.

148

But today, on his own, he decided to draw/create/color some graphics for an Incredibles game. I was blown away and so happy to see! I don't even remember the last time he drew anything.

We had a busy day ahead so I threw a pot roast in the crock pot and off we went!

He occupied himself well today while Boston and I spent many, many hours turning an overgrown corner of the yard into a future extended raised veggie garden for next Spring.

His excellent idea, he knows how much I love my gardens but I'm wondering how much he's regretting that idea after the work we put in today.

Tilled, shoveled, leveled, ground cover, hauled rocks, mulch, galvanized tubs, many trips for supplies and pick-ups. I looooove working outside! A good 7 hoursish later with a break for a down pour we about finished but ran out of energy.

Finishing touches tomorrow when it's not 97 and humid.

For me, there's a great feeling of accomplishment to do your own hard work and be able to see your efforts pay off.

As I've said, my yard, nature is my Zen. Where I find peace and mindfulness. Time to reflect and even listen to some music and sing and dance - thank you for appreciating my backyard concert, Lucie.

The thunder is rumbling and wind has picked up. Gypsy is nervous and always wants to go outside when it's storming - it's as bad as fireworks for her - I just chased her around the kitchen table to catch her (how's that visual for ya?!) - she's in the powder room with a blanket and the fan on until this passes or she just barks to go out.

I'm tired, a rewarding tired and hoping this storm passes without incident.

LIFE IS SO IRONIC

It takes sadness to know happiness,

Noise to appreciate silence,

And absence to value presence.

Namaste 🙏

7/15/2020

Mindful Moments ....

We had a lazy Sunday after our yard work Saturday!

My 2 buddies lounged with me watching cartoons - they were very sweet - Gypsy doesn't typically sit close to anyone ... willingly.

William and I took a bike ride to the lake, played some Pokémon Go, watched the fluffy clouds pass over the vibrant blue sky and then a bug got on my screen! ... oh, wait that's an airplane ... ooops

Apparently, it was bike washing day - I remember washing my bike as a kid - shining it up and getting it ready for my next ride. I loved my bikes - I've always had one and would ride more if I had time.

As kids, off of Madison and 67th place - we'd ride our bikes all the way down Madison, on the road, no helmets - can't believe we survived lol - no sidewalks then - to the Convenient store, a little neighborhood grocery store next to a gas station - they had full service there! What a luxury! They even cleaned your windows and checked your oil - that was service!

We'd get some candy then ride back home. It was safer then. Madison is a much busier street now and has a side walk.

Annika cleared out her perennials and passed on quite a few to me which I also shared with Lucie.

I took a chance and planted some in half whiskey barrels - boy was I tipsy trying to empty those barrels!!

They brought the first butterfly I've seen in my yard for years!

I got some food prep in on Monday! Another of my favorite things to do! I won't bore you with details, just photos and a surprise visit with my favorite daughter Caitlin and Williams buddy Cody.

I don't want to get into a debate about masks so I'm just going to say I wear mine to protect YOU and I wish everyone would go back to taking this seriously and wearing theirs to protect ME and my family.

Not one person I came in contact with today wore one at work - they did in the beginning - I sure as hell don't want to end up like Fla, Texas and the other sun belt states but I guess not many care anymore, but I won't stop wearing mine.

A clients 4-year-old, being allowed to come near me and my van without a mask asked why I was wearing one???!!

I said to protect you and your mom.

He said but I'm not sick and you're not sick so why wear one.

I said we don't know that ...and I just came from 3 other people's houses who weren't wearing them - I don't want to bring it to you.

His mother rolled her eyes and said "it's the corona virus son."

What the ever-loving F*%€???

stepping down ...

With talk of returning school and what that may look like has W a bit nervous and is my roommate tonight.

Whatever their final decision is, what I do know, is that our kids aren't going back full time so we need to be prepared for that for who knows how long ... the year that keeps on giving!

I call "Me Time" in 2021!!!! And aloooot of it!!!

Trina, I thank your boys for introducing William to "It's Raining Tacos" and Alexa for knowing what "repeat" means ... a million times - I miss you guys - had hoped to come out this summer.

Missing a lot this year but finding the silver lining in what we've been handed.

I wish you a peaceful evening, find the joy and be kind. ♡

Namaste 🙏

7/17/2020

Mindful Moments ....

So, William and I did a thing today and saved another baby girl Guinea Pig!

Let's just say Marshmallow would sooner eat Rocket for a snack than become roommates.

It wasn't a matter of them getting used to each other and Marshmallow has already decided that she hates Rocket. The teeth chattering was normal but the aggression and attacking and this morning coming back with some fur in her mouth was the end to that!

Rocket is just a baby and needed a friend. Maybe when the little girls get bigger Marshmallow will be more accepting ... maybe ...

No name yet but now we have a raccoon and a skunk.

They needed each other they were both lonely and they bonded almost immediately. When I saw them in one house together cuddling up against each other - I knew we made the right decision. Be still my heart ♥

We'll just have to do separated play times and be sure to keep Marshmallow part of the family.

My little apprentice helped out with Tasha and Lady yesterday. Presley however (not pictured) had been skunked and William wanted nothing to do with her (nose).

We made it out to visit mom for an hour and a half chat yesterday! We laughed and enjoyed each other's company while William enjoyed blanket time and his trucks.

Thankful that she's on the first floor and at least we get "screen time" the old-fashioned screen time.

William was sporting his musician mask in Walgreens - he's good about wearing it and understands the importance of protecting others - he leads by example. ♡

"The best love is unexpected

You meet them by fate and

it's an instant connection."

Namaste 🙏

7/18/2020

Mindful Moments ....

Today I said my final farewell to my BFF.

Mixed emotions of course. Heartbreak and yet in reflecting after he passed, I have so many friends in my life I wouldn't have without him and I saw a few of them today.

Fun stories, tears, laughter and sharing 40 years of everlasting memories.

See you on the other side my friend. Always in my heart and that of many. ♡

Lucie thank you for hanging with William today so we could be away worry free! He loves you and went to bed with the blanket you made him.

Grammy Barb struck again with front porch donut delivery - William will be a sugary happy guy in the morning.

You are both so good to all of us - we are blessed with your friendship.

I bought a couple of cool toys recently that I decided to play with a little tonight!

This around your neck reading light is as good as I thought it would be! Three brightness levels and adjustable! Now I can read and do my crossword puzzles while someone else is asleep.

I had also picked up an Omron blood pressure monitor for William.

Since the rona hasn't allowed for our monthly psych office visits where he is always weighed and blood pressure taken since February, I decided to do it here.

Of course, with my crazy life, I bought this 2 months ago and just now opened it.

And I had to play with it.

My BP is always low! I'm interested to check his tomorrow - he's been a bit off lately with stomach issues and tunnel vision (he's seeing his optometrist Monday) could be dehydration but we'll see what a professional says. 🙏

"Grief only exists where love lived first." ♡

Namaste 🙏

7/20/2020

Mindful moments ....

Well so far, the district has voted down a return to school with remote learning with another meeting to make decisions. With all due respect, parents have jobs and need to make plans, make a darn decision please so we can move forward this holding pattern is frustrating!!

Marshmallow had a special one on one yesterday. As much as she doesn't like the little ones, she needs attention too! William misses his cuddle bug Hershey. I'm hoping one of our new babies turns out to be a cuddler for him.

There was an hour and a half riveting game of chess yesterday. Moreover, and hour and half for ME!

A pretty little lady opening her eyes to the sun this morning on our walk. I don't see as many colors as in the Spring but if you look hard enough, they're there.

Gypsy has had some tummy issues the last few mornings. Early rises for both of us. I think she's feeling better tonight. Ate a whole bowl of food and is sleeping on the landing in her usual spot. Hoping for a good night's sleep for both of us.

William colored today!!! Being home must reeeeaaalllly be getting to him! But who doesn't love coloring in a coloring book as cool as this one that your uncle gave you?!

He's been having some health issues lately. Most recent concern has been tunnel vision so we started with an eye exam. No pathological problems thank fully BUT I enjoyed his eye exams! This is his eyeball! Looks like a planet! Pretty cool!

With his other symptoms I'm thinking potassium deficiency - a bit more research to do.

After For Eyes - who was quite efficient with safety protocols I must say including temp ck at the door and hand sanitizer - we went for a long bike ride. Actually, went to a park, no one there and hand sanitizer in my backpack. Something a bit "normal" was nice but always on guard for safety.

Took a few brief stops to enjoy the beauty of nature and to breathe in some fresh air, watch a few fishermen, read a book, relax to the sound of a waterfall and the cat tails bouncing in the breeze. Peaceful.

We have beauty all around us - we just need to be open to it.

Preston your talk yesterday was perfectly timed - our angels are always with us - and want we've got! So how blessed are we?!!

Namaste 🙏

7/22/2020

Mindful Moments ....

Diggin deep tonight!

Some pretty flowers from yesterday's morning walk - seek and you shall find.

Got some baking in yesterday afternoon while William's para was here. Sorry guys it's healthy stuff.

Blueberry Yogurt "Cheesecake" and Zucchini Brownies - my own non-guilty pleasures!

On the advice of my friend Shelley, I ordered William Raddish subscription, a monthly cooking kit for kids.

Each month is something different - this month we lucked out with his favorite foods! In his kit were chop sticks, a sushi roll, apron, recipes, grocery lists, directions on using chopsticks and some Asian history!

He loves it and although we don't have the ingredients for these recipes yet he hopped right into putting on his apron and cutting veggies for our Tuscan Salmon dinner last night! Which he had 2 helpings of.

Today started off a bit rough. After ending our last day of summer school, we ran some errands and went for a bike ride and relaxing chat at our favorite spot.

A trickling waterfall, light breeze and busy wildlife can bring serenity to troubled minds.

The cat tails remind me of when I was a kid and we'd walk over to the "swamp", a block over, and cut down cat tails - "punks" we called them.

We'd dry them out in the sun and light them to keep bugs away and my brother would light fireworks in July.

The swamp, that we were certain had a swamp monster in it, is now a beautiful park with sprinkle pad, fishing, ports potties and picnic tables.

We used to ice skate there too, before that and not wearing helmets became an issue - the good old days ....

"And when the broken-hearted people living in the world agree

There will be an answer, let it be

For though they may be parted, there is still a chance that they will see,

There will be an answer, let it be ..."

Namaste 🙏

7/23/2020

Mindful Moments ....

Before heading off to work I took a few moments to breathe in some nature, clear my mind before a long day of work with William.

My flowers were awake and ready to be admired.

Mr. Squirrel was greedily munching away his pre-winter stash - a snack or devouring the evidence perhaps.

William tolerates going to work with me. He helps, gets paid, is learning the lessons of a hard day's work, pushing through when you're tired and want to quit and throwing in some dance moves and air guitar while poop emoji Bluetooth plays some Spotify.

We talk a bit, spat a bit, watch for cool cars, eat lunch on the run and are both glad ESY is over!!

He found out what it was like to put in an 8 hr day today, unexpectedly.

Make it a point to check out my friend Preston Klik on FB Sunday afternoons at 4 and Thursday evenings at 9 for his breathtaking, emotion filled live sound meditations - tonight's will be up for about a day - take 20 minutes of your day and find some peace.

The Miracle League, William's baseball organization, is putting together a cookbook fundraiser. I got in my recipes and photo under the wire. Can't wait to see the book put together for these special needs' kiddos with a bunch of great recipes.

"I'm starting with the man in

the mirror

I'm asking him to change

his ways

And no message could have

been any clearer

If you wanna make the world

a better place

Take a look at yourself, and then

make a change."

Michael Jackson

Namaste

7/24/2020

Mindful Moments ....

On our walk this morning Gypsy and I saw this SUV "securely" propped up in this driveway - I suppose it's a good use for dumb bells if you're not using them.

I had heard there was a coin shortage but found it hard to believe because we aren't at a loss for it, but here ya go ... coin shortage - so my clients are partial paying us in coins because they can't use them elsewhere. I guess there's no coin shortage and we may have to stop taking them because you can't deposit them at the ATM!

I needed bandanas for work I get at Hobby Lobby for .99 each ... shelves were wiped out! I took what they had and William scored a couple model cars and craft set.

We made a deal that all activities wouldn't be done in one day to keep him busy for a while - both cars, done today - going to be a looong 3 weeks before school starts again!

He did a great job though making them himself. I haven't seen model cars like this before. He's done several Snap-Tite models but these were Legoesk on the inside but looks like a regular model car on the outside. Pretty cool.

I think this Robin that landed on the fence post was annoyed with our music and squawking to have it turned down ... or hungry ... either way, valid.

Threw in some food pics for fun - this is the excitement in my life right now. I'm as tired of coming up with meals to cook as William is of 5 months of being home every day with the same toys and no one to hang with but me.

William was mortified with my dinner:

"You put cashews on your Brussel sprouts???? What a way to ruin cashews!!!!"

He loves cashews ... Brussel sprouts, not so much!

If you like some cream in your tea or coffee but don't use dairy, Nutpods are great! Made with almond and coconut milk, original or several flavors (find them on Amazon, of course).

Tension is rising in the Mateblatt compound. Running out of things to do, new ideas, too much "together time" although William doesn't think so 4 months 24/7 and counting.

Baseball is back so we've got that going for us.

When you think you can't fit one more thing on your plate BAM a pandemic hit and you become a teacher, therapist, entertainment committee leader and alone time consists of sleeping, whatever that is! Are you with me moms?!!

Good times!!

Welp, gotta rest up for another day at camp Mateblatt!

Namaste homies 🙏

7/27/2020

Mindful Moments ....

Yesterday we had the pleasure of celebrating the birthday of a special little friend with a birthday parade.

William loves to hang out the roof and sing happy birthday - it's nice for all of us to get out and leave home at home.

What a nice surprise to be given big bright smiley face cookies from the birthday girls mom - sure made William's day - guess which color he ate and what color his poop was today.

Since today was kind of rainy it was a good day to get some things done at home, as much as possible anyway.

Some laundry, some work, some food prepping, some puzzle puzzling and the highlight of my day was when William actually wanted to try my lunch.

The best part was as he was gobbling it down, he asked what are these noodles in here? (He loves Chinese food and noodles).

I had him take a few more bites and then told him they're bean sprouts.

I guess I'll be sharing my prepped lunch with him and will need to make more - I'm so excited he's eating a bunch of veggies in there and doesn't realize it!! But I'm requested to add more of that "soy sauce stuff" to his plate - it's coconut aminos - glad he likes that too it's better for him!

Tried a new sweet treat recipe "Grasshopper Cookies" holy moly are they good!! They're already hidden - he's not getting my healthy cookies!!!

Highlight of Williams day was his monthly delivery of Hot Rod Magazine! Check out that smile.

Welp Dist. 202 goes back remote 8-31 - we'll see if it effects our school in the coming days ....

When life knocks you down

calmly get back up, smile and

very politely say -

"you hit like a b*tch!!"

Namaste 🙏

7/28/2020

Mindful moments ....

So, our walk today we discovered that apparently "eviction" means literally throwing out your home!!

William mastered chop sticks the modified way!

We both needed a visit from Auntie Paula other than to stay with William while I work.

A beautiful day to hang in the pool and thanks for helping to break up the monotony around here.

We had a little visitor at the pool. The little guy seemed to take a liking to William, hung around him and kept coming back.

Since William received his Raddish chef set he's been dying to cook but we didn't have all of the ingredients we needed for his Asian meal. So tonight, he whipped up chicken tenders, chicken flavored rice and corn pretty much on his own.

I had thawed out chicken for dinner and he wanted chicken tenders so we modified the meal, he sliced up them up into tenders, he shook them up in seasoning in a bag and then put them in the air fryer sprayed with olive oil.

He's learning to use a butcher knife which he's terrified of LOL thank God! But he's showing interest in cooking which I think is fantastic!

And because this turned out so tasty, he can't wait to cook again! Can't wait for him to be cooking dinner once in a while!!

Missing my family, a lot today - it's been a long time since we were together at Christmas - maybe we'll see each other for Easter 2021? stupid rona!!!

Namaste 🙏

7/29/2020

Mindful moments ....

Before leaving for work I needed a stroll around in the yard. A little serenity if you will. I've been waiting to see what flowers would surprise me in this center perennial planter. I am pleasantly surprised.

Paula thank you for always being so good to William. I never worry when I'm away.

I can't wait to use the "fits anything" lids - a genius idea!

Thank you, Terre, for the special surprises after Bohdie's groom today.

William LOVES his "hovercraft"!! Such a cool toy! He let me play with it too.

You are kind, thoughtful and have impeccable timing.

PSA outside is best for this toy.

Took these shots at Walgreens entrance - if it reminds one person to care about others more than themselves then I've done my job.

I first saw this woman with her bed on her roof on 55. That mattress is tied so loosely it was hovering 2 feet above the car and ready for launch!!! Always amazes me how these "attempts" to secure something in a car are allowed to happen - the spirits were on her side today!

"Be thankful for the bad things in life

They open your eyes to seeing

the good things you weren't paying

attention to before."

Namaste 🙏

8/1/2020

Mindful Moments ....

Certainly, a different kind of 1/2 birthday party for William, Oliver and Evi.

Masks, hand sanitizers, touchless foaming hand soap, Isopropyl alcohol, designated sanitized areas and rubber gloves among tasty treats and birthday gifts.

It's almost become so normal to be forever conscious of germ safety and distancing ... I miss hugging.

But to have an afternoon to relax, laugh and be with people you love is something you've truly come to appreciate.

Our usual large group down to a few. Very much missing our big crazy group but keeping it safe now ensures us ALL being together next year.

Our new world has kept up apart and togetherness is so good for the soul.

Trina and Jeff, we love you and the boys so very much and are forever grateful for your long journey to spend the day with us.

Thank you, Jeff, for "taking the wheel" so I could sit back and just be, that is rare.

Trina thank you for "seeing" and asking what you could do for ME - those words alone touch my soul at its core.

It was the perfect day to rejuvenate our hearts.

I will not miss this year when it ends nor will I miss its challenges and hardships but I will carry with me the lessons we've learned from those challenges, the many positives that came from it and the happy memories such as today to remind me that love prevails ... near and far.

Namaste

8/2/2020

Mindful Moments ....

Gypsy to left of me,

William to the right,

here I am stuck in the middle of a camp out again.

Someday I will sleep, today is not that day.

Williams Jeep pedal kart went in for surgery last week and is being returned tomorrow - he doesn't know - he'll be so surprised! He loves that thing, rides it hard which is why the chain stretched but my handy friend Greg fixed it and will discreetly deliver tomorrow.

It was pajama day here at the Mateblatts, well for William and I.

Boston finished straightening up, I caught up on 2 days of work and William played Minecraft, began a Lego set, drove around the most awesome 55 BelAir RC car ever, did his laundry and there may have been some napping during a Bruins game - understandable, who could stay awake during a Bruins game?!

Sometimes it's nice to have a day to just catch up, hang out with happy memories of a fulfilling weekend.

William is snoring and Gypsy is using the couch as napkin, I'm tired.

"Don't let the internet rush you,

No one is posting their failures"

Namaste 🙏

8/3/2020

Mindful moments ....

Sometimes it's the simple things that make a wonderful day. 🤍

Boston earned huge brownie points surprising me with a 5# bag of my favorite Guatemalan coffee. The green beans travel directly from the fields in Guatemala to The Coffee Lab at North Central College for roasting. This bag was roasted July 28th and, in my hands, today - I can't wait for morning.

It's a rainy cool, open the patio door, day to do some food prepping for the week, finish the laundry, keep, it chill kind of day.

I do this every week so we have healthy food choices even when we're pressed for time.

I'm in a group, actually a couple of groups but this one, who has weekly mindset/nutrition zooms for a few more weeks is energizing, validating, educational and uplifting. Today was one of those zooms.

An amazing group sharing vulnerabilities, wins, challenges and getting answers. I've met and connected with several wonderful women over the years and have created lasting friendships from this group ♡ Landa, Shelley, Linda, Liana, Jody, Kristy and Katie just to name a few

Find your tribes, like-minded people, your people and embrace the connection ♡ they make me a better person. ♡

William finished one of his birthday Lego kits while I prepped. He folded and put away his laundry, brought in the grocery bags and caught up on Minecraft - his Zen kind of day - except for the chores.

People come into our lives for a reason, a season or a lifetime - find their purpose and what they're here to teach you - learn from them.

Namaste 🙏

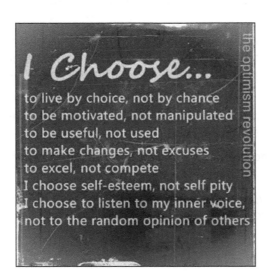

8/4/2020

Mindful moments ....

My day began with a fresh brewed cup of Guatemalan coffee on the deck while Gypsy enjoyed the cool morning air.

I welcome temperatures like this after 100-degree heat indexes. Warm in the sun cool in the shade ... perfect!

William had his Jeep pedal cart returned from surgery and loved taking it for a ride this morning. Fun to see my van hard at work at a neighbor's house while out for a walk.

The highlight of our day was a necessary trip to Honey Bee Gardens.

This is another Zen place for me and William. The serenity, hospitality, welcoming animals, self-sustaining farm, waterfall, paddle boat, baby chicks and nature ... so much nature - you just breathe it in and feel renewed.

Our paddle boat ride proved lucrative in discovering sun bathing turtles, diving ducks, mysterious figures under the surface and tranquil aerating waterfalls alongside this beautiful well-kept home.

Sometimes you need to leave your safety zone to venture out and find what soothes your soul.

If you're local, make an appointment with Cindy to spend time at the farm - you will never be greeted with more acceptance and carefree nature - except when I'm there to groom the dogs - they run in the other direction deep down they love me.

The Honeybee Households painting nights, children's nature exploration and crafts, small parties etc.

Check out the photos then set up an appointment - do your soul a favor and forget about your troubles for a while.

Thank you, Cindy, we needed this peacefulness - it's the first night in a while William fell right to sleep.

Namaste

8/7/2020

Mindful Moments ....

With school starting the 19th we're trying to get out a little ... before everything shuts down again.

We made our reservations at the zoo, parked in the south lot (nice!) and headed on in.

I am extremely impressed with how Brookfield is handling their safety procedures!

No contact everything! No exchange of money just debit or credit, the playgrounds are closed, the indoor exhibits are closed, indoor restaurants are closed but there is plenty to do out and about in the zoo!

I was however pretty disappointed in quite a few of the other attendees of the zoo not wearing masks and not keeping social distance. Why, why, why???

There are signs everywhere, every zoo employee is wearing a mask and gloves, there are zoo employees walking through the zoo with a loudspeaker telling people "You are now entering a crowded area please make sure you have your face coverings on and keeping social distance". I can't tell you how many families I saw without masks or even better yet the parents were not wearing masks but the kids were?? ... What??

I would love to know how wearing a mask has become such a big deal and such a political statement! It's everyone's responsibility PERIOD!

I am proud of William, an 11yo child with ASD, to voluntarily wear a mask for 2 hours at 85 degrees outside, take it down when no one was around and knew when to put it back up - he's an amazing example to rebellious adults.

They have Dino's on display which is a nice distraction for kids like William who prefer to play on the playground at the zoo which are all currently closed.

There are giant green dinosaur foot prints throughout the zoo that you follow from dinosaur to dinosaur. And then there's a huge dinosaur display where they had the Lego display a while back.

The children's petting zoo was open and free to everyone so we took a stroll through there and saw the wallabies, the alpacas, the reindeer and the goats although you could not go in and socialize with the goats but it was nice just to be among the animals.

I'm not sure that we'll go back after what we saw today but it was nice to get some fresh air and do something "normal."

Thank you to those of you who are living life but doing it safely to protect my family and yours.

Namaste 🙏

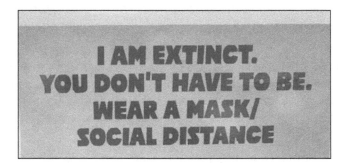

8/8/2020

Mindful Moments ....

We went about our weekend routines today as usual.

A ride out to moms for a window visit with a dedicated William lunching on a blanket and playing a video game. For some reason the bees were attracted to him giving him a sting on his finger.

The moment was pleasantly interrupted by his friend Jack zoom calling him.

He and Jack are buddies and haven't seen each other since March.

When Jack initiated a zoom last night for the first time William was literally in tears. He's missed him so much.

William is a hugger, a social people person and like a lot of us miss people, hugging and connection - as annoyed as I get with video games, thank goodness for other uses of the technological variety at a time like this.

Wherever we go he says hello to everyone and wants to pet every dog - I've seen people's frowns turn to smiles and pleasantly shocked looks on people's faces that a young person is so kind and welcoming.

A simple spoken hello and smile only seen with your eyes above your mask can change someone's day.

A lot to be learned from a compassionate, loving, empath like William - I learn from him every day.

When we came home William and I went for a bike ride, well he rode his Jeep pedal kart, and played some RC stunt racing in a school parking lot.

While I was out changing the oil and filters in my generator, Boston was prepping a special dinner he had found to give me a night off.

I couldn't help but think about how we've always shared household responsibilities in our own ways. He always cleans up the kitchen with whatever is left to do after I've made dinner, cleans bathrooms and vacuums while I'm doing laundry and other household chores. Some days those responsibilities riding heavier on one of us than the other but always pitching in to keep things rolling.

I believe, in well-functioning households with 2 people working full time, it's not about one "helping" the other it's about shared responsibilities. It's not about gender expected chores, it's working as a team.

That dinner was amazing and he was rightfully quite proud of himself especially since William asked for 2nds of chicken. All fresh ingredients for Bruschetta Chicken with foil packet potatoes, shrimp, zucchini and 1/4rd corn on the cob.

While the boys watched old reruns of Batman and Robin I got in an uninterrupted shower, hair mask and exfoliation - Seriously, when you have a lot on your plate everyday those 25 minutes are like a vacation!!

We enjoyed dinner, "Trolls" and off to sweet slumber - the house is quiet, we are content ♡

"Coming together is a beginning; Keeping together is progress; Working together is success" - Henry Ford

Namaste 🙏

8/9/2020

Mindful Moments ....

I think we're mask ready for school.

He looks adorable as a guinea pig doesn't, he?!!

I told him to smile when I took his photo. He said "why?? I have a mask on!!" I said because you smile with your eyes and I can see that, so he did.

School supplies purchased and delivered - I love on line shopping! (I even scored Clorox Wipes shhhhh).

If you're a foodie, a healthy foodie, you'll like tonight's photos otherwise scrolling on is an acceptable option.

We had Shipt delivery today and although William's job is to bring in the bags he had "better things to do" and was not pleased with the interruption, oh well, welcome to life responsibilities young man!

I have acquired many hats over the years and I won't list them but today's hat included barber.

I've been cutting William's hair for a year and a half and when shut down hit I became Boston's barber.

So, both boys had haircuts today, one more cooperative than the other ... I'll let you figure out who wasn't so cooperative :-)

You would be surprised how different it is to cut a human being's hair as opposed to the coat on a dog!!

We had a very lazy "leave your pajamas on all day but get a whole Lotta shit done" kind of day!

I had another much-needed break from dinner tonight!

Boston's Sunday creation was Stuffed Flank Steak with asparagus and provolone cheese, seared and slow cooked in the crockpot – YUM!

My day was spent food prepping, doing laundry, piggy playtime, piggy cage cleaning, haircuts and work. So, we're good to go for Monday

"I'd rather be completely exhausted from the hard times which breeds success ... than well rested from achieving nothing."

Namaste 🙏

8/10/2020

Mindful Moments ....

The cray cray started at 6:30am with a text from my groomer needing a complete work schedule change upcoming because her kids are getting out of school early every day. Thanks, Covid - rescheduling work days and clients over 4 months is a "little" time consuming.

My dad always used to say "and this too shall pass" a quote that gets me through many days. I even have it burned into a plaque in my living room as a constant reminder.

But that quote can go two ways.

Most look at it as it was meant to be read as persevering through tough times.

I also relate to it at times as life is short, slow down, take the time to be with family ... friends (even if it's just virtual for now) walk away from stress, take a walk, a bike ride. Leave the housework until later, it'll still be there even when we're not.

Maaany years ago, living in a different town, I used to pick up some dogs in my neighborhood for grooming whose owners couldn't around well.

After I dropped off a dog one day, she asked me what I was going to do on that beautiful summer afternoon when I left. I mentioned I had cleaning to do. The house needed dusting, vacuuming, etc.

What she said to me has stuck with me these 28 years ....

She said "my mother cleaned everyday of her life and you know what? She died and the dirt is still there."

Seize the moment.

"Because, this too shall pass."

2020 decided to throw another curveball at us today. Severe storms, tornado warnings and 85 mph winds blew through our neighborhood late this afternoon.

As a true Midwesterner I spent a lot of my time watching the sky outside while William and Gypsy were tucked in the powder room with water and blankets - until the craziest storm with hurricane like winds blew through us uprooting, trees, downing power lines, igniting fires and leaving over 14,000 out of power.

Wowza 2020 - I'd like to skip anything else you have up your deviant sleeve! I think we're good!

"And this too shall pass"?

From this storm and a post about the local power outage on a private page (which spans the globe btw) I found 2 amazing moms who live within miles of me - Coincidence, I think not!

Since being introduced to Raddish, William jumps into action whenever he can to cook something. When I said I'd make him a grilled cheese for lunch he ran to get his apron, so I stepped aside, coached a little, we danced and sang and voila - Grilled Cheese ala William!! With a side of Tostitos of course! Proud of him!

The only thing I'll say about Chicago of late, and its unrest right now, is that it's very sad.

"And this too shall pass"?

This phrase is not from the Bible. It is a translated Persian adage that was also employed by Abraham Lincoln before he became president. A little history lesson with a lot of meaning. 😊

"Never say Impossible ... the word itself says I'm possible."

Namaste 🙏

8/11/2020

Mindful moments ....

I'm happy to say our damage was minimal from hurricane "2020 Just Stop it Already" yesterday. Branches and limbs down, sweeping off the driveway and sidewalk and raking about covered it.

My local friends who were so harshly hit and remain out of power, possibly until Saturday in parts, I hope you are staying cool and for any special needs' families nearby, we have electricity for charging devices whenever you need it!

Phew that was somethin'! It has now disproved that major cities are clear from tornados and microbursts!

My veggies and flowers roughed it out! Sweet peas were hangin' sideways but pretty as ever - there is always a rainbow after a storm.

I've never made rainbow trout so I thought I'd give it a try! Great source of Omega 3. Coated it with olive oil, rubbed in fresh minced garlic, pink salt and pepper, parsley and rosemary - baked with lemon and asparagus for 15 minutes on 400 - easy and delicious!

Our school supplies are coming in a little at a time but we are both ready. Williams biggest challenge will be NOT hugging anyone! He hugs his bus drivers, teachers, everyone!! We're already working on that and he's not happy - he loooves to hug.

My list of self-care is growing for when I have time for hair appointments, Dr appointments and such coming up.

I love William dearly - 5 months of 24/7, literally, has been a bit smothering for both of us. Sometime apart will be good for both of our souls. ♡

Mr. William goes for his 6th grade physical next Monday - 6TH GRADE! How did that happen?! I'm not telling him about the shots, I'll let the Dr do that I'm calling it a physical with "boosters" since he loves cars so much that sounds like a good thing.

Cindy, William has "invented" Oreo Cookie ice cream smothered in honey from your farm! He's an entrepreneur! He wants to patented it! Could make you both a profit.

Most importantly - I believe our new piggie Snoopy is going to be a good snuggle replacement for Hershey we're doing socialization / snuggle training and for being as young as she is, she stays still for a good 10-15 minutes.

It's helping to mend his heart and calm him. ♡

"Sometimes self-care looks like locking yourself in your room while the kids destroy the house."

Yes!

Namaste 🙏

8/15/2020

Mindful Moments ....

Shout out to Lucie for helping out today - I love our old-fashioned values of helping each other without expecting anything in return - we were blessed when you and Grammy Barb graced us as neighbors who then became family.

While William struggles to fall asleep for many consecutive nights, I thought highlighting him was appropriate.

A child with many challenges he faces daily, out of all of them, I believe severe anxiety cripples him the most.

He feels with EVERY ounce of his being. Takes to heart things he can't ignore. Has the heart of an angel that shatters at the slightest turn. Becomes hurt and angry when teased and antagonized. He's an empath of the highest regard.

He worries about things children shouldn't have to think about. How can he help it with a year that has challenged his resilience to his very core? Things most don't know about

Most recently we've been planning on going back to school in person 4 days per week, one day at home to remote learn.

I'm not looking for judgement, everyone has difficult decisions to make right now. Ours was NOT taken lightly.

In a school of about 80, only 30 were returning, the rest remote. Only 4 kiddos in his class. His team is remarkable beyond words, he wants and needs to be there.

Special needs kiddos NEED routine, services, ABA and William is social. He's been depressed and going back to school, although scary, brought excitement and something to look forward to - his people! People who get him.

We purchased school supplies, cute masks and astronaut face shields. Weve practiced and timed mask wearing and he's a natural at hand washing.

We provided some face shields to his teachers, a gallon of hand sanitizer and touch less sanitizer machines. The school did not give the teachers their expense money this year, I don't understand that. Always pay it forward - We were as ready as can be under the circumstances.

Until last night when we were informed plans changed. A staff member, already having been present at school for meetings, tested positive for Covid exposing many other staff members. We are now shut down until October 20 at the earliest.

PLEASE wear masks! This person may or may not have but if others around them weren't ... here we are.

Our decisions affect those around us ... More than you know.

He's devastated, I cried - you have to understand Autism to know how detrimental this loss of routine, structure, progress and social interaction has been for 5 months and now to continue for at least 2 more.

So after yesterday, today he was quite dysregulated. I took him in the pool to regroup this afternoon. Water is calming. I pushed him on floatie while he relaxed and we quietly talked about whatever he wanted which was Batman and Robin the 1960's series, his new thing.

We then went in, changed and cooked dinner together.

He prepared one of his Raddish recipes Terriyaki Chicken Skewers - they were amazing! His choice for him and his dad as a side were tater tots, I had pea pods and roasted butternut squash. There are much better uses for potatoes Caitlin.

He was proud of himself and faced working with measuring cups, whisks, measuring spoons, a sharp knife and strange new things with hesitation yet confidence - he persevered. ♡

He puts everything he has into what comes quite simply to others and gains new pride in himself whether he sees it now or realizes it later.

So, while it's now after 10pm and he continues to try to find sleep right next to me for security, I wonder what runs through his 11yr old mind that troubles him so much at times, especially at night when our minds relax, his continues to turn.

I'm so very proud of him and the resilience he continues to have and the kindness and love he keeps in his heart despite his hurdles and challenges.

He's a gift to this world and an inspiration and I will never cease to be amazed at his accomplishments and the awareness he continues to strive for in himself to be a better person at such a young age - we should all be that determined to be better human beings.

Namaste 🙏

8/19/2020

Mindful Moments ....

I honestly don't have the energy today but this is what remote learning looks like while working at the same time.

I know it will work out eventually. For now, the entire system has been changed and it's so overwhelming trying to figure out how to navigate a completely new way of RL and trying to work and all that nonsense.

It works differently on an iPad than laptop. One app doesn't talk to the other and work done doesn't get submitted. Now the kids get assignments under their own email address, which needed to be set up. The links aren't working like they should be - overwhelmed is an understatement.

For anyone who's been trying to text, call or email me I will get back to you when I finish treading water and get to the shore.

May I say, homeschooling is NOT remote learning. HS is your schedule, your plans, your curriculum as you'd like to present it and when you want to present it. RL ... WOWZA is all I have to say. This is not the remote eLearning from last 1/4 or summer school and we haven't even started academics yet!

So here are some pretty flowers and now back to trying to catch up on my own work.

What doesn't kill us makes us stronger?!!

Namaste 🙏

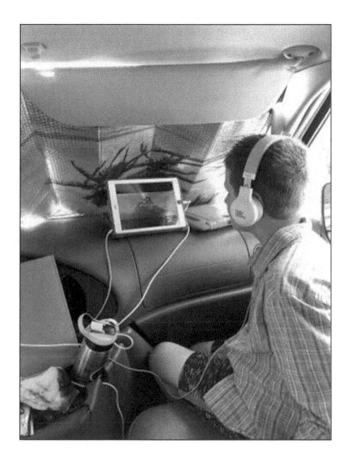

8/20/2020

Mindful Moments ....

There are perks for William coming to work with me. Pooch love of course!

Some assisting to earn some money.

Yesterday, from a friend who dates back to kindergarten, a big bag of snacks - perhaps too many caramel candies devoured!

Today a dream come true! A special cruise in a Porsche 718 Spyder convertible by a very kind-hearted incredible family - he was on cloud 9!!!

It's these little things that make all the isolation more bearable and tangible evidence that there are good people out there who are just plain kind.

Between zoom meetings, special treatment and work he had a pretty full day.

A very resilient, tough young man!

I am grateful to be off the road tomorrow, test out the remote learning protocol, catch up on some work and maybe just fit in a little bit of fun over the weekend.

Our piggies have been neglected so they had playtime and a little snuggle time before bed - I think they and William needed that time. ♡

William crashed hard tonight, didn't sleep much last night, so I came in the bedroom to finish folding laundry I started Sunday (it's been a week).

Much to my surprise Boston surprised me with a t-shirt from my favorite show and a favorite scene - made me laugh.

Been a long day.

Look for the helpers and find the joy.

Namaste 🙏

8/22/2020

Mindful Moments ....

On this beautiful summer, low humidity day we dropped top and headed out for an adventure!

Dinosaur Adventure Drive Through at the DuPage County Fair Grounds to be exact!

A well guided tour by DuPage County Fair Grounds and audio through our prehistoric eras with sound, movement and many history lessons.

A Kids Adventure Pack for William with adorable stuffed baby dinosaur, t-shirt, fossil dig, cotton candy and crayons with coloring sheets - pretty exciting!

Oh, and a window delivered funnel cake.

These opportunities have died off over the past few months. I've missed doing something different to get out of the house and distract from 2020.

The weather was so beautiful we decided to dine outdoors under the tent at B-Dubs. Haven't had dinner out since Father's Day.

Kudos to the restaurant workers hustling in and out to take care of their patrons and managing the uncooperative ones with class - tip your servers well and don't complain if your food takes 5 minutes longer.

The kitchen is serving indoor and outdoor diners as well as pickups and deliveries tip, tip, tip, wear your mask and be kind!!

Only 2 other tables filled until our favorite neighbors just happened to have the same idea and sit close by! Yayyyy

Along with a few chores and the daily mundane it was a nice day out and about!

William ate enough for 3 people at dinner and now at 11:45pm still can't sleep - lesson learned, probably not!

Namaste 🙏

8/26/2020

Mindful moments ....

We keep the house closed up for William during RL to reduce distraction.

At lunch I took a quick peak out the patio blinds to see what might be happening out in the world ....

I was pleasantly surprised by a visit from Lucie's hummingbird friend just outside our window checking out my barely alive flowers.

The photos came out fairly clear with an iPhone and a very fast-moving visitor.

After RL I taught William how to make our own GF Oat Flour.

You see we have a venture we are entering into and William is learning different techniques to build and succeed in this venture to be announced at a later date.

He thought it was cool how the simple process worked!

Our new raised veggie planters were filled today and ready for planting next year - that's all I asked our landscaper to do but he always goes above and beyond.

He trimmed some low-lying branches out front, finished off my stone landscaping frame in the back and added compost to my existing gardens as well - oh and he rolled up my hose for me.

Just in time for me to unroll it so I could put the sprinkler on.

Hub Landscaping, Jon - highly recommend them!!

Saw the new RL schedule for next week ... I'm just going to keep my mouth shut and hope this nightmare ends sooner than later! The kid can't sleep as it is with THIS schedule and Williams poor teacher is ready to jump off a bridge and I've threatened to send the laptop swimming a few times - Boston isn't fond of that idea.

Let's turn our attention to the adorable hummingbird, shall we?!

Preston I'm looking forward to tomorrow night's sound meditation - MUCH NEEDED!! Although I may need to slip William a micky to get him to sleep before 9!

Well, better rest up, for tomorrow is another day!

Namaste 🙏

8/31/2020

Mindful Moments ....

First day of new remote learning schedule lesson one:

"Responsible Day Drinking 101."

Namaste 🙏

9/2/2020

Mindful moments ....

After school William and I had the pleasure of a face-to-face visit with mom today.

Weekends are packed with visit reservations at the rehab facility and Remote learning and work doesn't leave much time for the pleasures in life. Grateful for 1/2-day Wednesday's to be able to get in a visit, without a window screen dividing us, while the weather is still agreeable.

One day a hug would be nice.

I want to send a shout out to all teachers right now.

They're spending their evenings, early mornings and weekends lesson and schedule planning while heading 4-5 zoom calls per weekday with overwhelmed, frustrated, unfocused kiddos and stressed-out parents. Unreliable, overused internet connections.

If you feel the Remote workload is unreasonable, as we do, take it up with administrators who work with the planning teams.

The teachers are doing as they're told, not as they feel is best for their families. They know the demands being put on kids and working parents is unreasonable.

They are advocating for their students and families with requests ignored. They are as aggravated and stressed as the parents who are complaining to them.

They have some parents who are very involved and some who hand their kids a computer and send them off to manage it on their own.

They have remarkable patience in zoom with unsupervised kids who are playing video games and musical instruments and talking to each other in chat while they're trying to teach a lesson.

Show a teacher some love today,

an encouraging word,

email of appreciation,

keep your kids focused while they're trying to teach under really crappy circumstances ....

Most of all ... BE KIND

Namaste 🙏

9/5/2020

Mindful Moments ....

Life boils down to perspective.

You can either allow yourself to wallow in a black hole of self-pity or use life challenges as lessons.

This was, well ... a week. I blame it on the full moon and I'm sticking to that!

It was a domino effect really.

The week beginning with a very emotional day of a new overwhelming RL schedule and has ended with a wasp sting to the arm pit, yes that's true!

A first client losing track of time on a back-to-back work day and needed to put the "dogs out for potty" as I saw her walk out of the house and around the corner with them for a walk ... ran me 20 minutes behind. Then returns to say btw I forgot to tell you I need you to park down the street behind that truck, they're still working on our yard. And the day slid downhill from there.

A forgotten appointment needing to be squeezed into an already tight day.

Remote learning issues at home, corresponding with the teacher etc.

A little stink of a 4# pooch pulling out his Sid Vicious on me.

Notice of a possible Covid issue with my contractor's daughter spelling out a potential shut down of my business resulting in canceled appointments.

A shattered phone screen quite obviously not protected by its screen saver!

The week hit hard today. Catches up with you after you've been running to catch up with yourself to stay on top of every issue. I'm tired, drained.

The school schedule and working full time and managing RL issues leaves no time to actually be the parent that the kids want you to be because you don't have time working 2 full time jobs.

I hit "I can't keep up, I'm not even going to try anymore, I don't give a crap about anything," mode.

Ya know what, whether those around you feel uncomfortable with it or not, it's OK not to be all rainbows, unicorns and sunshine all the time, that's not real life. It's ok to feel your shit, process it, manage it, just don't wallow in it. Get up and kick that shit to the curb!

The school issues worked out, had a face-to-face visit with mom, the phone screen is fixed, the work day ended up fine, I won with Sid Vicious whoop whoop, muzzles are king, I hope the wasp died, a happy little squirrel joined us for dinner, William picked a peaceful, serene background for his chrome book (pretty cool for a kid) and snuggle time with Rocket Pig and Snoopy is pretty awesome.

No pity, real life - get it out, go for a drive, work it off and move on!

Gain perspective.

Namaste 🙏

9/9/2020

Mindful Moments ....

Gypsy's getting older, slowing down, she has her puppy moments but her paw on my foot at dinner will always be my favorite thing that she does ♡

It's more of a reminder that she's there just in case I happen to get full or "accidentally "drop something but I'll pretend its pure admiration ♡

I notice things when I'm out walking or driving. I try not to hurriedly move from place to place letting things with meaning to me or someone else go unnoticed.

Mindfulness.

This little squirrel in the tree plays hide n seek every morning I walk Gypsy and boy does he/she tell us off when we get close to the tree! It runs up the tree as soon as we're seen and peers down at us screeching until we go on our way. Apparently, that's his tree and guests are not welcome to use it as a porta a potty!

My urge to decorate for Halloween continues to be validated by lovers of the day or maybe everyone is just in a hurry to end this "unprecedented" year! As am I.

My new favorite sign popped up recently - I intend to "vote Kindness" - enough fighting and hate in the world - it's time to unite and close the divide. Stop being nasty to each other!

I've been able to get to work alone lately but while I'm out I always seek out the classics for William. Saw 2 today he was pretty excited about.

The past couple of months I've booked a lot of new clients. What I've noticed is the huge number of puppies. Tons of new furry family members.

I can surmise, as I feel the same, that we've all had it with this year. The challenges, the financial strain, the isolation. What better way to bring smiles, company and happiness while keeping ourselves sane, with some sleepless nights, than with a new fur baby.

Today's new pup is Phoebe - a 3-month-old Westie owned by the daughter of a client of mine. She was an angel, not common with puppies and their first grooming's! A pleasant surprise.

We fall.

We break.

We fail.

But then.

We rise.

We heal.

We overcome.

Namaste 🙏

9/10/2020

Mindful Moments ....

Sept 11, 2001, 19 years ago tonight we routinely tucked ourselves and our families into bed.

We took for granted the normality of that day. A normality that would change with shock and devastation just hours later.

Before you put your head to pillow tonight, remember how quickly and unexpectedly life as we know it can change.

Remember to appreciate the roof over your head, your loved ones, tell them you love them - we are not promised tomorrow.

Remember to recognize the sun, the air, the trees.

Remember to appreciate our freedoms.

Remember to care about others.

Remember to be kind.

Remember ....

Namaste 🙏

9/12/2020

Mindful Moments ....

It's amazing how there's always more things to do than hours in the day, isn't it?

But thanks to a rainy day we managed to get some things done, fit in a game of Pokémon - I caved under duress from a lonely face! Not my favorite game to play.

The boys played some Beyblades while I ran out to have an uninterrupted chat with my favorite girl Caitlin and get some Benadryl Cream for Gypsy.

You can curse the rain but everything was thirsty. The hay brown grass has given way to a lush green and flowers decided to bloom just a little longer.

We started a new series on Netflix called "I'm Sorry" - hysterical crude humor (although episode #2 was edgy and uncomfortable during current times) but we will return for more - haven't laughed at a tv show that much in a long time!

William decided overeating homemade spaghetti sauce over cheese tortellini followed by a 1/4 of an apple pie was a great idea - until his stomach retaliated at bedtime - time for Tums!!

A new gigantic guinea pig blanket, soft, freshly washed and snuggly with some quiet conversation while gazing at a rainbow brought a peaceful sleep.

He said it looks like the Aurora borealis. I didn't know he knew what that was. I guess he IS learning something from school.

Time to shut down and prepare for another exciting at the Mateblatts tomorrow. ♡

Namaste 🙏

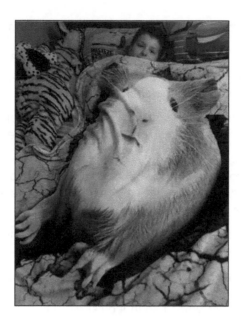

9/14/2020

Mindful Moments ....

Looking at our smokey sky today I can't help but think about our friends in California.

How horrific this must be to be able to be taken by the wind so far! Unimaginable ... sending solutions and peace to ravaged homes and businesses.

Jodi, you need to wish for rain for them, it worked for us!!

Chicago came out on top this weekend!

The first season opener win in 7 years for the Bears, another Sox win retaining our 1st place AL Central position and yes let's mention the Cubs pitcher Alec Mills pitching the 1st no hitter since 2016!

Way to represent, Chicago!!!

Our #1 Bear fan "Bear Man" is not letting the neighborhood down sporting his new Ford sponsored Bear mobile and fully decked out garage!! Very nice!

William endured torture of horrible proportions during remote today!

We're in a duplex and our neighbors are selling but fixing up the place.

Their deck is about 10' from our patio doors "kitchen school," so we listened to the power washer blasting the entire morning.

At 3 we left for a Dr appt William was just informed of an hour earlier - he wasn't pleased because he had to get a shot apparently needed for 6th grade now.

He walked out before me and, unbeknownst to me, told off the worker for ruining his school day. Apparently, the guy said he was sorry - which was nice considering he was just doing his job!

One thing I won't worry about William's future is taking shit from anyone, but he's going to have to choose his words more carefully!

Then the remodelers proceeded to work in the kitchen, attached to ours, apparently sledge hammering the walls and ripping out the foundation until 7 tonight - at least that's what it sounded like.

We may need to move "Kitchen School" to "Guinea Pig Room School" upstairs tomorrow!

He took his shot like a man, running away and cowering ....

He sat in my lap and sat still for a sucker - he got extra dessert tonight to go with his sore arm and I'm sure will milk the sore muscle for all it's worth.

There's already talk of an inability to type his work tomorrow because he "can't lift his arm" ....

I'm very resourceful, I'll find something to prop it up.

And with that the neighbors are quiet, William is asleep, the last load of laundry is in the dryer and I just had a conversation about watching the tv show Zoom when I was a kid - anyone else?!

Time to recharge for another exciting day at the Mateblatts tomorrow!!

Namaste 🙏

9/15/2020

Mindful Moments ....

In the darkness there is

Always light

In the light there is

always

Hope

In hope there is always

Love.

Namaste 🙏

9/19/2020

Mindful moments ....

This bed here that Queen Gypsy is perched upon was neatly made an hour before her redecorating - comfort is of the utmost importance for our girl.

Batman and his new neighborhood friend had some soccer, bike riding, Pokémon card playing time - I'm so happy he has a friend close by. Years ago, the neighborhood kids tripped him, called him names, teased him, pushed him off of his bike - he just wanted a friend. They get along so well ... it's a first.

While doing some much-needed decluttering today William decided to pull out all the loose nails between the wooden planks on the deck I've never noticed them, lived here 17 hrs, they're gone now ... how does he see this stuff.

3 weeks ago, we noticed a small bloody area on Gypsy's hip. Her biting irritated whatever was there.

The vet said it was an insect bite after shaving the area and finding 2 additional spots. Gave her some steroids for a few days. One spot reduced swelling and the other stayed the same and two more areas flared up.

So back to the vet yesterday. Now she looks like a patchwork quilt with a penis shaved into her hip, antibiotics and allergy meds. I think they could've been a little less creative with the clippers?!

Still don't know what's wrong - recheck in 2 weeks.

Have any of you been to the vet lately?? The walk-in waits are up to 4 hours daily and to book an appointment is a week or two out! What's going on?? Did everyone get pets over the past 6 months?? I mean yayyy if they're rescues but holy smokes!

Boston had a meeting at work yesterday on mental health awareness during this trying time with remote learning and isolation.

William and I made a background for him. He used it but they never put anyone but the speakers on screen! Maybe they don't like our sense of humor - I thought it was creative - Isolation and comedy, not a good combo lol.

3 more minutes to Sunday better get some shut eye.

Namaste 🙏

9/23/2020

Mindful Moments ....

There were many moving parts to today, but these 2 moments captured a lot in a couple of photos.

These simple moments of friendship, unconditional love and freedom from judgement is what life is about.

There isn't enough of it anymore.

Perhaps these past years of our countries decline in acceptance has allowed some of us, maybe many of us, to take pause.

To see these moments as precious and rare is sad, yet heartwarming.

Sad in that it should be natural to see past skin color, religious choice, political preference, choices in love - love is love ♡ - people are people with pasts, challenges, wins, heartaches and joy.

And yet it's heartwarming to know that the children are our future and if this is what our future looks like, then it's bright.

Shouldn't friendship, kindness, love always be free from judgement?

I know some adults who can learn from these 2 boys. Learn what it is to see past color, age, background and just be a good friend, a good person. ♡

The world will change, and can change, when we stop tearing each other apart and turn it into building each other up.

Straighten your friends crowns instead of knocking those crowns off because of your own internal turmoil.

It's very simple - just decide.

Namaste 🙏

9/27/2020

Mindful Moments ....

It was suggested to me today, and one other time, that I compile my Mindful Moments posts into a book one day. A memoir of an unprecedented, challenging year if you will.

In fact, 3 times in the past few weeks I was told I should write a book, that I tell a good story ... I suppose it's a matter of perspective and interest.

I'd not thought of that when this began.

For me this was merely a way to reflect, look for the positives in a rapidly declining year. A year of treading water just to stay afloat one day after another in what has seemed a never-ending cycle of challenges. Where ARE those murder hornets anyway??

I didn't think my writing to be anything profound, just survival through incredible isolation ... but who knows. Maybe one day I'll be on the book shelves.

I can't tell you how many times I've fallen asleep writing these. Stress, exhaustion, never ending days. Waking up with iPad in hand and a stiff neck but finishing just the same.

Some days the positives are hard to find. But there's always, always something to be grateful for ... always. Because if there isn't then there is no hope and without hope there is no future.

Make a list everyday of what your thankful for, even if it's one thing.

One thing as simple as running water, your toothbrush, food on your table, a warm blanket ... there are some who have none of those.

These beautiful flowers pictured were at a client's house last week. The colors were so vibrant and fresh I had to stop and look at them a few times. It's amazing what beauty our earth creates. Admire it, appreciate it while it's here.

I was honored to attend baby Jacks shower today honoring this lovely lady pictured. Kristi in all my years of being in the company of mamas to be I have never seen a baby so very loved even before you lock eyes for the first time.

He is going to live a life filled with love and happiness, that I am sure of!

I haven't seen these friends since early March before the world changed. With masks and a breezy, lovely outdoor visit my soul was filled.

I missed our welcome hugs but they will be back with time and patience. There's nothing like in person laughter, commonality and conversation to pick up your spirits.

I went home with a full heart. 💜

Thank you for your hard work, Robin, and loved having time to chat with you before I left. 💟

Today I am grateful for unconditional friendships. 💟

Namaste 🙏

9/28/2020

Mindful Moments ....

This passage came up on my timeline today from 2016 ... conveys the same message today as it was meant to 4 years ago ....

As I've gotten older it's become more apparent, or I am just more aware, that you are judged by some by your religious or political affiliation rather than who you are as a person, in your heart and how you treat others.

I find that to be really a shame because we are all just individuals with different things that are important to us in life - so how does that make someone unworthy? Perhaps it's one's own internal turmoil lacking in acceptance of those who follow a different path?

We weren't created as robots programmed to follow a strict norm.

We were created to be individuals with minds of our own to believe as we wish and find our people with whom we connect.

I've found some great friends who we may not see eye to eye on some things but we see inside our hearts instead - those are my people.

William, nearly 12, has compassion and empathy to the highest degree. His heart swells with love of animals, every toy, rock and leaf has a soul that needs saving and he's going to do it.

An ASPCA commercial came on today and I couldn't get to the remote fast enough before his face sunk and his eyes filled with tears.

He wanted to save every one of those lost, abandoned souls - he relates to them all in many ways - it's heartwarming and heart breaking all at the same time - we are empaths and feel others pain as our own.

Whereas I am often snuffed for being the eternal optimist, others issue not mine, I find pessimism energy sucking and for every negative I can find a positive, but you have to know when to walk away from negativity for your own mental health. You can't change anyone; you can only lead by example.

It was "a day" that began with a squirrel vs Gypsy showdown. I guess you could say the squirrel won since Gypsy's advances went no further than an attempted initiating glare, slight harness tug and a short while walking away!

I'm still pondering the cereal bowl on the car. It was either a tired diner or an offering to any passerby that may need a meal ... I'll pass thanks.

Gypsy's 3rd trip to the vet for an allergy recheck. She appears to be healing well - we'll be watching her for relapse. ♡

It's always still an eye opener to me when you're going about a routine activity and our current world affairs smack you in the face.

The vet's office set up is nicely executed, well run and organized - just like everything else, our new norm but still surreal.

And people, when there's a tape line on the ground to keep you 6 feet away, with signs instructing you to do so as well, from the employees who are masked and trying to help you - don't step over the line and lean across the table and let your children run behind the table to see what's going on. These procedures are being done for everyone's safety and it should be appreciated and respected,

Gypsy did enjoy her first ride in the new Wrangler, albeit a ride to the vet. Spacious back seat, rolled down windows ... she was stylin'.

Another packed day didn't allow for some things I wanted to do, like eat. So, with William in slumber land I whipped up one of my favorite desserts (yes, it's healthy, GF and amazing!!) Keeps my hands out of the naughty treats!

Try it, I freeze them and they taste like strawberry ice cream shortcake!

The wine bottle ... well like I said it was "a day" so why dirty a glass when you can finish off the cheap stress reliever from the bottle?! Are you with me?!!

If you're still with me - I love you my friends and family. You inspire me every day with your individuality, honesty and kind hearts - keep being you, unless you're an asshole then stop it!!

Namaste 🙏

9/30/2020

Mindful Moments ....

Last night's frightening display inspired me to stir up my own favorite frightening display of this season!

I like it much better than yesterdays! Bring on the ghosts, goblins and scary movies!

The cool weather inspires me to make soup.

This week's is a healthy Albondigas Soup. If you haven't tried it, I highly recommend it! Recipe is included just in case you're enticed - I garnish it with slivers of fresh avocado.

We've been doing a lot of decluttering, organizing and picking up some new, to us, furniture (credenzas Cody).

I'm going through ALOT of treasures from 18years of living here and in an end table I came across this book, pictured.

You see I was taken to Vegas for my 40th birthday.

Among many special events and surprises, on the actual night of my birthday, one of the best surprises of my life had been planned and expertly executed.

We were waiting outside of our hotel for what promised to be a great evening of fun and frivolities. I was told our ride would be there soon and we seemed to be waiting forever with cab after cab and limo after limo pulling up, loading their fares and leaving. It was a chilly night. That's what happens even in Vegas in February.

I wasn't paying attention when a stretch limo pulled up. I was escorted to the door which was being gentlemanly held open by the driver.

To my astonishment my best friend Tom and his partner were sitting inside, drinks in hand, yelled out surprise and the festivities ensued!

I was gifted this book and my all-time favorite coffee cup that I still use frequently. I had forgotten about the book until it appeared in my cleaning yesterday. All of those memories came rushing back in.

We spent the evening cruising the strip stopping from one roof top party to another, Freemont Street and ending back at their resort, who knows when!

While our dates passed out, Tom and I went downstairs for a little more roulette and a trip to In N Out Burger conveniently located in their resort!

It was a memorable evening and as we entered our own hotel, with the sun rising, my heart was filled with love and friendship.

My friend passed away this summer but what remains are the memories of some of the most amazing times together starting with Freshmen year of high school. Basement parties at his parents' house, concerts ... many many concerts (he/we loved music) bus pub crawls, parties, Farm Stock, weekends at the cabin and farm ....

It's no coincidence that he came to me in a dream last week and now I come across these gifts from that Vegas trip. He walked toward me smiling and gave me the biggest hug - I miss him. ♡

And with that ....

When you walk, walk;

when you eat, eat; and

When you sit, sit.

This is the way of Zen.

Do what you do fully in each moment.

Namaste 🙏

10/4/2020

Mindful Moments ....

Today was a perfect day to leave behind work, technology, decluttering and video games!

A beautiful day to meet up with Caitlin and Cody for fun at Kuipers Farm in Maple Grove.

We climbed and slid - ate and drank.

There's soooo much to do and a nice change from Cottonwood or Bengston's. About 50 minutes from Plainfield, just past Elburn.

Everyone was respectful in distancing and a good 98% wearing masks except to eat or drink. ♡

Hand sanitizer everywhere, including in my pocket.

Autism awareness represented - LOVE!! 🧩

Animals, apple picking, train rides, pumpkin patch, play areas, BBQ, a shop filled with homemade jams, donuts, taffy apples, cake and pancake mixes, honey, pies, lotions and Christmas tchotchkes ....

I can't wait to make some apple sauce and apple slices - William wants me to make a caramel apple, walnut pie - the boy knows what he likes.

I'm an observer. I love to people watch. What I loved about the day was not only enjoying the fresh air and beautiful weather with the ones I love but looking around at all the other families.

They left their troubles at home, put on a mask, laughed, played and enjoyed an afternoon away.

This year has been too much and it's not over yet.

Get out while you can. Go for a drive, a walk, bike ride - there are things to do and places to go where safety is taken seriously.

Don't let life pass you by, grab your mask, be safe and go live it.

Time is like a river.

You cannot touch the same water twice, because the flow that has passed will never pass again.

Enjoy every moment in life. ♡

Namaste 🙏

10/7/2020

Mindful moments ....

As a mobile dog groomer, we travel to hundreds of families over the course of a year.

We see our repeat, loyal clients fairly often. Their dogs become our family and we get to know each other like family.

When we lose one of our fur babies our hearts are broken along with their loving devoted humans.

Today one of my favorite big guys for years crossed the rainbow bridge. Bijou was such a good boy who was blessed with the most amazing family. My heart goes out to you all Leslie, Phil and Jantha.

I will miss him.

A shout out to another of my seniors who celebrated a big 15th birthday today. Happy birthday to this old girl Bella.

As always, I see interesting things throughout my day.

Laura, I think you need to up your game with hedge designs. Had to stop and grab a photo of this creation today.

So many views on politics, many confused confirmed by this backyard sign admittedly throwing in the towel.

We have a big day in the family tomorrow. A day we've waited and planned for, for 8 months.

Tomorrow we bring mom back to her home with 24hr care from family. ♡

She proved the Drs. wrong that she wouldn't survive a serious life-threatening surgery at the end of February at 92 years young.

Mom has come back fighting from so many accidents and illnesses that should've exhausted her resolve, but did not.

She not only survived, but 8 months later is going home from what we thought was surely going to be the rest of her days to be spent in assisted living.

She can celebrate her 93rd birthday next month, at home - each day is a gift.

EVERYTHING HEALS.

Your body heals. Your heart heals.

Your mind heals. Wounds heal.

Your happiness is always going to come back. Bad times don't last.

Buddha -

Namaste 🙏

10/8/2020

Mindful Moments ....

I will just say that today the stars, moons and planets had to be aligned.

My day began with a text from William's teacher that she's giving the boys tomorrow off from academics because they've done a great job with remote learning, they need a break and so do the teachers! 4-day weekend!! SCORE!

William, for one, deserves it! He's been working his butt off despite some challenges, loneliness and push back!

Next a visit to Fine Skin Dermatology, thank you for the push with your post Ken. A couple of trouble spots I've been putting off that turn out to be nothing to worry about! A measurement and future check to stay on top of it.

♡ ♡The piece de resistance ... MOMS HOME!!♡ ♡

I don't think I've seen her this happy in a very long time. She's come a long way in 8 months from nearly losing her life to taking those steps back into her house on her own two feet!

She is grateful and cried happy tears, as did we. Hoping her road ahead proves to continue to hold her high and strong at nearly 93 years young.

Her first meal at home ... her favorite ... PB&J!

Annika and I left her a little surprise in her bedroom - it's our sense of humor, I get it from her, Annika comes with it, she'll laugh when she sees it! To know us is to love us.

Tom and Annika will stay with her until we can figure things out for her care down the road.

It seems like forever since she went in for surgery end of February, then to rehab just as Covid hit and we've been unable to be with her since this all began. Having her back in her house felt as though she had never been gone - that first hug ... priceless. ♡

To enhance the good fortune of today's events, after 7 months on the market, with many bites, my old faithful Jeep drove away with some guys who are going to "off road ready" her more and want to take her out this weekend!

That's exactly who I wanted to carry on her legacy! Someone who would enjoy the reason she was created. She kept us safe and having fun for 15 years and now she can enjoy the trails! Bye bye Racey (William's name for her) thanks for the road trips, trails and parking lot donuts!!

They promised to send pictures - I hope to run into her on the trails one day.

Now if we can just get our re-fi complete ....

Laying our head to pillow tonight with a lot of lighter heart and soul.

"Ceasing to do evil, Cultivating the good, Purifying the heart: this is the teaching of the Buddhas."

Namaste 🙏

10/9/2020

Mindful Moments ....

Breathtaking is the word of the day.

The first photo, top left, is just outside our bedroom window.

For the past week I've watched its transformation from summer to autumn and soon to watch it shed its history.

The deep reds, golden yellows and burnt oranges are enhanced by the sun dancing off of the leaves in the early morning sunrise.

Hoping to get out on some trails this weekend to see the trees brazen with color before the colder winds blow.

On my walk this morning I found this suspended leaf seemingly just dancing around my camara as if showing off a bit before dropping to the ground.

I also found empty boxes waiting for the recycling truck on garbage day- they're mine now.

William needed his Nana hug and he got it today - these 2 are tight as thieves and he's about to tower over her tiny self - a well arranged outdoor visit, 6' apart with masks was perfect.

Heartwarming. ♡

Our ride home had us searching for Alfred Hitchcock at the Weber Rd entrance ramp. We could've made our own version of The Birds they are gathering for a warmer Air BNB for a few months.

Thank you, Kathi, for the front porch contribution! I truly appreciate you!

Looking back at this year I can only feel how slowly it flew by so fast - if you get what I mean.

The challenges we've all faced, our country in a disappointing divide, friends disrespecting friends for a differing of opinion - it's just surreal to me but I'm that optimist just wanting everyone to respect one another and get along - I'd rather be this way, like it or don't.

Preston your latest release Caravan of Dreams was another successful relaxation sleep inducer. He was very escalated tonight and within minutes of hitting play on Patreon he was out!! You have a magical gift my friend ... Cello, violin amazing!!

Keep your energy positive.

"What I give out, I get back. I give out only goodness and, in turn, only goodness comes back to me."

Louise L Hay

Namaste 🙏

10/12/2020

Mindful moments ....

Our weekends have been filled with decluttering and "redecorating" the house. Picking up furniture, selling furniture ....

First floor nearly done, started on the second floor yesterday.

When you're in a home for 17 years accumulation of non-essentials seems to creep up on you. Especially when you are raised by parents who lived through the depression years. A house full of "Let's keep this we may need it one day."

My dad used to clean and reuse foil and my grandma painstakingly removed wrapping paper and ironed it for future use - they were the original recyclers!

Taking action to reach goals is quite rewarding and satisfying!

Williams latest Raddish project was Halloween related and delicious!! Yesterday he made Mummy Enchiladas. We substituted fajita prepped ground chicken for beans.

There was ALOT of prep work and he stuck with it pretty well. The Enchilada Sauce was homemade also. He did a great job but was disappointed that you couldn't pick them up like a burrito.

A great way to get your kids to eat veggies! Leftovers today were just as good!

We all have gifts. It's up to us to figure out what they are, learn from them and use them to benefit others.

I've always had a natural ability to "see" into people's minds and hearts and feel their feelings. A self-imposed empath. Some may refer to it as analytical or intuitive. I tend to know things before they happen and know why someone is behaving in a certain way without a word spoken.

Through that ability I've always had an interest in psychology as well as the spiritual world and did take some classes regarding both back in the day.

William has taught me many things and one of those things is to stick with what you know, what comes natural to you.

In advocating for him all of these years and spending every minute of every day analyzing behaviors and emotions, learning from hours spent with his therapists, psychiatrists and team at school I want to learn more to understand him better. In doing so giving him the support he needs to succeed.

Autism is complicated. It comes with daily struggles, challenges, accomplishments, tears, laughter, frustration, love, fear for the future, fear of your child being misunderstood, judged, rejected, etc. The more you understand and absorb the more you can assist in a person's village to help them live their best life.

Life is short on this earth. I intend to spend my time diving into knowledge of anxiety with autism - HUGE in our world, CBT (cognitive behavioral therapy) and DBT (dialectical behavior therapy - mindfulness, emotion regulation, distress tolerance).

This is another positive to this pandemic and remote learning. With our autistic kiddos everyday has academics BUT also everyday includes Mindfulness activities and DBT activities. I get to do them with him and am learning a lot which has relit my fire - it was the interruption I needed, we all need interruptions to open our eyes to greater things.

Not in a formal setting, I mean when the heck would I attend classes, just on my own. Right now, to help William, I'm sure myself and maybe later, others, who knows ....

I have my books and dove in head first!

Finding positives and figuring out how you can give back in life is important.

What's your superpower?

You can sit back and complain or you can take action!!

"Do not dwell in the past, do not dream of the future, concentrate the mind on the present moment."

(Mindfulness)

Buddha

Namaste 🙏

10/14/2020

Mindful moments ....

Who woke up to this beautiful sunrise today?? Gorgeous!

Hand delivered ballots - Don't vote, don't complain.

A bit of a rough day today. Some work issues, Wi-Fi issues like we couldn't connect at all, frustration, anxiety ... phew we're about burnt out from 7 months of remote learning! The next 6 days feel like an eternity!

Most of the kiddos checked out weeks ago. Either don't show up or don't have their video on, they watch tv or play video games during zooms, use chat with classmates during zooms, no supervision. William is just done, focus is gone, anxiety high, I'm done trying to run a business, 1:1 teach, advocate, entertain, console, stand in therapist!

When someone says "Make sure you get some self-care" ohhhhh sure I do, I get to use the bathroom alone for 3 minutes a few times a day, maybe more depending on how many cups of coffee I've had, sleep for 5 or 6 hours and if I'm lucky get in an uninterrupted workout and if I'm really, really lucky I get to shower! How's that for self-care?!

Chewy was the highlight of Williams day. Kissed his face and hung over him when he was getting frustrated with the internet - leave it to a fur baby to bring a little smile through the storm.

This past weekend Gypsy was groomed and I cut Boston and Williams hair - yesterday was my turn! The best part was the cool Halloween decorations my stylist has and how well-behaved William was for having to sit and wait for me for 1 1/2hrs - I look forward to going to my next appointment ... alone!

Knowing this week was just going to be insane I made a huge pot of Chicken Tortilla soup over the weekend. Recipe acquired years ago from Tom T.

We don't put any tortilla chips in it but the boys like cheese sprinkled on top and I like to add jalapeños in mine. It's delicious!! When I can make something, everyone will eat it's always a success!

We did manage to get the pool covered albeit in the dark, in the wind - we don't turn our backs on a good challenge!

I am soooo grateful for that pool this summer. It gave us hours of escape from our reality when there was no place to go and not much to do. Warm water, blue skies, sunny days, diving for dollars, music, laughter - some natural medicine to soothe the soul.

Now she sleeps for the winter.

It is not how much we have,

but how much we enjoy

that makes happiness.

Namaste 🙏

10/15/2020

Mindful Moments ....

As a blessing in disguise, school zooms cancelled today. Let's just say another result of 2020 chaos!

Next week we start a new routine, another new schedule but man are we ready for some change!

Monday off, Tuesday new routine!

I made a comment to William's teacher today, after yet another mess she was dealing with, that I'm quite sure she and her team are as tired as we are.

She said "We are so tired and one day is not going to change the world. It's like I unbuttoned my pants this week! We'll get back on it next week!"

Just goes to show that when things get chaotic, and your plate runneth over, it's time to kick that shit to the curb, shake it off, take a deep breath and move on!

It always warms my heart to see how William interacts with animals.

He took advantage of a day off to schmooze with the fur babies - they are unconditionally caring and loving. They don't care what color you are, what religion you follow or who you love.

I was serenaded from the front seat by a composition via Garage Band. Sounds a little Metallica Enter Sandman don't ya think?! So proud!

Robin the ginormous box is already under construction, supplies pulled out but cut short this afternoon, we were just tired - thank you - We have another 3-day weekend to create! I will be sending photos!

We are all yearning for change. For unity, for something to be normal again, whatever that is. Instead of sitting around, waiting for someone else to create it or wishing for it to happen, take action and ....

"BE the change you want to see in the world."

Namaste 🙏

> **"**
>
> **It is not the strongest of the species that survive, nor the most intelligent, but the one most responsive to change.**
>
> Charles Darwin

10/17/2020

Mindful Moments ....

As the days get cooler, the daylight shorter and the trees shed their leaves we reach to find things in our new normal to enjoy.

Remaxx in Plainfield sponsored a drive by parade fundraiser to buy meals for first responders at the Plainfield Library with goodies for the kids.

I was happy that we could just drive through however the set up was quite different than expected.

Turns out the visit was much more eventful for William with Star Wars companions to chat and take photographs with.

He needed this distraction today. A distraction from the unknown expectations of the upcoming couple of weeks causing some excitement with lots of anxiety.

While William worked on his, soon to be revealed, project I was able to play in the kitchen.

Those apples from the orchard a couple of weeks ago rendered some delicious cinnamon apple sauce and enough extra to freeze for apple slices in the coming days.

The Spaghetti squash was roasted, the snow peas and green beans steamed for meals this week along with a pot of homemade spaghetti sauce.

I was half way through complete confusion trying to find the strings to pull from the snow peas when I noticed the packaging ..." STRINGLESS Sugar Snap Peas" point taken!

I was able to see my favorite daughter Caitlin at least for a few minutes. A late-night catch-up chat last night and a few minutes today ... every moment, whether brief or long, is cherished.

My dad said to me one day when she was little that when we have children it's like our hearts are walking around outside of our bodies - wise man.

Although it was grocery delivery day, we ordered out for Olive Garden. I've noticed we do this a lot. Haul in a week's worth of groceries then order out for dinner - It was delicious!

Boston and I then proceeded to reminisce about our sorted pasts and laughed until we cried. Man did we do some stupid things! Meh, it was before smart phones, hell it was before cell phones.

"We are shaped by our thoughts; we become what we think. When the mind is pure, joy follows like a shadow that never leaves." Buddha

Namaste 🙏

10/19/2020

Mindful Moments ....

This quote was taken from a good friend's post that said much more but this nails it.

With the impending, yet another severely controversial, election on our heels I've been thinking a lot about this subject.

Although I will comment on a political post, I won't post anything political. I learned my lesson 4 years ago that you can't have an opinion without being ridiculed and berated and you shouldn't have to defend your convictions to friends, so just don't go there.

I don't have room for that negative energy in my life of those who've decided to dislike me because I don't follow their beliefs, of any kind.

I've never walked away from a friend who walks a different path unless they treat people poorly, but I have had some walk away from me. That's not my loss, it's theirs.

I'm clear on who my friends follow and if we don't agree we just don't go there.

You see I think the problem is that some have forgotten to look at what's inside someone's heart.

What kind of person are they? How do they treat people? Would they hold the door for you if your hands are full? Would they give you a shoulder to cry on if you needed it? Do they respectfully disagree but love you for you? Would they bring you a bottle of Titos and listen while you vent? No? then you don't need them!

I continue to learn who my friends really are and appreciate all of you who accept me for who I am with my strong convictions, my delightful weirdness, my open armed acceptance of every race, religion and background, my support of my LGBTQ friends and family, strong support of women's rights and those who entertain these posts. ♡

I love unique, eclectic, individualism, sound bowls and flutes, guided meditations, spiritual awareness, the West and all it has to offer, hikes in the woods, bike rides, people watching, laughing, music, singing, dancing, analyzing and fixing ....

We weren't cut from a cookie cutter. We were created to be different, unique. It would be a pretty boring world if we were all the same.

My wish over the next month, is that no matter what happens, the ugliness of a divided country begins to mend.

The healing is up to us, not a politician.

Namaste 🙏

> If you are losing friends over politics were they really friends to begin with?

10/21/2020

Mindful Moments ....

Well ... today almost felt "normal."

Aside from my entry way displaying supplies for hand sanitizing, temperature taking and masking up before the bus arrived, it was ... normal.

Wow, does a taste of normal feel amazeballs!!

William found that after alllllll of the worrying, uncertainty and catastrophizing of the unknown, being at school was a pretty darn good thing!

He had a GREAT day!

I have reflected in prior posts that for most, this inconvenience, this pandemic, has brought to the surface those things, places or moments that were taken for granted.

We've been guided through a cavalcade of emotions these past months from fear, to disappointments, to missed mile stones, doubt, anger, depression, financial stress, lost loved ones but those who use those feelings as a reminder to appreciate every little thing that life has to offer will come out of this on top.

It's those interruptions in life that reminds us why we're here and that we all have a purpose. Find your true purpose and expand upon it. You have a wealth of personal wisdom and experience to offer someone, one star fish at a time.

There were some people recently who jumped at the opportunity of a simple request.

I needed empty boxes ... just that simple.

Attached to this post is the joy and creativity your thoughtfulness brought to some weary kiddos and their teachers. They have more building to do but the smiles make it so worth the effort - thank you Todd, Kathi, Mary, Nina (for your offer) Robin and I'm hoping I'm not leaving anyone out - if I did, please forgive my Rona jelly brain - it's been a looooooong haul!

The "Minecraft / Dino Mec" suit box was a secondary pickup from Robin - he had a great time creating that one at home!! Thank you!!

And me ... I got to sit, in the quiet, sipping coffee (I was exhausted) and catching up on paperwork after work ... allllllll alone for an hour and a half! Whoop whoop!!

Good day was had by all. 😊

Namaste 🙏

11/3/2020

Mindful Moments ....

Do you know what I did today?

Well, I didn't vote ... because I did that weeks ago.

What I DID do is feed my soul.

Wasn't it a beautiful Fall Day??!! Warm, bright sunshine with the promise of more beautiful days ahead.

William has spent time each day painstakingly going through Target, Mind Ware and Amazon toy catalogs circling about EVERYTHING.

I remember those days with the Sears catalog - we didn't have quite as many choices back then and you were happy to get one or two toys you asked for along with clothes and fruit with socks in your stocking (I never ate the fruit 😕).

I spent a few hours outside taking down Halloween decorations, cleaning out my flower beds, where I do my best reflecting.

William rode his bike with his neighborhood friend and I played in the dirt. 💗

I found this tomato who decided to grow despite being gently dropped between the fence posts - that's determination!

It's amazing what a little time in nature can do to restore your energy and nourish your soul. Put me in a better mood pretty quickly.

I put farrrr in the back of my mind what the days ahead may hold and stayed present.

You know I've spent my life as an optimist - not everybody likes an optimist - I've been ridiculed for it - but that personality speaks for itself.

I still believe there is good in everyone but they have to believe it and find it for themselves. I've come to have very little tolerance for lack of kindness. I have no room in my life for it and it wears down my energy.

I thought of a post I commented on yesterday that made me a bit sad.

I follow several special needs families' blogs who are putting themselves out there to advocate and educate about Autism.

I've thought about starting a blog for many years. Telling our story, our journey, our challenges and our wins. To educate.

I've actually wanted to do many things to educate about Autism. Speak to police departments (we've had issues!), schools, libraries, wherever I could get someone to listen.

Here's what stops me. Hatred. Judgement.

These families I follow have an amazing following of supporters - it's a community I've come to rely on - but they have also been ridiculed, threatened, their children berated and called the "R" word, fat, ugly, that they should be put to death because they're worthless. A child! I kid you not.

They are strong people who have to be strong for their special needs' family member and strong enough to fight past the ugly people in this world who are so unhappy that they berate and threaten children.

I have wonderful family and friends right here although you never hear even half of our story. I just don't go there because I don't look for sympathy but if I did it would only be to educate.

So, while I've seen such awful things being said in general FB conversations, especially these past few months, I still believe, deep down somewhere, there's hope for a better, kinder world.

That blog ... maybe someday when I learn to desensitize because I have seen some of the worst and I don't want that for my family.

For now, I will keep high hopes for better days, renewed friendships and the return of kindness and acceptance of EVERYONE, every race, religion and sexual orientation.

We are all born unique and to make our own imprint on this world - how do you want to be remembered?

A special mention to Boston who recognizes me and because we've all been quarantined at home for nearly 2 weeks, sees and hears what I manage here every day - thank you for the flowers and wine - both are much appreciated.

I plan to wake up tomorrow to blue skies and sunshine and welcome a new day with hope for a better future.

Namaste 🙏

11/4/2020

Mindful Moments ....

I woke up today, Wednesday Nov 4, to sunshine, blue skies and mild temperatures ... another lovely day!! The sky was an amazing brilliant blue without a cloud to be seen.

While today has been filled with anxious anticipation of election results, I took note of a few things.

Facebook - pretty darned enjoyably quiet and free from judgement, preaching, hate and rhetoric. NICE – see, we can be civil or perhaps we're all just tired of trying to change everyone?

In fact, I saw some humorous engagement with amusing non-political memes, needs of advice and some expressions of gratefulness ♡ WOW

I saw a country, yet still sadly divided, exercising their right to vote, express themselves and their convictions in RECORD numbers!!

That's what this country is about - now let's grow up, be kind, find the joy and get along.

The lack of politically slamming commercials was a breath of fresh air!

There was a sense of a different kind of calm in the air and it was refreshing.

Perhaps foes are hiding in the trenches waiting for their attack or in their private groups scuttling about over this number and that - staying in the moment I will enjoy the peace before us as if it will last forever.

There has been some enjoyment in tv ads for me lately - I'm easily amused.

I can't help but stop what I'm doing and watch every Geico "Wild Thing" commercial that it comes on. The trip to the DMV and the Tailor crack me up - something to laugh about - thanks Geico for the comedic relief of late! Much needed.

William found excitement in a Buick we saw on our way to work this morning and soon after an older model Stingray. Oh, happy days!!

I won't soon forget these many months of working while teaching and entertaining. There have been many hard days with some fun and amusement thrown in just at the right time to stumble through into the next day. A bit of a Twilight Zone episode that has lasted nearly a year, and too long at that.

Even poor Gypsy has run out of steam - we had to plug her in for a recharge.

"Breathe. Breathe again.

Breathe in acceptance, breathe out criticism. Breathe, breathe again. Breathe in love, breathe out hatred. Breathe, breathe again. Breathe in whatever you want, and breathe out whatever no longer serves you."

Namaste 🙏

11/5/2020

Mindful moments ....

Well, I enjoyed and am thankful for the peacefulness of yesterday because boy oh boy has the tune changed on here today.

Back to name calling, everyone's assumed lazy or in fear who didn't go in to vote, the democrats are cheating, the post office is hiding ballots, there are shenanigans going on - UGH!

Goosefraba!!!!! From "Anger Management" a movie many should take the time to see right now!

I've also learned today that apparently posting peace and kindness to each other messages is offensive to some. Well, I believe if you can throw one star fish back into the ocean then it's worth it.

Take a deep breath people! Turn off the tv and radio. Take up a hobby. Stop assuming you know everyone's situations and for love of all that is FACT CHECK before you post ridiculous accusations. Be adults!!

So, how's everyone's day going ... I've had a great day!

I had some awesome clients today with great conversations, laughs and kindness to William with candy, homemade cookies and Capri Sun.

I was told "he's a real gentleman and a pleasure to be around, he's smart and his inquisitiveness is appreciated." HE appreciated how nice my clients are, he said. As am I.

I would like to thank the makers of the Nevada ballot counting memes today ... good stuff ... now that's worth posting.

After work, I've never been so thankful to be distracted with remote learning and then watching the millionth episode of Amphibia and Big City Greens today. I even let William watch unboxing YouTube videos, which I think are a mind-numbing waste of time, because it was better than anything else.

I dusted and started my next decluttering project and then sat down to get some client communication done before I made dinner.

I was able to have a nice phone conversation with Caitin now that her hectic days are behind her for now and will be able to spend a little time with her this weekend. I miss my girl and as few as they are, cherish every moment we have together.

Tomorrow is a new day. Live it like you won't have another.

BE KIND!

"May silence make you strong."

Namaste 🙏

11/7/2020

Mindful moments ....

On this beautiful day I took the advice of a wise woman, Annika, and created space for some much-needed self-care.

After such a tumultuous, stressful week I went out to our local Forest preserve for a nice long peaceful reflective hike by myself.

I thoroughly soaked in its beauty, peacefulness and friendly fellow visitors.

No hate, no politics, no mudslinging, no disrespect - just a handful of people, like me, looking for solitude and place to clear their minds.

I watched geese announcing their flyover as they flocked in groups overhead.

I watched a beaver playfully flopping around in the water looking for his next snack.

And for some reason today the heron and egret preserve appeared like a lonely ghost ship through the branches of the fall trees.

The bright sun reflecting off the lake from a clear blue sky brought serenity.

After my hike I went home and put Christmas lights up outside - don't judge it was 74 degrees - I'm not plugging them in I'm just taking advantage of the day, carpe diem, not freezing my rear off this year!

A person behind a desk in an oval office doesn't have control over our behaviors.

It's up to each and every one of us to take responsibility for our own actions and put an end to the negative nature in which our country has turned.

RESPECT one another - just because our values are different doesn't make us wrong or right, it makes us individuals.

There are many, many people I know who my heart is full for today, you know who you are. We all matter, we are all valued and it's time that it's recognized.

BE the change you want to see in the world.

Namaste 🙏

11/8/2020

Mindful moments ... post Sunday edition.

Last night The Fear and TWD World Beyond took priority BUT this was our afternoon yesterday.

Taking advantage of the beautiful weather for an outdoor visit with mom.

Watched a family across the street enjoying an outdoor, socially distanced, Bears game in the garage, piñata for the kid's, afternoon - William wanted so badly to join in on the piñata fun but of course he couldn't.

One of the boys put some of the candy in a bag, with mask on, brought it to moms' driveway and set it down for William to go get.

THIS is how kindness shows up!

Be kind!

Happy Monday - putting my teacher hat on!

Namaste 🙏

11/10/2020

Mindful moments ....

Without realizing it, in a blink of an eye, time just flies by.

These 2 photos are 8 yrs. apart. She was nearly 4 on the left and is nearly 12 on the right.

A little saggier skin, grayer muzzle, lumps and bumps and slower stride, like the rest of us, but still the aloof, fearer of personal space invading, poop munching, bark face cutie pie. ♡

These photos reminded me of how quickly life passes by.

And it passes whether we're fretting over trivial things or taking a step back and soaking in the precious moments.

The older I get, the less I tolerate - not in the sense of INtolerance but in removing negativity, judgement and lack of acceptance of differences from my life.

I no longer have the desire to be in a circle where this type of value is the norm. I have no room for it.

Also, the older I get the smaller my circle becomes and changes yet the larger the benefits that it provides because I keep those close to me that feed my soul with positive energy, spirituality and peace.

I no longer linger in the company of those who don't.

The important things in life change with age and life experience.

What was once important, like material things that were momentarily a necessity, are long gone and now just trivial pieces in time in comparison to healthy, nurturing relationships with good people.

"We are shaped by our thoughts; we become what we think. When the mind is pure, joy follows like a shadow that never leaves."

Gautama Buddha

Namaste 🙏

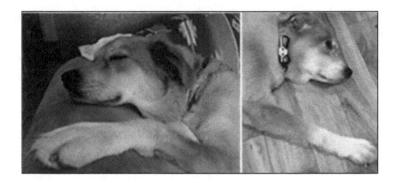

11/11/2020

Mindful Moments ....

Meet Henry, Fisher and Leah! 3 of my subjects for today.

Wolfy is not pictured as just getting through the appointment with this big guy with all my fingers in tact was top priority, and Chewy, I will see your cute little face next week!

I wasn't going to write tonight. It's been "a day" today, like many this year. Not a bad day, just a lot.

What came to mind today was how life throws us curve balls to keep us on our toes. It's a test you know. How we handle them gives us a passing grade in a life lesson or has us repeat until we get it right. Some lessons take longer to stick than others.

Have you ever looked at the "big picture" and get so overwhelmed with the whys, how's and what will happen that you forget to stay in the moment and breathe?

This happened to 2 people I know this week, at different times. They both looked at everything that was being tossed to them at once and couldn't breathe. They panicked, wanted to shut down and crawl in hole. Ever feel that way? I have.

I found myself talking them both down from the proverbial ledge and redirecting thoughts to ... breathe, one step at a time, focus on priorities, we'll get through this ... stay in the moment as worry and stress don't change the future outcome.

Sometimes it's easier to help someone else through a difficult time than help ourselves when we need it most.

Staying in the moment can be so hard when anxiety and panic overwhelm your thoughts. But does it solve anything? Does it change what the future holds? Is it good for your well-being? No. No and No.

Thanks to a few soulful people in my life and remote learning, a certain benefit for us, William and I have practiced a lot of self-soothing, emotional awareness and relaxation techniques provided by his team at school, through technology.

Deep breathing, muscle relaxation, 5 senses awareness, music, meditation - there are so many ways to bring your mind into the present. It's ok for it to wander, as long as you can bring it back. Awareness.

The last 3 nights Dreamcatcher "Water of Life" (native flute) by Preston on YouTube has lulled William to sleep and relaxed my thoughts with its calming tone and gentle stream. I'm listening to it now.

Check him out on Patreon and YouTube and follow his Sunday evening at 4pm live sound meditations. He has a gift of magical, peaceful music for you to open in your heart and mind.

Life is not promised to be perfect. It's not promised to come without challenges BUT if you open your mind to self-awareness, with practice and dedication, you can find peace and tranquility.

Tonight, I find peace in knowing that many months of mortgage refi hazing has come to an end and we can look forward to a little less financial burden in the coming months - thank you Lucie for coming to witness even though it turned out that you didn't need to - it was nice to see your "face" and chat for a bit. She didn't arrive until after 7 so I'm glad you didn't have to wait.

Our past is behind us, our future not promised, breathe and stay in the moment ....

Namaste

11/14/2020

Mindful Moments ....

A little food porn for my foodies today.

It's not often I'm able to do the simple things that make me happy but thanks to Cody hanging with William while Cailin was grooming, today was that day!

There are soooo many things I'd like to do I never know where to start when I have a couple of free hours - I decided to spend it in the kitchen!

The crock pot was filled with fresh ingredients for a pot of Cilantro Lime Chicken for dinner, rice steamed on the stove and corn bread made yesterday.

While the crockpot prepared dinner, I made some of my favorite healthy goodies! Recipes available upon request.

First up Almond Butter Cups - one of my favorites!

There are unhealthy fats and healthy fats - olive oil, avocado oil, coconut oil (yes, I know there are doubts about coconut oil but way healthier than butter, corn oil or lard) are a few of the healthy ones.

These are made with organic unrefined coconut oil.

While those were chilling, protein balls were in the works - another favorite quick, tasty, healthy snack!

Some beautiful avocados were delivered yesterday soooooo what else do you make but guacamole mole mole!!!

In the meantime, I threw some boneless chicken thighs in the air fryer, seasoned, for lunches.

Dinner was served, topped with fresh, sliced avocado and Avocado Serrano sauce (my new favorite hot sauce) - rice and corn muffins for everyone else.

Most of the time I laugh when someone says "you really need to take care of yourself so you can take care of everyone else" well I'm already taking care of everyone else so there isn't any "me" time!

But those few hours that are gifted are soooo appreciated!!

I'm already missing my family for Thanksgiving this year - heck I'm missing them from the entire year! We haven't seen each other since Christmas last year.

With caution now, we can have tomorrow with those we love.

I'm not a risk taker. I'm not a fighter. I'm not competitive, except within myself. I don't let chance lead my way. But I DO live life with purpose, activity, caution, my own and others safety and wellness at the forefront so that we may all be together once again.

You have within you,

Right now,

Everything you need

To deal with

Whatever the world

May throw at you.

Namaste 🙏

11/17/2020

Mindful Moments ....

Some random things today, because I'm feeling random and haven't written in a few days.

I'm grateful for MeWe and Parler - nuff said - FB has been so peaceful and pleasant.

Back to family photos, memories and nice job with the memes lately, they're great!! I've found myself laughing out loud many times! Most people's sense of humor is returning and the atmosphere is relaxed.

Things to laugh at, bring your blood pressure down and try to relax a bit.

Here's something I'm still trying to digest.

Back in late Spring, scientists, not politicians, said that if the public didn't wear masks and stay away from crowds, we were headed toward a second round of a Covid breakout, much worse than the first, leaning toward a dark winter.

Sooooo, most went on not wearing masks, defying science, going to/having parties, concerts, beaches, etc.

And here we are.

And those who didn't participate are the ones complaining the loudest about returning to tighter restrictions.

What still doesn't compute with some of you? It's disappointing and sad.

My family has made a difficult decision to stay in our respective homes this year for Thanksgiving and will enjoy each other's company, cocktail time, food and laughter from a safe place via zoom in that we hope to have another year with all of us together and healthy.

Was that an easy decision?? NO! We haven't been altogether since Christmas last year - that sucks, and it's ok to say that. I miss everyone, I miss people BUT not bad enough to risk their wellness or mine at such a high-risk time.

If I leave the bedroom door open when I'm showering, Gypsy is always waiting on the bed for me when I come out. As hard as it is for her to jump up these days, she's still there waiting - something normal. ♡

William was privy to his first viewing of a live successful rocket lift off. He was amazed with the excitement and power of the historical SpaceX Falcon 9 rocket launch blasting off to the International Space Station on Sunday the 15th.

I recalled being out there in person years ago to observe a launch that had to be scrubbed due to weather. It was still exciting, just the same, being there in person.

He said he'd love to go one day; I'd love to be able to take him.

At the risk of making this any longer I've captioned some of the photos instead - some interesting things I've seen on my walks this week and other random musings.

Oh, and please stop hoarding toilet paper, no one poops any more often whether we're in a shut down or not.

Namaste 🙏

11/18/2020

Mindful Moments ....

I took this video last week while out walking.

I'm no ornithologist but it "appears" to be a downy woodpecker, probably female. Correct me if I'm wrong because I probably am.

There she was just hammering away either looking for food, constructing a nest or calling for a suitor. ♡

Just in pure natural momentum, survival, as the winter looms.

How similar our lives are in some way's. Housing for our families, warmth and food in their grumbling tummies.

And yet so different in that their world is small in basic necessities and comes without materialistic extravagance, desire for purposeful vengeance or spiteful gains.

Just survival.

I was thinking about this video at work today while enjoying a lovely sandwich consisting of chipotle lime avocado oil mayo and ham with a questionable expiration date.

Since I forgot to bring my breakfast protein shake, slightly, possibly spoiled ham was going to have to do / the grapes were delish and I feel fine!

I digress.

This brought me to our current status of a pandemic.

They are oblivious to the isolation, depression and frustration.

They freely fly from one project to the next with one thing in mind - Survival.

Isn't that what we're trying to do? Well, most of us? Just make it to the next day?

As another disappointment hit the emails today of an extended "adaptive pause" for school, as they're calling it now to make it less daunting, I just felt numb.

One disappointment after another.

Return on Oct 21 ... 2 days in school cancelled due to a staff member testing positive until November 9.

Return November 9 for hybrid ... cancelled due to staff positive covid exposure.

Return on November 30 for hybrid ... cancelled due to exponential covid numbers that need to stop!

Next return date ... January 4 for full 5 days ... remains to be seen.

The kids, the teachers, the parents are fried. None of us have much more remote learning in us - I've wanted to throw in the towel more than once, just give up. But we can't.

After a very emotionally exhausting day for William today and a tearful call at work when his counselor broke the news to him, I felt like a parrot.

Just repeating the same things I've said for 8 months - we can do this! We're tough and strong! We can't control what other people do, we can only do our part! We'll have "fun" with it! We'll find fun things to do at home ... movie nights, game nights!

All the time knowing I was trying to convince myself we'd make it without losing it as much as trying to convince him.

Oh to be that bird flying freely through the crisp November air just searching for the next sturdy tree to build a home and to survive one more day.

Christmas lights, bows and garland make me happy and hopeful and need to be a beacon to forge ahead. So, it shall be very soon.

Find something to keep you going.

"Free Bird."

Namaste 🙏

There is freedom waiting for
you, on the breezes of the sky,
and you ask "What if I fall?"
Oh but my darling, What
if you fly?

-Erin Hanson | Quotes 'nd Notes

11/19/2020

Mindful Moments ....

I seriously almost typed Mindless Moments! - shows you where my brain is today!

That's the 9:45pm I was staring at last night projected onto my ceiling while lying on the bedroom floor.

Nooooo I wasn't drunk - I didn't fall.

William wanted a "sleepover" last night after his emotional day but couldn't relax, stop fidgeting.

We worked on meditation, muscle relaxation techniques and breathing techniques for over 2 hours when I decided to just give him space.

Autistic kiddos have a tough time with sleep and relaxation. Most are riddled with anxiety and brains that are wired to stay in constant motion. It's hard to watch him struggle. He has several medications to help but sometimes that doesn't even work.

Every night I lay with him and talk to him, play flute or gong meditation music, coach him through relaxing ... sometimes, RARE times, he's out right away. Most nights it's a half hour to 3 hours of being unsettled, unable to relax his mind and body, it won't allow him to. It just depends on what occurred during the day. The calmer the day, the quicker to rest.

I know the nights I need to be near but move away and then he settles and falls asleep. Last night was that night. So, I laid on the floor next to the bed from 9:30 to 10pm when he finally fell asleep. I continue to try to understand his struggles.

The mind is very complex and difficult to figure out so you just roll with the differences of each day.

Autism has been compared to the behaviors of dementia. I'm finding this to be quite true with mom now. Interesting. Something I'd like to look into more.

William has a couple of comfort foods. Sweets, sweets and sweets oh and bread ... yes bread and lots of it!

Top right was his dessert tonight. A delectable creation of layered Oreo cookie ice cream, a slice of apple pie, drizzled with fresh honey and topped with Reddi whip! My thighs just grew an inch typing that!!

Dinner was a healthy homemade burrito bowl of slow cooked flank steak on a bed of lettuce with cheese and avocado drizzled with avocado Serrano sauce - William ate 2 burritos made similarly, with rice and then the dessert! ah to be young and have a strong, fast-moving metabolism!!

I received the most heartwarming messages from a couple of friends today - I'm honored that we can touch each other's lives every day. ♡

As we close on Friday Eve, I wish you all a peaceful sleep with dreams of better days to come, hugging everyone you see (well for the huggers anyway, like me - we're not ok!) and future gatherings filled with laughter with family and friends. ♡

To quote one of my mom's favorite authors:

"Seize the moment. Remember all those women on the 'Titanic' that waved off the dessert cart." Erma Bombeck

Carpe Diem

Namaste 🙏

11/20/2020

Mindful Moments ....

Short and sweet.

William was up at 3:45am today, for the day - after a rough night the day before.

He rode the struggle bus through 5 zoom calls and 5 assignments - I'm proud of him for trying his best!

So, his teacher sent me this tonight.

Sweet dreams bitches!

Namaste 🙏

11/22/2020

Mindful Moments ....

I ran across this amazing little nursery Saturday while running errands, The Fields on Caton Farm.

I've lived out here 18 yrs. and never knew it existed because all the big box stores stood out more.

These photos are from their outdoor nursery area set up with a cracking fireplace, comfortable seating and beautifully peaceful decorations for photos or just to take 5 from life.

I want to just go hang out there for some quiet, alone time!

There were so many beautiful, FRESH CUT trees but this 9ft Frazier fur was calling my name.

Their service was amazing from dressing the tree, wrapping and performed the most secure tie down on the Jeep I've ever seen!

Customer service bar none!

Support small business!!

I have to say until yesterday morning I was very excited about setting up Christmas.

Something to look forward to ring in with glimmering, soft lights and colors pleasing to the eye.

A couple of things shifted that excitement. I allowed others to get into my head and bring that excitement down.

It made me sad and day dreaming of years ago when Christmas music filled the house while decorating, working together and having fun to get the job done with enjoyment but swiftly so the fruits of our labor could be enjoyed ....

I spent the day decorating inside and out, eating while I worked but my heart wasn't in it.

My back, feet and legs ached after 7 hours. It was exhausting.

However, I've "decided" to turn that around for ME.

Everything is done and I can take pride having done it myself and enjoy the sites for the next month

Lesson re-learned - don't let anyone steal your thunder!

William chose the outdoor decos a little Charles Brown and company - he helped decorate his tiny real tree and added one new ornament that he gets to choose each year - this year, a motorcycle.

Those lights will be lit every day for my enjoyment!

Alexa will be serenading me with an occasional Christmas tune, just enough so as not to over saturate before Christmas.

Be true to yourself ....

Namaste 🙏

11/24/2020

Mindful Moments ....

Brings you random Tuesday!

We finished school work early and ran out to get some errands done.

Gypsy has been showing her age quite a bit lately and just doesn't seem comfortable anywhere.

William and I saw these dog beds on sale and grabbed one for her.

I laid it down at 1:15pm and she was still sleeping on it at 530; I loved seeing her so content. ♡

I did not intend to keep it in the middle of the hallway - so when she finally got up to get a drink, I moved it into the living room where I wanted to put it originally.

She finished her drink and went and laid back down in the same spot without even looking around for it. I think she thought it had been a mirage or in her dream.

We'll see if she decides to occupy it again in its new location ....

Anyone else's dogs having skin allergy issues this year?

Gypsy has never had allergies until this summer. Little itchy bumps and that she bites at, they get bigger and some form a larger lump.

Allergy meds "seem" to stop it but a few weeks later it starts up again. hmmm

Even more adorable was Marshmallow's fascination with the musical Christmas tree - so cute!

Little things make me happy.

So, the item pictured in photos 3 and 4 is a quiz.

Who knows what this is? No fair guessing Paula. ☺

I cannot WAIT to hear my perverted friend's answers - Insert Jeopardy music ....

Productive, busy day and time to chill.

I'll be looking for prize winners!!!

Namaste 🙏 at home!

11/29/2020

Mindful Moments ....

Other than staying healthy this weekend I had some goals to keep my mind off of missing my family.

1) to complete 95% of my Christmas shopping (brown and blue have been here several times already)

2) to make out my Christmas cards and have them addressed, stamped and ready for mailing

With my family, friends and my amazing autism family the card pile stacked over 120 cards. It's a good feeling.

It's sad that not many take a little time to send cards anymore. That personal touch really makes a difference.

I decide to add to that pile and want to start a crusade of appreciation.

If each of us who send cards add to our list our local P.D., Fire Dept, hospital ER's and ICU's and maybe adding in your local food pantries we could all make a difference. ♡

Let's show our Healthcare workers, first responders and volunteers who are spending their time away from their families, putting themselves at risk to help others on a daily basis know how much they are appreciated for their selfless acts. ♡

It's a card, a few kind words, maybe a few dollars to a food pantry. How about joining me in doing a simple act to show appreciation? My cards are ready to go. ♡

We can sit at home and feel sorry for ourselves and be disappointed that we can't be living our typical lives or we can turn that around and do something positive with it. I choose the latter.

We had 2 wonderful zoom calls with both of our families this weekend. We may have missed the hugs but we enjoyed each other's company, laughed and caught up ... safely.

Namaste 🙏

12/3/2020

Mindful Moments ....

Child on the dog bed ... dog on the couch for attention.

I'm glad both are being used.

Today I want to talk a little about the "hard", the voodoo of talking about real life, real emotions, real feelings.

Not what we happily post on FB but what's "really" happening in our lives.

Headliner today swept me off my feet:

"11-year-old boy dies after shooting himself during zoom class"

Wow, gut punch.

William is 11.

William is having a VERY hard time lately. So are a lot of people.

He's done with remote learning, done with zoom classes, done with sitting in front of a computer 5-6 hrs. per day. He WANTS and NEEDS to be at school.

He's losing his mind. And so am I. Staying sane while advocating for a special needs' person is a feat in itself. No kudos, it's just the facts. Dedication and sacrifice.

Sure, lots of us are.

But we don't all live with Autism and other labeled emotional disorders that make all of this isolation frustrating, overwhelming, out of much needed routine, lonely ....

His Autism and severe anxiety turn into meltdowns, not tantrums, I'm talking self-injuring, aggression, depression, frustrated melt downs. Inability to fall asleep, it can take hours and he needs me there by his side the whole time.

Anxiety.

He looks for material things he thinks will make him feel better. Do you ever do that? "If I just buy this one thing all this pain and anxiety with just POOF, disappear" - nope.

Dig deep and figure it out.

Lately all the coping skills and relaxation strategies we practice daily don't make a difference.

It's the hard that happens here daily and in many homes with emotional illness that no one talks about right now while some boast about going to parties and "no one is going to tell me I have to wear mask" which keeps us isolated longer. Isolation is depleting.

What I want to say is for those who are struggling:

I hear you.

I see you.

You are important and your feelings are valid.

Ask for help, lean in and reach out.

Look for the helpers.

I have found my tribe and thanks to them and their kindness tonight I'm a little lighter, hoping William and I sleep tonight and tomorrow we get up and do it again.

We are 261 days into this.

We've made it this far.

With hope, stamina, perseverance and positivity we can make it a bit longer.

You are not alone in your struggles. 🫶

One day at a time, sometimes, One minute at a time.

Namaste 🙏

12/4/2020

Mindful Moments ... (from last night).

It's amazing how a day away from what troubles you can change the course of the future, albeit short term.

No zoom calls - stress reduced 90%!

Finished academics by 11.

Brought in groceries and took off for a few hours of fun in the sun today.

He was calmer, patient, soulful and helpful. Just listen to him sing Christmas Carols while, slightly begrudgingly, emptying the dishwasher while I shower.

It was a Culver's flavor of the day ice cream for lunch kind of day.

Followed by some Jeep ducking! What is this you say??

It's a group of Jeepers spreading joy all this year with little rubber duckies left on other Jeeps.

We've added first responders to the list and any other vehicle we'd like as well because everyone needs a smile right now.

We had fun! It feels good to make someone else smile, get out of the house, leave tech at home.

William "ducked" his first Jeep today and loved it! We even handed one to the inhabitants of one which is even better than secretly leaving one. You actually get to see a smile on someone's face!

We must've hit almost a dozen today and almost got a couple of squad cars at Chipotle but they left too quickly!

The afternoon was peaceful, bedtime was easy, right to sleep, not hours of struggling.

So, tell me these incessant zooms aren't causing emotional distress!

Anxiety can rule your life - sometimes you have to step away from responsibilities, take the bull by the horns and nip anxiety in the keester!

I'll take the couple of days of calm and hope some of that calm slips into Monday - I am realistic not negative. When those zooms are back it's game on.

Since it's Saturday, and Cody is entertainment committee so I can have some free time while Caitlin makes the donuts, I have baking on the to do list ... and lots of it!

We're all struggling in some way feel your feels then find the joy.

One day at a time.

Namaste

12/5/2020

Mindful moments ....

Seemed like a good night to light the fireplace - sending peace and healing energy to those who need it, peace and love B.L. ♡

Serenity!

Namaste 🙏

12/6/2020

Mindful Moments ....

My main goal this weekend was to finish the baking I had planned.

Christmas goodies aren't complete without Peppermint Bark, Chocolate Chip Cookies, Kifli Cookies - Apricot and Cherry, regular and gluten free, GF Peanut Butter Cookies (best PB cookies EVER) and a new one this year Coffee and Milk Thumbprints.

Sometime over the next week there are a few more goodies I'd like to complete.

I had some great taste testers here and they passed with flying colors.

Some powdered sugar sprinkled on the Kifli's will complete them.

I woke up this morning with a lot on my mind. Something that came up over the weekend was grating on me. I was disappointed in something I have no control over.

I grabbed my coffee and started working.

Self-employment doesn't run from 8 to 5, M - F. There is NO rest this time of year for groomers, hair stylists/barbers and nail techs! Props my friends I feel you! We will rest on 12-25!

We are booked solid through Christmas with requests coming in hourly. I am grateful but exhausted!

William came down as always bright eyed and ready for action trying to dip his toes in my coffee being silly.

As my mind swam with having to get to laundry, book work, baking, generator oil change ... I couldn't help but think that these past 9 months I just haven't made much time for fun anymore - because there hasn't been much time.

I've just been surviving.

I realized that my time spent with him this year has been teaching him, guiding him through daily chores, finding entertainment without friends and managing his anxiety while working.

So, I dropped everything and played Pokémon cards with William for 2 hours.

Everything else was still completed, later, regardless of the break. But kids aren't kids for long. Relationships change so enjoy it while you can. They get older and move on, they are not ours to keep.

You hope that when they're young you create a bond that brings them back over the years.

I introduced William to the dreaded violent Bugs Bunny and Friends. I haven't heard him laugh that much in a very long time! I laughed more than I did when I was a kid and saw them originally.

He looked at me after about the 4th time Elmer popped Daffy in the beak and said "Daffy's really stupid, isn't he?!"

I couldn't stop laughing!

In text convoing with my sibs today one of my brothers brought up a subject which accurately labels our emotions right now ... Acedia ... look it up - it's a little dark but just might make you feel a bit validated and normal in your emotions under our circumstances.

Tomorrow brings the first of the last two weeks before winter break.

Two weeks doesn't seem long but the last 9 months have been the fastest, slowest 9 months of my life! It's like pouring ice cold water over ice cubes and waiting for them to melt.

Like the Little Train that Could we will climb this hill and get past it!

Gypsy was tired from helping me in the kitchen.

To better days!

Namaste 🙏

12/8/2020

Mindful Moments ....

Until today I, almost, thought we finally squeaked past the judging and name calling of political preference and mask wearing.

I was wrong.

I thought the word "sheeple" crawled back under the rock it crawled out of.

I was wrong.

I thought everyone crawled into their private FB groups to bash one another privately instead of publicly.

I was wrong.

I thought friends started to respect friends in their personal beliefs without childish name calling and judgement.

I was wrong.

I've learned ALOT about people I thought I knew well this past year. Sadly, a lot I no longer care to associate with because if I'm not accepted for who I am and I fall into a name calling category, I don't need the company.

On the flip side, I've learned ALOT about people I know, that I already knew.

Friends who I can respectfully disagree with or, find commonality with, continue to see the good things in them that first drew us together before I knew their politics or stance on a pandemic. Those are my people. ♡

I don't meet someone and say "hey what political party do you follow?" I don't even THINK about that. I see the traits in someone that appeal to who I am and who I like to keep company with. Period.

This past year has changed a lot of folks. Or maybe just brought out true colors?

We grew up knowing that politics and religion were off the table topics. It's no one's damn business because everyone has their own reasons for believing the way they do and those reasons don't merit back lash or judgement.

Weren't we born into a "free" country? Don't we have the right to carry on our lives as we see fit as long as we're not hurting anyone?

Again, I was wrong.

These days there seems to be so many unhappy people out there. You get slammed for the clothes you wear, the house you live in and the technology you choose to use

I am RIGHT, however, in standing firm in my beliefs, keeping company with those who respect that, nurture my soul and finding the joy in every darn day I'm blessed to be a part of.

And I am blessed!

I have an amazing family, amazing mother-in-law, brothers, brothers in law and sisters in law who are kind hearted and genuine. Extended family I don't often see who have hearts of gold.

I have a 93-year-old mom, who even having spent 7 months in assisted living recovering from surgery during this pandemic, was kept safe with proper PPE, sanitization, 3x daily temp and oxygen checks so she could come home. And we have the ability to carry on those precautions.

Yep, blessed beyond words, without judgement and with respect.

Namaste

12/9/2020

Mindful Moments ....

Today was ... interesting.

It was a work day but much different than many others.

My first client, who has been with us for over 20 years, has an old golden who is suspected to have cancer.

The whole grooming gig is hard on him now so we do nails, de-shed, ear cleaning, a little trimming while he lays comfortably on the living room carpet.

He has a little trouble getting up but has no trouble looking in my pocket for his expected treats.

These appointments are always difficult for me because I know animals. I know aging and I know that each appointment could be the last time I see them - going to people's homes for 10+ years, monthly or even more often, makes them like family.

While driving down my second client's street I see a brown dog just off the roadway in the grass milling around right across from the house I'm headed to.

Upon closer inspection, it IS the dog who I'm headed to groom! He sees the van and comes running toward me. I stop and get out to coax him in so he and I both can safely head up the driveway.

Fisher decides my approach is an invitation to engage in playtime and starts running all over and puppy play position stance ensues (He's 9 mos. old).

He runs up the front lawn and into the backyard at which time I contact mom to tattle that Fisher is on the loose. He apparently did not have his invisible fence collar on and decided to venture across the street. Fisher safe, grooming done, another success!

My third house is the most interesting.

I pull up the long driveway to then make a 3 point turn on a small parking pad to be facing forward.

As I'm ready to text the owner that I've arrived, I see the garage door open, see her sitting tying her shoe, so I thought, grabbed my mask and start toward the side doors of the van.

I see her get up holding her left eye and staggering toward the open door with dog in hand, blood running down her face and arm.

I jumped out, sat her down, grabbed the dog, put the dog in the van and grabbed a towel for her head.

Her dog is a sweetheart but a bit overzealous and pulled her down the garage stairs where she fell, said she hit her head on the concrete floor, I think it was more the bumper of one of the parked cars.

It was not good - huge gash above her eye, her eyebrow literally relocated, Immediate swelling.

I called for her husband to come out and when we helped her up, we saw a softball size hematoma on her shin, another cut with a golf ball sized hematoma just under it.

I don't know what she hit but it wasn't soft - Her husband took her to the ER, I finished the grooming and moved on. Just checked in waiting to hear how she's doing.

I believe the universe places us in situations at the right time.

My last house, my girls, my Rosie the Llama and her goat and sheep friends. ♡

Although my presence was insignificant today lol, they usually come to the fence for a scratch and to look for the possibility of a carrot offering. ♡

I love the farm, so peaceful and welcoming! Girls were great as always and I LOVE the dozen eggs! I'm a simple person and gifts like this make me so happy! Fresh farm eggs!

This beautiful sunset ended my day (it was only 3:45 with the sun so low!), although driving into it was difficult from the glare but what an amazing gift - a huge, bright ball of days end.

William in bed tonight reaching under his shirt to his arm pit "IM GETTING MORE HAIR THERE!! IM BECOMIMG A MAN!!" While rapid fire farting yes you certainly are!! Oh, glory days! Lol

On that note, stay on your side of the street, watch your step and enjoy nature.

Namaste 🙏

12/12/2020

Mindful Moments ....

This girl has been my office assistant, dinner companion, sous chef, walking Buddy and confidant for nearly 12 yrs.

She may be slowing down but boy can she move when she hears the crumpling of a deli meat package, she gets her pills in! Like lightening she is.

I had the pleasure of spending the day with Caitlin and Cody today. Although both a bit out of sorts today, they're fine! We were able to hang out while they relaxed, Cody played with William, Caitlin helped to pack client gifts and well, I just go non-stop all day.

I had my to do list today that went incomplete. I couldn't get to some things I needed to get sorted out for Christmas as making a dinner I didn't anticipate taking the time to do got in the way.

As I've mentioned Cody is a lifesaver to my drowning self.

I have one day per week with William occupied and cared for so I can try to catch up from the backlog of the busy week.

Most Saturdays I just don't know what to get done first because once the day is over very little aside from work and remote learning get done!

I believe that life has a way of interrupting our path when necessary. Slowing us down if you will.

Allowing us to take pause, step back from the hustle bustle of life and spend time in the moment, being mindful.

Sometimes we're so busy trying to keep up with this and that, work, laundry, shopping, decorating, planning, working that we forget to enjoy life for a while.

When our dad told us to enjoy our youth because time flies and soon, we are filled with responsibility, we baulked and continued on with our play.

Now here we are many decades later looking back at those simpler times wishing we had taken more time to "be".

It's never too late to screech to a halt and appreciate what each day brings rather than stressing over what we can't control.

I feel as though this year has flown by while we treaded water to keep our heads above for air with the multitude of challenges and responsibilities thrown at us, one after the other without a moment to breathe.

And yet we now have a light at the end of the tunnel. If more would do their part in staying distanced, mask up and keep anyone out of their homes that don't belong there, and stay out of other homes and establishments you don't belong in, we could get through this with more lives saved, maybe your own.
♡

Years ago, when I lived in a small neighborhood and would take my groomed dogs to their homes I was chatting with a client at her door.

She asked me what my plans were for the rest of the day. When I said I had cleaning to do at home, she said "honey, my mother cleaned everyday of her life. She's dead now and the dirt is still there!"

Whenever my life gets overwhelming, and that happens a lot, I always remember what she said to me that day and smile.

Sometimes I continue with my work, thinking about her, and sometimes, yet rarely, I drop everything and take 15 minutes to sit and be.

Life is shorter than you think.

Namaste

12/13/2020

Mindful Moments ...

I just watched a Geico commercial and now I want to take up clogging! It looks like fun and good exercise!

Although the highlight of my evening was watching Christmas Vacation! Too many classic moments to list, one of my favs.

Even when I finished up some baking and laundry it was kind of a William day.

We played some Pokémon and then saved by the bell! His friend came over from the neighborhood.

This Rona situation is hardest on William. I have a million things to keep me busy but he's lonely and bored.

I won't allow them to play in the house right now but couldn't deny outside hang out.

He taught his friend how to play baseball in Grammy Barbs backyard since ours is all POOL lol- he misses his baseball team. Both seasons cancelled this year.

I made them hot chocolate and fresh baked cookies to warm cold tummies until they couldn't stand it anymore and went their separate ways for the day.

When William came in, he built a fort to snuggle up in, turned on his DVD player and watched some Bugs and Friends. He has a great self-awareness when he needs some decompression time and takes it.

I'd love to have a cozy little fort to disappear into sometimes myself.

Chef William was on board for dinner and whipped up a lovely Chicken and Dumplings recipe. It was delicious!! A double batch is in order next time for leftovers.

I was happy to see him enjoying something other than tech. He has so many more talents and interests than that but it's been easier for him to crawl into a fantasy world gaming screen than face our current reality.

It's time to start living life again despite our restrictions. There are so many things to experience in life, so much fresh air to breathe and sights to see!

A lot to look forward to this last week of the school year. Spirit week with daily fun activities.

Thursday evening drive through Christmas event in the school parking lot. We've decorated the Jeep, gotten out our ugly sweaters, light up necklaces and Santa hats!

I had enough magnetic decos to go around the whole Jeep. What a surprise to learn that the only metal on this JL in the rear quarter panels, the rest, aluminum! What then?

With dreams of spirit week, his upcoming birthday and Christmas he is in sweet slumber resting up for a few weeks of events to bring some sort of normal to a life that's been very abnormal for much too long.

Moments to archive in our minds to take us through a few more months.

And this too shall pass ....

Namaste 🙏

12/14/2020

Mindful Moments ....

I was going to skip this tonight but decided to jot a few anecdotes from the day.

First and most important a happy heavenly birthday to our dad. He would've been 95 today! Hard to believe he's been gone 15 years.

Many moments crossed my mind of dad today but not of sadness, except that he's no longer here, but of moments that make me smile and memories I hold close to my heart.

Miss you every day dad - until we meet again. 🤍

I went out to get the mail today and felt quite let down when the porch wasn't decorated with Amazon boxes - I think we've had daily deliveries since the day after Thanksgiving - I hope they haven't broken up with me!

These top two photos are a hoot.

Those coy goofballs behind that fence are silently poised almost every morning when I walk Gypsy.

They sit ever so still, not a sound or movement, and watch us walk by.

On the occasion Gypsy notices them she loses her mind, as she does every time, she sees another dog, and there they sit silently still, mocking her lunacy.

These two separate occasions Gypsy didn't notice them but they locked their sites on her until we were home.

William was on the struggle bus today so during a break from zooms I made him some hot chocolate with yummy marshmallows in the cup pictured.

He called to me from the front room, in a concerned voice.

"Do you really need coffee to survive???" I responded that it depends on who you are and was impressed with the fact that he read that.

The boy is LITERAL! We're working on gray areas but for now careful choice of wording in explanations is a must to avoid misunderstandings!

Thankfully there are 4 more days until winter break. No unwanted zoom calls for two weeks. No melt downs, tears, negotiating, bargaining, time schedules.

Four days of all remote after break and then back to hybrid on January 11th.

To say that this household can't wait and needs it is an understatement!! My heart goes out to William and kids like him who NEED to be in school. Whose emotional stability is being tested by the day and that of their families.

They've tried to make this last week fun with holiday themed days. Today was tree topper day, we wore Santa hats, tomorrow decorations, Wednesday, ugly or festive sweater day, Thursday ... no idea lol and Friday PJ day!

Thursday evening the school is having a parking lot drive through event with lights and music. Staff will be out handing out gifts to the kids in their cars and vice versa.

It's nice to have something different to look forward to - the kids and staff deserve the recognition for the most difficult year of their lives.

Even in the midst of life's many storms

We have the capacity to

Stand in the center

Of our own Peace.

Namaste 🙏

12/15/2020

Mindful Moments ....

William, Lisa and the Terrible, Horrible, No Good, Very Bad Day!

First a blow dryer problem with the van - this time of year ANY issue disrupting the schedule is NOT welcome! So that had to be attended to in between school.

This was not a proud mom day or proud boy day.

He lost it and fell apart; I lost it and fell apart.

There was yelling, foot stomping, storming off, crying, work avoidance, throwing things (that might have been me, sigh) and wine at noon, that was me too! I'm out of wine btw, just sayin'.

I've learned a lot about Autism, severe anxiety etc., but the one thing I have yet to completely understand is gut wrenching anxiety when we are in the last week of school with fun things thrown into each day and 2 weeks off ahead. I thought this would be a good week.

He just can't let go of things. He holds on for dear life to past events and lives in perpetual motion of impending doom around each corner.

He's had a lot of disappointment, abuse and abandonment in his short 12 years, I soooo understand.

I miss the happy kid who didn't have a care in the world, smiled and laughed all the time enjoying activity and exercise.

I figured out that we've had return to school dates ripped out from under us so many times, he's already stressing over January 11th getting cancelled as well.

It's sooooo frustrating!!

ALOT boiled over, out and oozed everywhere today! And you know what, that's ok dammit!

It's impossible to be Mary Poppins 24/7 in a year like THIS with a challenged kiddo with so much upcoming yet to do and very little "me" time to do it.

This weekend is it for accomplishing anything and everything. I've made a list and I'm on a mission.

The saving grace was starting the day with "Shine bright like holiday lights" day! Even Gypsy joined in, much to her dismay.

The teachers are running out of ways to keep the kids engaged. Some teachers started putting stickers on their face for every correct answer - brilliant!

So today Emily covered herself with a string of garland for the same - see circled photo - it worked - I've never seen the kids answer so many questions willingly!

They need some fun, something to distract from the mundane, boredom of 9 months of screen time!

After that is when the day went skiing downhill at top speed and crashed hard late afternoon!

Oh, if anyone finds an antler, probably smashed to pieces, on I55 north just before 355, it's my Jeep's.

We're both spent - he crashed quickly, thankfully and I need to recharge for a long work day tomorrow.

Every day is a new beginning. A chance to start over fresh.

Tomorrow will be better.

Namaste. 🙏

12/16/2020

Mindful Moments ....

Wednesday random addition!

I left for work at 7:15 anticipating calls and texts from home today.

A simple text from an understanding teacher at 7:30am changed everything.

She said he was doing so amazing on his work, has already exceeded his IEP (independent learning plan) goals for next Spring despite his struggles so he could skip 2 of his zoom calls today - "Merry Christmas" she said.

Emily said she's so proud of his progress. 💭

Auntie Paula said he gave a sigh of relief!

I saw the best yard sign of 2020 today! Simple and to the point with R2D2 supervising.

I was disappointed to see a for sale sign in front of an old stomping ground "Tracy's" in Westmont on 55th St.

They made their money at the bar although the food was always perfectly greasy at midnight!

Lots of memories - another loss to covid.

My boys today have quite the personalities! Personal profiles under photos.

I thought this yard and house decorated like a ginger bread house was adorable - had to stop for a photo op!

Every year I see some beautiful light displays.

THIS year I feel as though some have gone all in to shine a light, so to say, on the end of a challenging, heartbreaking year.

Some of the decorations have had heart, soul and love put into them.

I'm going to take William out a few nights to see them in different neighborhoods with requested Christmas music playing.

We need it.

It was a long day, I'm tired but everyone had a good day today and that's all that matters! Even bedtime was a rare breeze.

I'm thankful for the good days as they get us through the hard ones.

2 more days until winter break.

Sooo, hard to believe Christmas is 9 days away - it doesn't feel like it without our usual family tradition to look forward to and plan for but we'll make it a good day none the less -

I'm sure a family zoom call will be in order.

My work day ended with this Hawk perched overhead by my house and one flew above the Jeep yesterday.

The best was a huge hug from William upon walking in the house while he presented me with a picture of a horse, he did a "sticker by number" for me, reluctantly, but done just the same.

A much better day today.

Moods are kind of like the weather in Chicago, wait 5 minutes and it will change.

Tomorrow may be different but I'll tuck today away in my memory banks for future use.

Remember to pay it forward whenever you can.

Time to rest up for another day in paradise.

Namaste 🙏

12/17/2020

Mindful Moments ....

Tonight, we set out.

To leave stress behind.

We decked out the Jeep.

Started to unwind.

Dinner was fast food,

Cooking was not in my mood!

We set out our sights.

To see our GLA family and lights.

A special drive thru event was the plan.

For a tired, overwhelmed clan.

We didn't expect a grand display,

I mean the teachers are just as exhausted and frayed.

Upon our arrival a grand arch led the way.

To rows of decorations and cheering hurrays!

Bright lights, Christmas Music and eyes smiling above masks,

Our hearts filled with joy from the loving labor of their tasks.

Gifts and holiday salutations were exchanged.

With therapy pups present and, in a row, they were arranged!

This is where love shows in times of despair.

In a very short time, our lives will be in repair.

We have endured a year quite like no other.

We have found peace and solace in the kindness of one another.

Until our new normal, keep spreading the love.

Together we will be one again and rise above.

Namaste 🙏

12/22/2020

Mindful Moments ....

I've been running to catch up with myself the past 4 days!

Friday late afternoon a very dear friend sends me a text to see if I'm home.

As I looked down at my extreme casual wear, "I said yep I'm home!"

She said great I'll be ringing your doorbell in a minute!"

"I'm in my jammies "I said - she replied "PERFECT! Jammies are my FAVE" how can you not love someone who loves you as you are?!

As promised, Denise rang my bell toting a box of gifts for all of us. I was nearly speechless, I know, hard to believe!

It's been challenging here lately, she saw that and showed me that we are seen, supported and appreciated. I cried.

When you're in the trenches and bare your soul, you don't do it for any reason other than to advocate and educate for special needs kiddos, offer support to others in the trenches and bring positivity in a tiring day.

We talked on the porch for quite some time.

You shined a light in a lot of darkness. You put a smile on our faces and tears of gratefulness to our eyes, hot chocolate in our tummies and vodka in our glasses.

I value you my friend, you accept me for who I am and I look forward to a time we can spend more time talking our stuff and taking our Jeep's off roading! – Preston, we need another meditation friend! In good time!

Thank you to Brad and Phoenix for their patience and Caitlin for your covert info.

The rest of our weekend was filled with gift wrapping, errand running and last-minute checking into "what did we forget and what do we still need?"

Boston your gift-wrapping assistance was much appreciated - you can tear tape and keep track of the scissors like nobody's business!

While we were busy being elves and Caitlin was making the donuts ...Cody and William turned our front room into the coolest fort ever!

I'm ignoring the tack holes in the wall because they had fun and William needed the companionship and quiet place to feel secure. You can hardly see the holes (and Cody promised to help us paint).

When you have bigger fish to fry each day you don't sweat the small stuff. I mean aren't we supposed to make the best of the life we have, while we, have it?!!

Today we went out to spread some love at Aunty Flos house and Nana's house. Leaving goodies and Christmas cheer since we won't all be together this year

It's been an eventful few days with more to come.

Be compassionate.

Be a messenger that delivers compassion to everyone – not through some esoteric practice, but through the kindness of your eyes.

Namaste 🙏

12/23/2020

Mindful Moments ....

I was happy to be home from work relatively early today, still so much to do before tomorrow.

While Paula and I chatted, William's cake was frosted and groceries put away.

For a moment it had slipped my mind that this kind hearted man had said he was stopping by after work today with a gift for William from he and his wife.

I told William that Big Jeff's dad, Paul, was stopping by to see him for his birthday - he was elated!!

We ran to the front door, masked up and set outside.

You see this friendship came from a connection with Paul's son Jeff who I met through Caitlin when they were in HS.

They were fast friends ♡ She became their daughter from another mother and Jeff became my son from another mother.

We all tragically lost Jeff last New Year's Eve but his memory lives on forever with all of us as does the family we gained through Jeff with Dottie and Paul. ♡

This is Jeff's truck that Paul fixed up and kept. William eagerly asked if he could see the engine, as he does with everyone's car, but this one is special and although it was raining Paul obliged without hesitation.

We shared some memories, laughs and tears and will forever be grateful for the kindness bestowed upon William from his extended family - Thank you Paul and Dottie.

Another way love shows up.

Birthday surprises are set for the morning, judging by Williams extreme excitement tonight, morning could mean 3am - so off to get some sleep I go!

All good men and women,

Must take responsibility,

To create legacies that,

Will take the next,

Generation to a new level,

We can only imagine.

Namaste 🙏

12/26/2020

Mindful Moments ....

Update - it took 8 hours for this to post but here it is.

On a peaceful Christmas day.

Yesterday was filled with excitement, surprises, love, revving engines (Williams favorite), friends and family.

It was a day I had hoped for, for William.

A day that wiped away the past 9 months of challenges with surprises, smiles and special gifts for a pretty darn amazing kid if I do say so myself.

I feel like it's an award show but so many specials thanks to Caitlin and Cody for expertise organization.

Tree for leading the parade on your bike in 15-degree weather, outstanding! Tori, smart move staying warm in the car!!

Sarah for your amazing depiction of a Pikachu mobile and my gift will be used this evening.

Denise, I saw that red beauty around the corner! Pikachu is part of the family now.

So many friends who had the time to come out and show the love ... Allene and Eli with car club friends (he LOVED it!) thank them for us please, JoAnn and Jack / he was so excited to see his buddy, Jack!

Lesa and Dede - again, elated to see his cousin! Caleb and Carli, your generosity and kindness is so appreciated! Mo and John have missed you both so much! My favorite part of your gift to him was the Axe deodorant maaaan does he need it, his cool backpack!!

Ståcey he wanted to chase your car down the street - we miss you!

Paula you are so loved!

Barb and Lucie thanks for coming out and hanging with us in the cold - we love you!! The car that drives on the walls ... amazeballs!!!

To our neighbor "Q" and his kids for cheering out the window.

The Fed Ex driver who waited so patiently with a great attitude for our craziness to pass!!

After we settled down and warmed up, we feasted on a dinner of Chinese food and off to see a Christmas display nearby - see the videos for a fantastic experience!!

On the way home, much to our unplanned surprise, Santa Claus was waving to passersby down the street from our house!!

And if you don't think it could get much better ... he stopped at our house first for a Christmas delivery!!!

Wrapping paper flying, birthday cake, singing and exhaustion setting in we all settled down for a long winters nap - after our annual shot of Cherry Kijafa!!

oh, and a shout out to satinchair.com for a really awesome, perfect birthday sign rental!!

I miss my family terribly today but I'm using the memories of past Christmases this week to fill in the blanks and I am filled with joy for a young man who so deserved it and relaxing today is ok - that's all I needed for Christmas.

Thank you everyone!!

Namaste 🙏

12/27/2020

Mindful Moments ....

These beautiful people here are the most selfless, giving, kind peeps you will ever meet and I'm proud to call them family.

They spent Christmas Eve through today with her mom and dad. From what I hear teaming up to cook, what I'm very sure, was an amazing homemade Chinese dinner and helping out.

My niece Trina, Jeff and their two wonderful boys Oliver and Evi took time out of their long drive back home to stop in for a short outdoor visit.

We dined lavishly on pizza and sweet treats, caught up on a few things, relaxed and peacefully enjoyed each other's company.

After a whole bottle of lighter fluid, we had a nice warm fire to chat by while the boys played! William sure needed his cousins!

I kept this surprise visit from William until today just in case something fell through. He's been wanting so very badly to see them.

Their beautiful souls are just what we needed today!

Thank you so much for making our weekend! We can't wait to see you again!! I'm packing the moving truck now; I'm about done here. ☺

You are appreciated and loved.

Namaste 🙏

12/28/2020

Mindful Moments ....

A couple of weeks ago I sent a message over to mom's house that one her favorite movies was on Ch 2 - The Sound of Music.

Annika put it on for her and mom didn't remember having ever seen it.

We watched that and The Wizard of Oz every year of my entire life. She looked forward to it and when I had grown and on my own, she'd call to remind ME when it was on.

It's equally as hard losing a parent to dementia as it is to lose one permanently. I've experienced both.

When they no longer remember the things that brought them joy as well as forgetting the people they love.

She called to wish William a happy birthday, a day early, but forgot his name and who's birthday she was calling about. They have always been close; he's named after my dad. It's heartbreaking.

So tonight, I made myself a cup of Peppermint Patty hot chocolate and turned on the Wizard of Oz.

I will always hold those memories close to my heart.

Christmas was disappointing although I spent it with 2 of my favorite people Boston and William. Left over Chinese dinner, games and Legos all day I miss my family but next year we will celebrate twice as much!

Today we started our first bathroom remodel project. We're doing all of them over time as we can afford it.

We shopped Saturday for our supplies. I'm not a shopper and agonize over decisions when you have so many choices and know it's permanent so it was painful! So many stores and options! Price helped keep options to a minimum.

When we began, I said "ya know it would be really cool to flip houses and do the work ourselves" until it took us 5 hours of back breaking tile demolition!

The builder slapped globs of glue or cement or whatever with no sub floor. We chipped, chiseled, hammered and swore for 5 hours (William helped for 30 seconds).

We've decided flipping houses is not on our list but this was a great 2nd workout for both of us today - great way to work off some emotion!

Tomorrow the chair rails come down and ceiling is painted.

We have a new light fixture, medicine cabinet (at a $30 clearance steal!!), and the slate tiles need to go down and be grouted after the walls are painted.

Saturday the vanity is delivered. Possibly a new toilet but current unexpected financial situation may make that a later replacement.

I LOVE the satisfaction of hard work, doing the job ourselves and taking pride in the blood sweat, tears, back ache and blisters that go with it!

Our hope is to work every day until it's finished which it better be by Sunday because Boston goes back to work next week.

Stay tuned for the finished product.

While we worked all afternoon William did an incredible job building this air plane and airport that Santa brought him, with some breaks from work to keep him company! Really nice job and really BIG!

We need an addition for all of his toys!

Hope everyone was able to make the best of what was a very difficult holiday for some of us. I'm glad it's over personally.

Namaste 🙏

12/29/2020

Mindful moments ....

I follow this amazing Autistic adult who puts his life on the chopping block every day to spread awareness of Autism.

I love that he stresses that you don't "grow out of Autism" just because you get older.

He describes life from the ASD point of view as this world is not designed for them.

I'm learning a lot from him and what to expect as William gets older.

Autistics are expected to adapt to and understand our world when we should be spending more time learning to adapt to theirs.

Whether you know someone with autism or not you should follow him. He is a wealth of information; I love his brutal honesty and his assistance in understanding the point of view from an autistic mind. Not to mention his photography is outstanding and his way of coping.

His post today hit home.

I often don't tell people how I feel to avoid conflict, hurt feelings and I often feel that other people's problems are worse than mine so mine are insignificant.

I recently let myself become vulnerable and calmly expressed my disappointment and hurt feelings for myself and William's feelings about something that was pretty quickly devalued because someone else felt that their situation was so much worse than ours. Which is why I most times keep my feelings to myself, not any more.

It breaks my heart to see a child's feelings crushed time and time again with broken promises and disappointments. If you have been treated like that or wouldn't want to be treated like that, don't do that to someone else. Resolve your past traumas before you pass them on to an innocent person. You deserve that and so do the people in your life.

"It is not a competition" I love those words.

Remember that you have value and no one has the right to devalue you or your family - they have not walked in your shoes.

You are important. Your feelings matter. Your opinions matter. And that goes for everyone.

Namaste 🙏

12/30/2020

Mindful Moments ....

I found it quite ironic today that my last grooming before the end of 2020 was this sweetheart, Rona.

If any of you remember my original post of her, she was adopted back in early April.

I thought they had named her Rona for obvious reasons however she came with that name so they kept it.

She's growing up to be quite a sweetheart and I'm very happy that she has her forever home. 💕

Of course, like most animals she took a liking to William and wanted to be upfront in the cab but then who wouldn't if they had a grooming they had to attend to?!

One of my favorite Christmas gifts is a phone holder Boston bought me for the van.

Other phone props don't hold up my iPhone plus which is large and heavy. This thing is the bomb!

I can have my phone poised right in front of me all day without worrying about it being dropped or kicked off the table! Not that any of these 4-legged angels would do that!

It's fantastic I highly recommend it for any of you who have your phone with you during the day and drop factor is a concern.

While I worked William kept busy with his tech and a Star Wars Lego kit with an occasional over the shoulder smile to the current grooming all-star.

Boston was home today doing some work on our remodeling job and had the opportunity to visit with someone who gifted us with this enormous bottle of Grey Goose and a couple of lovely glasses.

I believe we are now fully stocked with adult beverages to possibly get us through the next couple of days.

I have to say this is probably the first time in my life that I can't wait until the holidays are over.

Christmas is typically my favorite time of year with the lights, excitement, family time and gift giving makes me happy. I would rather give someone a gift that brings them joy than receive one for myself.

The simple act of giving can be gift enough.

I've said it before and I'll say it again how very much I miss my family and our traditions and even some of the new traditions we tried to build this year fell through.

I can only keep looking forward to a time when my brothers, sisters in law and my mother and us are all together again laughing, teasing each other and goofing off.

We are not a family who argues and gets into conflict at family gatherings.

Quite the opposite.

It's a time when we leave our troubles behind, kick back and relax and enjoy the day together until we can do it again.

We have a lot of making up to do from this past year and I'm counting down the days on the calendar until we can make that happen!

We have a zoom coming up soon I'm looking forward to since we couldn't zoom on Christmas.

I am grateful for the gift of technology to get us through all of this together.

You can't give up on hope, without hope we have nothing!

Namaste 🙏

12/31/2020

Mindful Moments ....

Coming to you from our bathroom debacle ... I mean remodel for the last Mindful Moments of 2020!

We've all been working hard, have accomplished a lot and look forward to our end result! Stay tuned!

I don't make resolutions.

It seems that this year many are choosing a word to carry them into 2021.

I have 2 words ... "Drama Free."

Now this doesn't mean there won't be drama - that's just life.

This past year, from my perspective, can be narrowed down to the word "drama".

Drama from hate, violence, mask wearing or not, republican or democrat or independent, disrespect, broken promises, misunderstandings ... I don't think I need to go on, we've all lived it.

This year, more than others, drama has caused anxiety, anger, frustration, broken relationships, lack of self-care, depression, sleepless nights and broken hearts.

My promise to myself is to not allow outside drama to get in the way of my self-care, my goals, my dreams, my feelings and my sense of good friendships, family and community.

Although I've encountered a lot of sad situations this year, I have found more kindness in people I would have never expected it from and pleasant situations that I may have never experienced without this pandemic.

You can find good in everything if you choose - we have choices, make the right ones.

Those who have reached out to help one another, offer a shoulder to lean on in hard times and have just remained darn good people regardless of challenges thrown at them has kept most of us going strong.

I will continue to strive for positivity and being a good person.

Hold your loved ones close, many have lost theirs this year, unexpectedly and too soon.

Show appreciation to those who have always been there for you now, people come and go, the ones who are important may not be there one day.

As we enter a new year do not live with regrets.

Live with purpose.

Make that phone call. Or text. Lend a hand. Apologize when you have wronged someone and refrain from repeating wrong doings. Actions speak louder than words.

Our Chili's has just been delivered, a charcuterie left from Christmas for later along with some cocktails and "unsub" will be just fine with us!

We miss you Mo and John we will celebrate double next NYE!

From our family to yours, farewell 2020 and the best of good fortune, good health and happiness to everyone in 2021.

These are the people I can count on.

Namaste 🙏

2021 PASSAGES

1/1/2021

Mindful Moments ... 2021 First Edition.

These people are my heart and soul! My family zoomed tonight and it was the best, most fun, soul cleansing 2 hours!

We shared, we toasted, we laughed (a lot) and mom popped in 4 times to tell us she loves us.

I can't wait to hug them all!! Thanks for hanging out tonight my brothas and sista! oh and Mia who made a "catmeo" appearance.

William had some money to spend on Legos today.

Have you been to a store to buy Legos this week? There aren't any. Empty shelves - delivery from Amazon 2 weeks out.

The owner of Leisure Hobbies was kind enough to give me the address and phone number of a place where Legos are life! I'm quite sure I'm late to the party but we now have connections!!

"Bricks and Minifigs" a hidden little treasure filled with new and used Lego kits, huge bins of misc. Lego pieces to buy by the container you fill yourself.

They have birthday parties and buy from you. William found some treasures and we will be back!

Boston left me this gift last night. I'm sorry babe, there's no help for this sock and I can't believe you put it in the laundry basket!!

I like to listen to music while I work. I was listening to my favorite oldies station while painting and the songs took my mind on a time travel to about 35-40 years ago.

They brought back memories of my buddy Tom who passed away this past June, unexpectedly and way too friggin soon. That rocked my world and turned it upside down.

These songs reminded me of him and the crazy shit we used to do. Made me smile!

The bon fires, pub crawls, house parties, concerts, cruising around, hanging out, pool floating, dunes trips ... 40 years of friendship brings a lot of memories.

A song can hold a story that no one can tell but you.

I miss him.

Our remodeling project is cleared of everything - our front porch is adorned by a plastic wrapped toilet and man was that vanity a beatch to get out! The mirror and light fixture however, cake walk!

Painting is done - tomorrow, new light fixture, sub floor install and I get to go shopping ... ALONE ... for accessories woohoo!! So excited, about the ALONE, not the shopping!!

When we have each other, we have everything.

Namaste

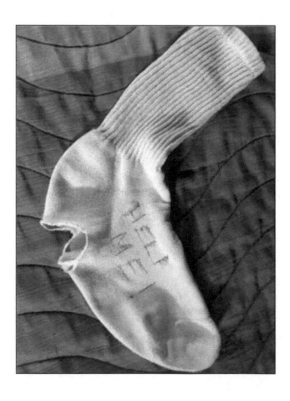

1/2/2021

Mindful Moments ....

Does anyone know what day it is anymore?? We sure as heck don't!

Such pride I have for William today!

Auntie Paula told us that channel 357 was going to start showing old shows today.

I turned it on this afternoon and there was a Twilight Zone marathon. Loved that show!

Turns out so does William! It held his interest over tech time! So proud! Having a Ghost Hunters and scary movie buddy is right around the corner!

Bathroom is coming along slowly but surely.

It's a challenge to hang with William and work but we've worked out a system while one of us works the other plays and then SWITCH! Unless we both need to get something done.

It's a small area so it's difficult to be in there together anyway and William has been so much calmer and sleeping well this week so it's important to make it all work.

Light fixture is up and sub floor is down! 2nd paint job of our "one coat" paint done also.

While the boys raced cars (which is all of our favorite new game!!) I got to go out ALONE! It was to shop for a new toilet and bathroom accessories and I loathe shopping but ... I was ALONE for a whole 1 1/2hrs!

Parrrrtayyyyyy!!

So tomorrow the tile goes down, toilet gets picked up and the vanity, that was supposed to be delivered today ... bastards, ... will go in probably next weekend since it won't be here until Wednesday even though it's sitting in the Lowe's store and we ordered it a week ago.

If I know Boston, he'll finagle a free delivery charge out of it since they promised it today.

Oh well - nothing goes without a hitch, and this has had a lot but we're having fun with it and excited to keep going.

We're crazy, because we're exhausted, but we're already planning our next project, but this one easier and in the living room ... what could it be.

Hard to believe that the holidays are over, but that's ok with me and remote learning begins again Tuesday.

My hopes are high that hybrid begins the 11th and sticks this time! We are just short of a year being home. What a fast, emotional, challenging year. It's not over yet, but we're rounding the corner!

If you want to

Reach your goals

You must shrink

The size of your

BUT!

You can do anything you DECIDE to do!

Namaste 🙏

1/4/2021

Mindful Moments ....

I don't like to brag ... BUT I took first place in Cars 3 Drivin To Win video game ... just sayin. 😊

We're working our keesters off here with this project! Withholding more photos until more is finished but William was quite proud to cut some tiles!

We've decided that we will earn our way into The Guinness Book of World Records for the longest time it took two people to remodel a powder room!

In our defense the geniuses that put in the flooring and the plumbing for the sink were obviously not quite sure what they were doing.

A plumber needs to redo the piping before the vanity can go in, which was promised delivery to us by this past Saturday and it isn't even at the store yet.

The plumber comes at 7am Thursday.

Boston worked his hiney off today laying tile. A borrowed wet saw was a life saver but still took nearly 10 hours.

I was busy kicking Williams ars at racing - someone has to do it.

Hopefully grouting tomorrow - we're getting our steps in running upstairs every time we need to use the facilities and with us that's about every 30 minutes if we can stretch it that long! Haven't had a toilet downstairs for several days and more to come.

We all learned something new today!!

Horror (Hoar) Frost - Skilling threw this one out today and we had to Google it! He's a wealth of weather information that guy is and so excited about his career! Enjoy the info.

I'm happy to report that although my groomers kids have tested positive for Covid, she tested negative yesterday!

They all wear masks around each other, sanitize and the kids are quarantined into one room. It can be done!

All clients are rescheduled and we are rolling again! Woot woot! Staying positive for no more closures!

Hope.

Faith.

Peace.

Love.

Believe.

Namaste 🙏

1/5/2021

Mindful Moments ....

I've always believed that things happen FOR us not TO us.

I also believe in events in life, people you meet or walk away from happen for a reason - everything to help us grow and teach us something.

It reminds me of when I'm driving somewhere and there are different ways that I can take and for some reason my conscience tells me to take a certain way. I believe that is for a reason.

What we learn from every event in our life and how we react to better our lives is up to us.

William finished school work early so I was running around trying to get some things together to go run errands. I wanted to leave the house by 12:45 and ended up leaving at 12:50.

We took a right out of our street and came on this scene a 1/2 block away from us.

The corner house is our friendly neighborhood Hemp Farm which always seems to have some sort of issue with the police there.

Last summer some teenagers jumped the fence with machetes and bags thinking it was a nice crop of the devil's lettuce only to be chased off the grounds with the owner shooting his gun in the air onto our neighboring street.

The owner of the house was arrested for illegal discharge of a firearm in a populated area … Idiot.

This however, as we found out as the day unfolded, was a car to car shooting in front of this house where some of the bullets entered the home of the hemp farm. A half block from our home.

This occurred at 12:45 as we were leaving.

Forgetting mine and William's water bottle at 1245 and running back in to get it happened FOR us!

We haven't had problems in our neighborhood in over 15 years.

We've had a nice quiet neighborhood until this but if you watch the news, it's Naperville, Burr Ridge, Joliet, Bolingbrook, Willowbrook, Oakbrook etc. etc. etc.

There is no escape from violence albeit rare here.

These shooters don't live here and they're still being looked for.

It's up to us to create a better world for ourselves and our children's future.

Negativity and anger breed more negativity and anger.

Peace and love create more peace and love.

You choose your future.

I will no longer get aggravated with myself when I am not running on time on my self-imposed unimportant schedule!

We did make it to our errands and as you can see William thoroughly enjoyed his 5 Layer beefy cheese burrito from Taco Bell, well, at least what made it into his mouth.

And Gypsy dined on her peanut butter treats Christmas gift on her comfy bed.

Boston came home from work early to grout the bathroom and I believe has passed out already.

Work will be a vacation for him tomorrow.

You can sit back, complain and wonder why there's hatred and violence and say that someone should do something about it or you can take action and do your part in creating a peaceful world.

My positive attitude irritates some people ... hmmm wonder why that is?... Makes me want to be even more positive!

Try smiling at someone and saying hello, you could change their day.

Hold a door, compliment a stranger, help someone load their groceries, give a weary friend a break, run an errand for them, shovel their driveway, watch their kids so they can get away, cook them a meal, donate a few dollars to your important charity, hug a senior they may not have anyone to hug them, tell your kids teachers how amazing they are, tell a friend or parent how much they are appreciated - kind words go a long way and can change the course of someone's day without realizing it. 🙏

The world can be changed one-star fish at a time. ☆

Namaste

1/6/2021

Mindful Moments ....

I sit here tonight in emotional turmoil. I live for positivity and yet I haven't been feeling that today.

We all watched unbelievable attacks on our government while other countries sit back and take note of those weaknesses.

I'm not a hateful person. Nor a judgmental person. Nor a controlling person. All quite the opposite.

Nor do a I love politics. However, over the years I've paid much closer attention to government because it affects my children's future.

I don't want to be angry and hateful for what was played out and encouraged today but I won't say it's not difficult to ignore those feelings. Purposeful, hateful, incited attacks on our freedom to vote and have those votes counted is unforgivable.

It's desperate.

I've been watching the speeches of the certification process, something I would NEVER have entertained before this despicable act today.

I've seen both sides of the aisle reflect a need for the governed process to be followed through with.

If you look at this from a different perspective, perhaps this senseless, violent attack on our government has actually worked in the opposite as intended. It changed a few minds.

It brought doubt to an end to several and the importance of voters' rights to both sides of the aisle which are not to be overturned by a chamber of politicians because they may not like the outcome of those voters.

Most important - and I preach this nearly nightly here - WE NEED TO UNITE AS A COUNTRY!

Our division makes us weak; our unity makes us strong and able to accomplish anything.

Hurt people, hurt people. Peaceful people create peace.

We have to take responsibility for ourselves in creating peace, strength and unity among ourselves.

We have to live amongst our neighbors not amongst a cabinet of politicians.

Some need to take their heads out of the sand and start fighting for a better life, a better country, a better union.

Remove negativity from your circle.

I think I speak for many when I say we need to move on. We need a fresh start. We need a peaceful transition into the next phase of our country.

Less hate, more peace. ⊕

I wrote in my prose yesterday - "you can sit back and wonder why there's hatred and violence and say that someone should do something about it or you can take action and do your part in creating a peaceful world."

Choose peace.

Namaste 🙏

The old year is worn and tired.
Time now to kiss it goodbye.
Take with you its wisdom – the authority
and the power of all you have learned.
Remember the past year with love,
but let go of its despair.
Live the year that lies ahead
with fresh energy and hope.
Be strong, have courage.
It is time now for something new.

1/7/2021

Mindful Moments ....

Today we celebrated what we hope to be the last full week of remote learning.

Next M-W-F in person, Tu-Thurs at home. I am cautiously optimistic it will hold this time.

It's been nearly a year of one let down after another. Enough is enough!

It's time to move on.

William is a social guy and needs friends and teachers in person and I can't always be all of that nor does he want me to be and that's ok!

We both need our time and our people.

It's been a hard week for a few reasons.

Mostly for William although he looks forward to school which is a blessing for him.

We returned his Kawano we gave him as a b-day gift, with his blessings, which was a total bust and got him a hover board that arrived yesterday.

He's going to do great with it and with its flashing lights and Bluetooth stereo he's going to have a blast! He's taking it slow but is a natural!

Thrilled to get him away from video games, thinking too much about life and doing something outside and fun!

This weekend we'll venture out to a parking lot and let him go!

Our next adventure was to Illumination at Morton Arboretum.

Thanks to Lucie who let me know weeks ago that they extended the event I was able to get tickets for tonight.

Well organized and the lights and music were beautiful and a much-needed relaxing event.

On the way home William was quietly staring out the window and then opened up to me about something he's been holding inside, but I knew was on his mind.

Broke my heart to hear his words.

What I am thankful for is his ability to talk about and get out his feelings.

He's a passionate, kind hearted young man who trusts too easily and gets hurt hard.

He doesn't understand why everyone can't be kind to him and love him - I wonder the same thing.

The only thing I could say is some adults have their own unresolved issues that get in the way of how they treat others. But he still feels it's him.

It's taken yeeaaars of therapy to help him find the right words to express emotion appropriately.

I'm proud of him - his compassion is a gift.

Took a while for sleep to come for him tonight but tomorrow is a new day and dad and I have fun plans for him.

I will forever advocate for him until he can do it for himself, and he will, he has a great future ahead of him!

With a new toilet in our front room and vanity on the front porch our plumber is due to install both and fix that redonkulous pipe!

The tile is finished and I'm hoping by Sunday everything will be done and ready for Better Homes and Gardens magazine or at least we'll be able to use it again!

My plea is to be kind to everyone especially innocent children. If you were wronged as a child, take responsibility and do your part in stopping that cycle 💔.

"Don't miss the best part of your CHILDS life

because you're out living

YOUR best life ....

your BEST LIFE should

be YOUR KID'S LIFE."

Namaste 🙏

1/9/2021

Mindful Moments ....

There's nothing like dog love to bring things into perspective.

My dog whisperer was with me at work today. He is so incredibly amazing with these dogs. His heart melts as soon as he sees them and their response is heartwarming.

The littlest one top right was shaking and scared. He talked to her and stroked her head until she calmed - he has a heart of gold and they feel it.

I've been contemplating getting William on a list for a support dog. It can take years as they are sponsored and take a while to train. It would greatly help his anxiety and give him the additional unconditional love he gets from us from his own buddy. We'll see how that works out.

Services are not handed out like candy at Halloween you have to fight for it, for everything, and I will fight for anything that will give him peace and boost his self-esteem.

While we put in a half day the plumber was at the house fixing the bathroom pipe, installing the toilet and vanity and fixing a leaky garbage disposal pipe.

Thank you, Terre, for the plumber referral he did a great job and was VERY reasonable!

Very excited, almost done. Mirror to hang and some incidentals and we're onto the next project!

Tomorrow putting Christmas behind us finally and getting everything put away.

After our last appointment I took William past my friend Toms' childhood home who we lost this year. I tell him stories about Tom all the time. We hung out with him when William was little.

A trip to the zoo, fun times at the cabin, an apple orchard (where there were no apples because there was a really bad season for them LOL) and Toms many visits to our home.

Just sitting outside his home brought 40 years of fun, happy memories flooding back - so many stories to tell.

Time goes by faster than you think. In the blink of an eye. One minute someone is there, the next they're gone - don't let time slip through your fingers.

After stopping for gas our hawk friend swooped across the van and perched himself at the buffet table.

William said "Now I'm going to have good luck today!" I hope so William, you deserve it. 😊

William spent the rest of the afternoon riding his hoverboard around the house.

We gave him errands to "roll" around the house lol "Here, throw this away please. Take this to the front door please. Roll this into dad, would you?" He loved it! Makes him happy and feels important!

It's like having a butler on wheels!

Tomorrow he wants a "William and dad day" (I just love it!) so they're going out to get some distance on his ride!

I love seeing him accomplish something, be proud of himself and having fun!

This boy was born with wheels on his feet and a steering wheel in his hands! Literally!!

We also want to get him back to archery. His teacher started taking lessons a month ago and sent us photos of her targets and the name of the place she's going. It may be closer than where we were going a year ago which would be nice!

Since Gypsy was up most of the night sick, she's taking respite on the couch by me - I love her. 😊

I'm tired too - sweet dreams all.

Namaste 🙏

1/10/2021

Mindful Moments ....

I had nearly an hour to myself today!!! You have NO idea how much I can get done when no one is here!!

William and dad had some time together out for lunch and then hoverboarding in a parking lot.

They had a great time.

This kid loves the hoverboard so much he rides it through the house all day and rocked it while they were out!

You see because of his impulsiveness and need for speed I am very cautious about allowing him to operate anything with a motor and wheels.

A lot of people don't understand that Neurodiverse kiddos have a difficult time with judgment, balance and impulsivity. It can be very dangerous. It's not like putting your average 12 yo on moving transport.

I'm incredibly proud of the caution he takes learning this and the confidence it has brought him in such a short time!

He had it by his side with a Lego break and battled with me after dinner to ride more!

Great way to get him off video games!! He was always an active kiddo until these past many months - this has given him a spark.

The first video made my week.

While they were out, I did the laundry and made a shrimp boil sausage bake recipe courtesy of Landa- our store didn't have old bay so I picked up a Cajun seasoning - it's soooo good and easy to make!!

William loved it too! Glad I made a double batch!

The crock pot took care of making Chicken Tortilla soup courtesy of Tom T. (double batch) while I stripped down the remnants of Christmas!

Cook once eat twice I say! Meals done for the week!!

The tree we picked up from the Fields on Caton Farm is the freshest Christmas tree I have ever had in my entire life. We hardly lost any needles from it or had to give it much water.

We've had it since the weekend before Thanksgiving and just took it down today.

Williams little Charlie Brown tree on the other hand had scarcely a needle left when we took the ornaments off today but left quite a puddle on the carpet.

Although I will miss the peaceful glow of its rice lights, I'm so glad Christmas is put away for 11 more months when we can spend it with my crazy brothers! I love and miss them!

We have a fun-loving family. No drama, no judgement. Our time together stays in the moment and always renews my energy and happiness.

Tomorrow is a big day. Another try at in person hybrid school.

Like everything there are many opinions about returning. You have to live in each household to know what the kids need and can do.

I'm extremely happy for William. This is what he wants, his life back, his socialization, his much-needed routine.

His teachers and school are ready and I pray they are able to sustain the plans this time!

"Many say that life enters the human body by the help of music, but the truth is that life itself is music." - Hafiz

Namaste 🙏

1/11/2021

Mindful Moments ....

I'm being honest when I say I don't feel much like writing tonight.

Sometimes I have things on my mind that aren't shareable but ....

My favorite part of today was how abundantly happy William was when he came home from school today.

He ran off the bus with the biggest smile, threw his arms around me and gave me a huge hug.

He didn't know how important that was to me. 💛

I haven't seen him this happy in such a very long time.

He had a great day at school with teachers and peers who value him, he needed that.

Treat our children well, they are our future and our future needs well adjusted, kind hearted, compassionate adults.

They will remember who has always been there for them, well most of them do anyway - always choose kindness.

Namaste 🙏

> "It's not our job to toughen our children up to face a cruel and heartless world. It's our job to raise children who will make the world a little less cruel and heartless."
>
> — L.R. Knost

1/12/2021

Mindful Moments ....

It's hard to see him but William and I had a visit from our cardinal today. 😊

I'm not sure who was swinging by to offer an encouraging nod but William would like to believe it's Hershey, Uncle Jeff and his grandfather ... I'd like that too. 💬

By the way Denise, thank you!

I want to be clear that when I write my prose, which I've been doing for nearly a year now, it is merely my feelings and experiences from my day and how it affects me and /or my family.

My thoughts are from my heart although sometimes speaking from your heart offends some.

If something I share resonates with you and stings then maybe it's something to explore. I never say anything to be hurtful to anyone purposely. That's not who I am.

I discovered recently that I've been unfollowed because someone feels the things, I write are to gain attention for myself ... I have no words for them other than, look within.

I use my words and thoughts to provoke thought.

If something I say brings a smile to your face, changes the course of your day in a positive way then my heart is full and my goals are met.

It's all about perspective - we see what we want to see.

I love my kids with all my heart, Caitlin and William. I'd give my life for either of them, as most parents would. I never want to see them hurt, like most parents.

I've spent my time sacrificing and dedicating my life and time for the better of them. Like most parents do.

I have nearly 57 years of life experience, more than some, less than others but experiences of ALL kinds just the same. I could tell some stories, but couldn't we all?!

Some really great memories and some poor decisions I've made that didn't work out but I learned from them.

Isn't that life?

It's not the mistakes we make it's whether or not we learn from them and change the course of our life for the better.

Take responsibility. Live with integrity.

I've learned my best lessons from the most difficult times of my life.

When life is easy, we tend to take it for granted.

We slightly older folks share our wisdom from experiences to try to make a positive difference for those who may need it, if they want to hear it.

Not to get attention for ourselves but to send a message of experience whether it's heard or ignored.

My Mindful Moments are not seeking attention but sharing experience.

I'll never make everyone happy, this I know, and have learned the hard way, but my hope is that in some way I can positively influence at least one person now and then.

I'm always here for anyone who needs me, family and friends, always have been. My life has gotten more complicated, but I'm always here.

Our cardinal was our much-needed angel today - I wish you visits from your angels every day. ♡

Namaste 🙏

1/13/2021

Mindful Moments ....

Why do kids get up at the crack of ridiculous and then say they're tired all day?

Why can't we just call beige...beige or off white? Why do we need to call it "biscuit"?

Have you ever seen an off-white biscuit? Then it's not done! It should be browned on top!

We now have a "biscuit" colored toilet… It's off white!!

PSA I started taking magnesium and zinc combo a few weeks ago and I haven't slept this well in a long time - worth a try if solid sleep is an issue.

I love starting my day with Rosies inquisitive stare when I pull up for the girls' grooming's. She was unamused by my presence once again.

Her goat friends were equally as unimpressed! I still enjoy them.

The bathroom is further along than this side-by-side photo but Boston did such a great job on the floor I wanted to share. I can safely say that tile setting professionally is not in his future - not that it's not great, it's just exhausting, back breaking work!

We hope to come "near" to completion this weekend.

I'll probably get in trouble for this but I have to say how proud I am of Boston for finally beginning his PhD work. Signed up, books delivered, on his way! You've got this!

And lastly a great email from yesterday - The Miracle League Baseball organization returning in the Spring, following the Covid guidelines and safety protocol, however participation is totally up to the parents.

Can't wait to get him back on the field and running all the bases despite a single base hit it's so exciting he just can't help himself!

Taken from a book of "Quotes That Will Change Your Life" that's kept at my bedside ...

"One of the deep secrets of life is that all that is really worth doing is what we do for others" Lewis Carroll.

Namaste 🙏

1/18/2021

Mindful Moments ....

Super random, boring, Monday, who really cares edition.

Spotlighting the princess on one of her many thrones.

She looked comfy so I covered her with my super awesome blanket/wrap I was gifted for Christmas.

William has a tendency to be impulsive and hurried with some things during the course of his day. So lately I've been a constant reminder of "haste makes waste" and explaining that to him.

As I found perhaps, I should take my own advice.

Last Thursday, with only about five minutes before his first zoom call, I was hurriedly unpacking the dishwasher and putting things away so as not to make noise during his call.

Apparently, I too "hastily" put away my cute little brandy glasses and two of them came crashing out from the top shelf of the cabinet and broke on the floor.

Did I learn my lesson? No!

Caitlin and Cody gifted me a grater/zester and fantastic knife set for Christmas.

You can imagine where this is going.

I have your basic kitchen necessities for your average person who does a lot of cooking at home.

I have always struggled to zest a lime or lemon on the grater well cuz it's crappy! - so from habit I of course was pressing as hard as I would have before and zested off a nice chunk of my thumb! (border lining on cannibalism but the zesting was just for a recipe for me - yum).

I also found out how great the knives cut when I sliced into 2 of my nails - disclaimer - they did not separate from the rest of my nail leaving those food sources clear of body pieces.

Practice what you preach perhaps knucklehead. ♡

With our remodeling project about 95% complete and passing the staining baton to Todd (Happy birthday again my friend) I finally had a day to kinda do some things I enjoy! So selfish of me.

I baked a loaf of Almond Egg bread (GF) and made mini almond and cashew butter cups - soooo yummy and healthier than processed peanut butter cups.

I also saw a FB video about cutting up avocados and freezing them for future use - GENIUS! So, I did that too!! Apparently, some stores sell them cubed and frozen - who knew?! Not me!

When I had my chicken tortilla soup tonight, I grabbed a 1/4 frozen avocado and tossed it in! Voila!

So, if that hasn't dazzled you enough, I shall end today with a quote from Martin Luther King Jr ....

"The quality, not the longevity, of one's life is what is important."

"An individual has not started living until he can rise above the narrow confines of his individualistic concerns to the broader concerns of all humanity."

Namaste 🙏

1/19/2021

Mindful Moments ....

Today was a bit of a bump in the road for William and I.

Bear with me.

I say both of us because although I know him to his core there are emotions that he can't yet verbalize and it frustrates me not to be able to help him, it frustrates him to be unable to voice them.

We had a pretty rough day. William found focusing, concentrating and complying extremely difficult from sun up to sundown. I watched him struggle, need numerous breaks, tried to sit and talk with him but I don't even think he understands exactly what's upsetting him.

Autism is such a complicated world.

It's amazing and full of imagination, creativity in many forms, humor, intelligence beyond what is written in books from minds that see the world so very differently than the neurotypical.

It's there that communication gets foggy.

Our brains operate at different speeds and levels of understanding. So to put those two different perspectives together to form a common thought is challenging.

Not only that but this world was not built for them and yet we expect them to understand and blend into our world.

You have to get into their world to truly understand their perspective.

It doesn't mean that Neurodiverse or Neurotypical is right or wrong it's just the perspective and point of view in which we both see the world and interpret and process life.

Even as well as I know William and knew he yearned to be back at school, I just assumed that going back to school after 10 months at home, even for three days a week, that those two days a week at home remote would be so much easier.

I was sorely mistaken.

For Autistic's transition and change is way beyond stressful and anxiety provoking. Adjustment can take weeks or months. I had temporarily forgotten this having him home every day for nearly a year.

We were in a routine and now, even though it's a good change, it's a new routine and not even a reliable or back to normal one. It's wearing masks and taking temperatures and keeping distance.

It's having desks separated at school and not being able to interact with your friends who are 6 feet away, engage in recess, PE class or field trips.

It's keeping kids like William who love and need hugs, unable to fulfill that basic need.

It's having half of your classmates at home remote learning on the screen in the classroom with you while you sit at your desk and try to learn with some of the other peers also having difficulty adjusting, regressing to behaviors. It's a snowball effect.

We made it through school, a haircut and folding and putting laundry away with a lot of pushbacks and need for redirection but he got it done.

You have no idea how difficult it is for someone with special needs to do even the simplest tasks when they are dysregulated.

PATIENCE IS KEY - yet something I'm running low on after 10 months together.

I don't know how many participated in this but there was a going dark type ceremony at 6 PM this evening in respect of the loss of life from Covid this past year. Tomorrow being the uncelebrated 1-year anniversary of the first day of the first Covid infection in the United States.

So, I sat with William and we turned off all the lights, the TV, the technology and we reflected on the last year.

We talked about the challenges we faced, the things and people we lost and the great things we learned and how we learned to adjust and appreciate things we may never have.

The kindness we saw in people helping each other, providing food, shelter, financial assistance and virtual love and support.

Turning back on the lights at 6:10 was symbolic of a renewal. So, we turned on the lights with the hope of a better tomorrow.

This photo below was in his counseling assignment today.

His self-esteem and self-worth need loads of uplifting so I had him yell these three times.

I copied it and will have him recite it every morning. Maybe you could do the same.

Positive affirmations can change your whole perspective and help heal your soul.

Learn from our specially-abled children - they have a lot to say just in a different way.

Namaste 🙏

1/20/2021

Mindful Moments ....

It was quite a day here in our country ... as it is every Inauguration Day.

The change of a President has not changed the negativity, judgement, division and rhetoric of those on social media. It has only changed the direction from which it comes.

If you didn't witness this inauguration because you are angry and disappointed with this elections outcome and are unhappy with our new President, then you missed this young woman's powerful message.

A message that doesn't involve political agendas but the need for change. And boy, does this country need change.

Amanda Gorman ... Wow.

It doesn't matter what you think of our current administration.

If this young woman's perspective written so eloquently in her poetry and the reading thereof did not touch you, move you and inspire you today then you have much to learn and I am saddened for you.

In her few years she is wiser and carries more hope and inspiration than those who are her senior.

She should be seen as a beacon of hope and message carrier to the down hearted that there is always hope, always room for change and always the need for respect in one another DESPITE our differences.

In her words "... a nation that isn't broken, but simply unfinished ...."

I am humbled by her words.

Namaste 🙏

1/21/2021

Mindful Moments ....

This is all I needed today. 🤍

Love the Holderness Family and if nothing else, Bernie Sanders has some people united for a while. He has to be loving this he has a great sense of humor!

Enjoy!

Namaste 🤍

Favorite Bernie Memes

On the Delaware

1/23/2021

Mindful Moments ....

I had to stop and get a shot of this sea of geese hanging out on the pond.

I've seen large flocks in various areas but I can say that I've never seen so many in one place at one time - we saw this twice today at 2 different spots. Interesting.

We, William and I, were on our way to Loki's house for his spa day today.

Loki wins "The Best Dog of the Day" award! Although reluctant to get in the van he was an absolute pleasure!

A much-needed break after our first appointment with 2 extremely hyped-up lab and pit-xs' whining, screaming and spinning, and that was mostly William A day in the life of a groomer.

Gypsy ... on the other hand wins "The Worst Dog of the Award" ... as usual - at least she's consistent! She really needed it and now maybe she won't want to go out all night long to lay in the snow and cool off - apparently, it's been too hot in the house with a thick pelted coat! My bad! The groomers dog never gets groomed.

Boston received "The Best-Behaved Human Hair Cut" of the day award. He was well behaved, sat still, didn't complain and wasn't upset when the only treat offered for good behavior afterward was a marrow bone!

Now that William, Boston and Gypsy have their grooming's done, I need MINE!

It's days like today that I'm thankful for prepped meals. Too darn tired to cook - a nice bowl of Albondigas soup warmed up hit the spot. ♡

I had to add in last night's dinner of Crock Pot Mongolian Beef over spaghetti squash (for me, boys rice) - it was soooo good!

Time to crash!

Hope everyone had a productive day!

I will leave you with this:

"Save the excuses. It's not about "having" time.

It's about "making" time.

If it matters, you'll make time." - TRUTH

Namaste 🙏

1/25/2021

Mindful Moments ....

Yesterday we had the pleasure of taking a ride out to Rochelle to celebrate Codys birthday.

The food was delish and company fun and entertaining from human to the D- Family Zoo inhabitants that reside in their warm cozy habitat!

Louis, Clark, Mew, Harvey, Midas, Penelope and the quails.

Apparently, the quails are quite the show for Midas. He loves to sit and watch them perhaps planning his next meal muahahaha!

The quails are interesting creatures reminding me of the clueless chicken Heihei from Moana - not the sharpest tools in the shed.

Penelope the turtle sits and waits for one of the cats to dare come near her habitat! SNAP off the beans!

I spent a few hours decluttering today.

William feels the coffee table is a catch all to set up his legos, matchbox cars and any other miscellaneous tchotchke that he can find.

I clean it up and within three days it's back to a disaster. But he came home from school today, took a look at the coffee table and said,

"WHAT HAPPENED IN HERE??" "Where is all my STUFF??"

Um put away where it belongs!!

We'll see how long that cleared, shiny coffee table stays shall we??!

Gypsy enjoyed her new fancy raised bowls! I felt she deserved something nicer than an upside-down plastic bucket.

I think I've lived in Illinois too long or maybe it's just me but I feel like everyone's kind of going overboard with worry with the snow that we're getting, at least near where we live.

Schools are closing all over the place already without even waiting till tomorrow morning to see what we end up with.

Where I live, we're only predicted to get maybe 2 to 4 inches of snow by tomorrow morning, the plows are already out so what happened to the resilience of Illinoisans when it comes to this kind of weather? Unless you have to work outside that's a different story!

Now we're talking a long time ago but when I was a kid in the late 60's through the 80's there was always snow on the ground and the chance of school getting canceled because of it was extremely rare!

We bundled up and crunched through the snow with our snow boots to the bus stop where we waited sweating underneath our scarves and heavy coats for the bus to pull up.

I had 2 clients text me Sunday suggesting cancelling for tomorrow.

Where I appreciate the concern, I've always been a pretty resilient, tough person and not only that but I also feel that the weather can change at the drop of a hat.

I discouraged both clients and asked them to just hang tight and wait. They obliged. As long as the van can handle the roads safely, we work inside where it's warm.

Let's see if the winds change, let's see if the plows are out all night salting making the road safe to drive on, I don't like to overreact.

In my experience of being on the road working for over 30 years, more often than not, the weather turns out to be much better than anticipated.

We all know how the weather people like to hype it up and if we do happen to have a treacherous day, THEN we cancel.

"Life doesn't

get easier

or more

forgiving;

we get

stronger

and more

resilient." - Dr Steve Maraboli

Namaste 🙏

1/26/2021

Mindful Moments ....

Today was a good day to step back a bit and be in the moment.

This past year seems to have flown by just keeping our heads above water leaving us to forget to appreciate all the little things that make it all worthwhile.

I rarely pass up an opportunity for some snowboarding and sledding on our berm behind the house.

Surprisingly it wasn't slippery snow but great for packing. Once we had it packed down the sled slid with ease but the snowboard, not so much.

A half hour of fun and back in for hot chocolate!

Gypsy loves nothing more than romping in the snow, eating it and going for long walks. Love to see her happy.

It always takes me back to when I was kid.

Those red rosy cheeks from the cold against exposed skin and always a good hunk of pure white snow for the munching or an icicle just waiting to be plucked!

We didn't last long but the fresh air and break from school, work and chores was welcome.

With laundry, school, animal care and some winter fun behind us I was able to do some self-care and attend a scheduled zoom for ME. 😊

The busy day came to a close with the van taking a nail to a tire and needing a tow to Reza - who stayed late and quickly took care of the issue so I can work tomorrow - thank you Reza!

The situation was interesting.

I mean nothing to fret about we got through the day of work before it happened, no one was hurt and it's repaired so that I can resume work in the morning.

The amusing and a bit scary factor is in the photo of the van being pulled onto the flatbed.

If you zoom in closely, you can see the front end of the tow truck lifted off the ground while trying to secure the van onto the back.

Now I've had my vans towed many times over 30 years but I can safely say that it's never been too heavy for a flatbed tow truck!

They had to drive slow so taking the expressway was not doable coming back out to Plainfield from Darien. They had to take back roads just in case the truck decided to leave the ground again.

Another eventful day in the books.

"You will never be happy if you continue to search for what happiness consists of. You will never live if you are looking for the meaning of life." - Albert Camus

Be in the moment.

Namaste 🙏

1/27/2021

Mindful Moments ....

Today wasn't particularly eventful.

An uneventful day is welcomed sometimes. ♡

I was able to catch this bright full moon out of our patio doors. Not bad for an iPhone but it never does it justice.

It had a peacefulness to it today. I think that's why I was drawn to it. Sometimes it creates an imbalance of the mind, but not today.

Most full moons create difficult days for those of the neurodiverse community.

Today it seemed to send a message of calm and hope.

Something, at times, which is difficult to muster when life shakes you to your core and spits you back out to renew yourself, refocus and gain strength and wisdom.

William and I sat in his room, in the dark, gazing for a bit before sleep blanketed his day.

There is always, always, always something to be grateful for.

Today I'm grateful to have the universe draw us in with its natural, majestic, beauty to send a message of peace.

Namaste.

1/28/2021

Mindful Moments ....

For Special Education Week ....

When you have a neurotypical child, you feel reasonably assured that class participation and decent study habits will result in good grades. These kids have close friends. They get invited to participate in social things like dances and weekend gatherings. They make the teams, auditions organizations and clubs.

But when you have a child with certain differences, this is often not the case. Learning may take longer, both academically and socially.

Despite their tremendous efforts, results are often a fraction of their peers and social acceptance is fleeting, setting them up for painful comparisons and bitter frustration.

Instead of a fun and fulfilling experience, school can become a breeding ground for depression and anxiety, and assignments a battle ground at home. It is exhausting for parent and child alike.

This is the week of SPED (Special Education), Autism, Dyslexia, and ADHD (attention deficit hyperactivity disorder) awareness.

For all the children who struggle every day to succeed in a world that does not recognize their gifts and talents, and for those who are walking beside them, please let this be a gentle reminder to be kind and accepting of ALL people.

Recognize that the "playing field" is not always a level surface.

Children who learn differently are not weird. They are merely gifted in ways that our society does not value enough. Yet they want what everyone else wants:

To be accepted!!

Our world would be far less beautiful without them.

Namaste 🙏

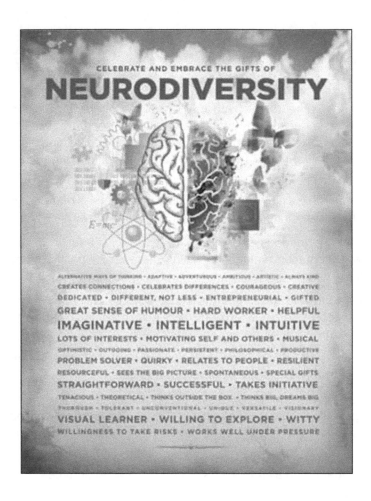

1/29/2021

Mindful Moments ....

I can't tell you how happy I was to receive a delivery in ... "certified frustration free packaging!!"

Life needs this label slapped on it.

On our walk this morning, and every morning we have snow, I noticed our neighborhood is very "all or nothing" with snow care.

There is either thoughtful scrapped free concrete with a bag of salt poured on it or ....

No effort at all "don't sue me if you fall and break something."

Trip to Rezas #2 today - simply a belt decided to stop providing service!

And again, Reza had it repaired and ready to return to work within an hour - you have my deepest gratitude!!

Now owning a mobile business and dealing with breakdowns is challenging.

Most clients are understanding and some drop you like hot coals and go somewhere else if they are inconvenienced. Oh well their loss.

However, the nail in the tire on Tuesday I look at as a blessing in disguise.

It happened at the end of the day, after all clients were taken care of.

Had that tire not come off the van I wouldn't have realized how bad the tires were and needed immediate replacement. So, the van is scheduled for new tires tomorrow afternoon.

The belt finally hit exhaustion just short of a nail clip today and did it self in just before pulling into the parking lot at Rezas.

With that being repaired tonight I'm still able to keep my tire replacement appointment for tomorrow, which I thought I was going to have to cancel.

We've been driving on a regular tire that was mounted on an aluminum rim which is rusted due to being stored under the van exposed to the weather.

I believe things happen for a reason and your attitude about it is all about perspective.

In the past after some breakdowns some have asked why don't I just stop mobile grooming or get rid of the van.

I don't stop mobile grooming because I love it. I don't buy a new van because I can't afford $80-$90,000 for a brand-new van and because of Covid all the used vans have been sold.

If you're driving a vehicle six days a week it's bound to have wear and tear that you have to keep up with along with maintenance. It happens to be a high maintenance business. So, you know that going in and you just deal with it until you have to weigh the pros and cons.

So thanks to good timing we have repairs done and new tires tomorrow! New tires will make driving through the snow we're getting much safer!

You have to look at the gains IN the losses in life.

Every situation provides an opportunity for a lesson, it just depends on what you take from it and then leave the rest.

Namaste

1/31/2021

Mindful Moments ....

Did anyone else get 12" of snow today??

No? Just us?!

This was our "shovelin' crew, shovelin' on down, doin' it for you" blast from the past!

It's times like today I'm reminded what great neighbors we have!

"Q" was shoveling our walkway and in front of the van by 8:30am.

When we decided to go out at 11 there was Lucie rolling down the sidewalk with her snowblower.

If not for the cumulative teamwork of shovels, snowblowers and some fun-loving friends we'd still be clearing plowed in vehicles and ends of driveways.

Cleared sidewalks are so appreciated to those of us walking our dogs and kids going to school now.

Slipping on ice and trudging through shin deep snow on a sidewalk is dangerous - be kind and considerate to others.

We had some fun, built a fort, threw some snowballs and were able to socialize with humans out in the fresh air.

William even learned to use the snowblower - as brief as the lesson was.

In between we managed to throw in some laundry, get paperwork done, make some meatballs for dinner, sweet potato and turkey breakfast sausages and tuna salad.

To Williams delight Auntie Paula shared a warm fresh baked apple pie this evening - thank you Auntie Paula!

With the van fixed and new shoes installed, van cleaned off and driveway cleared we are ready to start another busy week.

Despite what we tend to see and hear there are good people everywhere - keep them in your circle and negativity at a distance.

Snuggle under a blanket, be safe and warm.

Namaste 🙏

2/4/2021

Mindful Moments ....

I've had a wonderful day today!

It's not about this incredible surprise of a Cake Boss cake, a mini fridge for the bedroom and other lovely b-day surprises.

What makes today very special for me is the time my friends and family took out of their busy lives to send a message, a story and a smile.

Your words and gestures have truly touched my heart beyond measure.

I feel blessed and loved today and I thank each and every one of you from the bottom of my heart. You all bring great value to my life.

A dear friend posted a picture from my birthday last year of our giant Zumba class where we had a great time and went out for a relaxing brunch with friends afterward.

Who knew a year ago today where we would be a short month after that day?

It really makes you reflect on how quickly life can change in the blink of an eye.

I must say I can't wait to try this cake tomorrow! Carlos Bakery pulls no punches with their dry ice packing- that sucker couldn't be cut with a chain saw!

So, an overnight thawing is in order!

Boston was on the money with a new KitchenAid!

I've had my original one for 16 yrs, bought refurbished. Def got my monies worth!

I guess he noticed me smacking it to start the paddle turning when I'd turn it on and nothing moved.

I use it ALOT!

Paula my "Friend" love it love it!! You know me so well! Thank you for the fly by! Miss you!!

Lucie Grounds and Hounds! Coffee and donating to rescue pups all in one! Brilliant! ♡

Todd it's always a pleasure to hang out with you even if it's during your hard work and the amazing job you've done on our staining and touch up! Thank you for starting my day with some Jackie Gleason! Time On My Hands, a perfect selection!

I've decided that I'm continuing my personal birthday celebration through tomorrow since William will be in school - he and Gypsy kept me on my toes today!

William didn't want to do his remote learning and let me know it and Gypsy barked to go out all day ... to eat snow.

Gotta love these two. ♡

I took some time for myself to finish my latest vision board - if you haven't made one you should what you visualize comes to pass - it's my 4th one and many things have come to fruition and made the better part of Wellness/Nutrition/Self Improvement weekly zoom call.

It was a spectacular day!

Tomorrow I look forward to seeing my favorite daughter Caitlin and favorite son in law Cody! Let the fun continue!

Thank you all for enriching my life daily. ♡

"Be the reason someone believes in the goodness of people."

Namaste 🙏

2/5/2021

Mindful Moments ....

So, it's Cake Boss for the win! Thanks Buddy Valastro!

An overnight defrosting melted the temporary preservation of this delectable delight - no need for a chain saw today!

Wowza creamy dense frosting and light fluffy cake, abundance of sprinkles and mouthwatering goodness! Highly recommended!!

Of course, not to be outdone by Cody's professional rendition of a delicious Ahi Tuna Poke Bowl - holy smokes that was amazeballs! Leftovers are a beautiful thing.

Thank you for supporting my healthy food needs.

William was surprised when I picked him up from school early for these planned festivities - well, planned by us, can't tell him until the last minute, he gets too excited!

Despite the cold outside the warmth in the house could not be surpassed.

Everyone tucked in warm, safe and sound on this frigid February evening with full tummies and happy hearts.

Namaste 🙏

2/8/2021

Mindful Moments ....

"There are four kinds of caregivers in the world. Those who have been caregivers. Those who are currently caregivers. Those who will be caregivers and those who will need a caregiver." - Rosalyn Carter.

Today's mindful moments is dedicated to my sister-in-law, Victoria Mate, who lost her battle with dementia yesterday.

The endless selflessness of my brother Dave and the love and dedication of Trina, Rachel and Jeff, up until and through her last few moments were filled with the best care for her comfort and peace.

With all the challenges we have all faced this year let this be a reminder that dedication and love prevail especially in the most difficult of times.

You never know what someone is going through.

Be kind.

Always, always be kind.

RIP Vicky - peace and love to you Dave, Trina and Rachel

Namaste 🙏

2/9/2021

Mindful Moments ....

Marshmallow wanted to come out for snuggle time during cage cleaning today ... ok well that's a lie ....

William wanted to snuggle with her so I chased her all over the cage until I caught her evasive little furry butt and put her on William - that's about how it works with these 3.

She did, however, enjoy some sweet pepper while burrowing with William.

I had a phone conversation with a business acquaintance turned friend over the past 30 years.

We discovered that we are the same age and our birthdays are 6 days apart. We also found that we have quite a lot in common.

We've never spoken on a personal level before mostly because he's usually working on my van and I chat with his sister who runs the office. For some reason today he decided to ask how things were going with William through isolation and remote learning. I guess because he's feeling his age, as he alluded to and doesn't think he could handle it.

His kids are in their late 20's and he and his wife are living the good life. He wondered how I do it all because he finds himself so tired all the time at our age and not having the enthusiasm he used to.

We are both entrepreneurs and put everything into our businesses to make them successful. I've had the privilege of working with he and his sister for what seems like forever. They are amazing people. He says I'm one of his original clients still in business who hasn't retired or sold and keeping them in business. Retire? What's that?!

He wondered how we managed through nearly a year of isolation with a 12 yo old special needs child, at my age, no offense intended or taken since his kids were grown, getting engaged and buying their first house.

He also mentioned the properties he manages, along with his business, his 70 honey beehives, his hunting property, his Mead production, his gardens etc. etc. etc. and he wonders how "I" do it.

It was a refreshing conversation in similar yet contrasting lives.

I told him all the things we do and have done to keep busy, swimming, drive by car shows and birthday parties, bike rides, snow play, cooking and in my mind all I could visualize were the shelves of Lego projects that William is keeping Lego in business creating.

I intend to document them at some point when the time is right.

Pictured is the largest project William has accomplished with 1023 pieces of Razor Crest! It's a pretty amazing accomplishment!

I believe that no matter what our age, we can do anything we believe in and decide to do if we follow our passions. ♡

We have energy for what we want or need energy for.

Priorities.

Sleep well, let peace guide you and live with intention.

Namaste 🙏

2/10/2021

Mindful Moments ....

This top photo here is how you get kids back to school safely - some stay remote who prefer or who can't tolerate a mask and the rest are temp checked before getting on the bus and before entering the classroom, sanitized, masked, 6 ft apart and happy as hell to be back even if only hybrid for now. It can be done!

I haven't seen William this happy in a very long time!! He can't wait to go back full time and his teacher says she's so proud of how great he's doing!

They had a little birthday party for his teacher today and "Classroom grandma", his teacher's mom, bought them pizza for lunch and sent treat bags and chocolate in their initials. 💗 She does a lot for them - his teacher's sister is autistic so classroom grandma has a special place in her heart for these kiddos.

Williams initial just happens to work right side up and upside down.

I couldn't help but share this photo of the dog by the cake - that is ALL cake, even the dog! Talent!

I'm going to have updated progress photos of the great remodel project tomorrow - I know you've all lost sleep over it and just can't wait to see it.

There's one thing we need to wait for Spring to finish as its staining that needs to be done outside but the rest will be done tomorrow.

It's amazing how what's important when your 20 is much different than what brings you joy when you're over 50.

If you're a good learner, life experience teaches you many things.

It's the little things like having pride in a place to call your own and make your own, time with family, pajamas at 4pm, eating dinner on the couch watching a good movie, staying home and chilling on the weekends, a peaceful backyard fire, saving money for your future rather than spending it frivolously on things that don't bring memories or long-term happiness.

It's the little things that bring joy to your heart in the long run.

Keep it simple.

Live with intention.

Show kindness.

Lend a helping hand without expectation.

Notice the sunrise/sunset.

Notice the shape of the clouds and the breeze blowing through the trees ... the birds chirping.

From The Book of Zen ....

"Watch as others battle for fame and recognition. Let them have their glory - how long will their happiness last? Be silent and go unrecognized. Find your peace in the silence of knowing what you've truly accomplished. Pray for all sentient beings that the joy they seek be truly theirs."

Namaste 🙏

2/11/2021

Mindful Moments ....

I'm honestly too exhausted to put together a bathroom side by side tonight but I will share my most favorite addition to the remodel.

It's true ... when she's not barking to go out and eat snow we dish!

Gypsy joined me during my work out for an overview of the backyard and to be sure no one, and I mean no one, walked down the sidewalk unnoticed and without a shrill shout out from 2 stories above.

She hit my "mamas not happy list" today barking to go out every half hour oiy vey girlfriend give me and the neighborhood a break!

But then both 12-year olds were on my list by dinner time - it's so nice and quiet in here now.

Sleeping children and dogs is the universe saying "thank you for not losing your shit today mom, your stress hives will be gone by morning."

Shout out to Lulu for the ride to Batavia today and thanks for letting William hang with you while I was discovering the additional repairs found to be done while he handed me homemade Mead and honey, makes the news easier to swallow.

These are the people I spoke of the other day. Business associates turned friends. They're very good people, small business owners who respect small business owners! Looking forward to testing both gifts.

What better way to send my new Kitchen Aide on its virgin voyage but with Valentine's Day cupcakes for a well-deserved school party! With all the holidays and birthday celebrations the kids missed this last year they deserve a fun afternoon tomorrow.

With the vans new shoes, belt, generator gaskets, tune up, oil change, plugs and repaired exhaust pipe she is parked and a lady in waiting to get back on the road tomorrow - that maintenance needs to be paid for and a week's worth of clients to make up ASAP!

I am thrilled that I have such a great support team!

5:30 comes quickly so off to sleepyville I go!

Look for the helpers. ♡

Namaste 🙏

2/14/2021

Mindful Moments ....

As my son from another mother Jeff used to say ....

Happy singles awareness day!

I'm not big on Hallmark holidays but big on loving my family every day not when it's required - it feels insincere to me.

I'm happy to have spent yesterday with Caitie and Cody hanging out, laughing and goofing off while Boston gave me a break and cooked dinner.

Caitlin, Cody and I made sure to sample the caramel Mead - omg heavenly!!

Today a few hours to visit with mom, Tom and Annika and some sibling group text goof off completed the weekend perfectly.

Mom looked all cozy warm in her fuzzy robe and proudly showed us her artwork - what a great way to fill her long days and pour out some of her colorful creativity.

She doesn't completely understand all this isolation, mask wearing but to keep her healthy is of the utmost priority. ♡

Actions speak louder than words - give someone you love your time filled with memories - that is a gift that spans time. ♡

My boys were gifted these breakable chocolate hearts expertly prepared by Lesa!

Hard to believe Boston ate the whole chocolate heart and William hasn't finished his yet - so you know Lesa, I've bought chocolate goodies for Boston many times over the years and most of the time they get put to the side and not eaten.

He absolutely loved your chocolate and devoured it before I realized it was gone!

Looking forward to your next confectioners' creation!!

We ordered a Valentines dinner from Chop'd. Pizza for William, a chicken with gravy sandwich and a salad of quite the variety for B and me Macadamia nut crusted Mahi Mahi with fried cauliflower rice, numerous veggies and pineapple.

William's t-shirt was one of my fav V-day gifts.

It has certainly been a week of unexpected events from both ends of the spectrum but in staying positive I'll leave today with my new favorite quote ....

"There are 2 kinds of people,

The kind that loves Reese's Peanut Butter Cups,

And the kind that are dead to me."

Wishing you all the most important kind of love, self-love.

Namaste 🙏

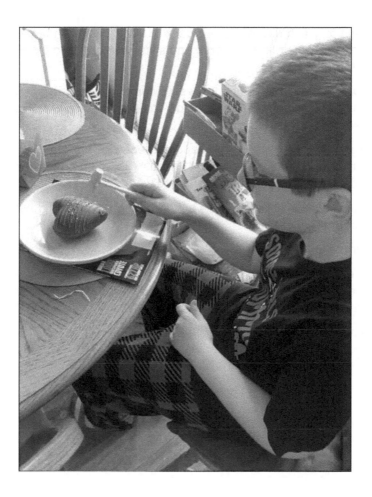

2/17/2021

Mindful moments ....

We've seen so much cold and snow lately I thought I would cover this post with signs of Spring!

I found these tulips that Caitlin and Cody brought me so interesting as they are opening. Their graceful beauty enveloping each pedal full of bi-color vibrance.

These need to planted close to our deck where I can see them each day, every Spring until their time to bloom and shine welcoming in the Spring has ended until the next year.

Every now and then in each of our lives we come to a cross roads where we need to make a life change of some kind. A change that weighs on our minds and yet we avoid it.

Because in avoiding making life changing decisions we stay in a state of safe, even though we aren't content. Because stepping into a new comfort zone can be scary and yet oh so rewarding when we do.

In the grand scheme of things life is actually quite short and I don't think we realize that until we get older.

Take chances in life.

What's the worst thing that can happen? It doesn't pan out and you move onto something else? You won't know unless you grab some courage, use your voice and follow your passions.

"Be the change you wish to see in the world."

Namaste 🙏

2/20/2021

Mindful Moments ....

Well, today I snuck out with my best girl and enjoyed a couple hours away from home. REALLY enjoyed a couple of hours away! My first time in a restaurant in a year.

Krema has done an amazing job of keeping patrons safe, distanced with disposable food containers, plastic wear, plexiglass partitions, distanced tables, masked employees and sanitized tables and counters, not to mention an air filtration system.

We enjoyed a lovely lunch of a GF sandwich of bacon, spinach and mozzarella cheese and a lovely coconut milk latte with a heart in the foam their menu is always filled with fresh and healthy options.

The stroll up Lockport Street was actually pleasant with the sun shining, warming icicles trickling off the awnings despite the 15-degree temp. It actually felt warm. I had my coat unzipped and no winter shrugged shoulders or hurried strides.

Our next stop was Be of Good Juju - I need to hit downtown more often because I didn't know this magical shop existed. I stocked up on sage and some crystals for my collection and a soy candle!

Green Quartz and Jasper to unblock some energy and move into a creative project so I can exit this stagnancy I've been in with some changes I desperately need to make for my sanity.

The house and my van are in for a much-needed saging - it's been far too long.

The soy candle labels are hysterical and naughty! I'm glad William is reading so well but I'll have to hide the candle I purchased if you're easily offended don't look at the last 2 photos.

I have been scolded by William for the towel I have in my doggie powder room "my dog and I talk shit about you" - Boston loves it.

I believe you have to have a sense of humor. You can't take life too seriously or it will eat you up. Sit back, find something to smile about every day, dance in the kitchen and sing all the songs loud and proud. ♡

Things don't happen TO us they happen FOR us and this pandemic has happened for me to make some business decisions, move on from unhealthy relationships and empower myself to move forward as I see fit for me, not anyone else.

Find your "real" people even if they are few, push the insincere aside. Keep those close who accept you for who you are and appreciate your uniqueness - you are valued, you are unique, you have purpose. ♡

Namaste 🙏

2/21/2021

Mindful Moments ....

Brought to you by "2020 forgot to end"!

Yesterday our attached new neighbors texted me asking if we had any water seepage in our walk-in closet in the 2nd floor master bedroom.

She sent me pictures of the water stain on their ceiling, the molding pulled away from the wall where it was wet and her husband's clothes were all wet.

I went up to investigate our closet and everything seemed to be OK.

This morning, however, when Boston stepped into the closet to get his clothes and came out with wet socks, we discovered that our carpet was starting to soak with water.

While knocking some icicles off the gutters today I noticed that a piece of our siding above both of our master bedroom closet windows is loose and flapping in the wind.

I'm wondering if this is the root of our leak problem somehow.

Needless to say, the morning was spent evacuating as much as we could from the closet, and there is a lot.

We found the wet carpeting to be in front of the door all the way to the wall under the window but didn't seem to be spreading anywhere else and wasn't coming from the wall or ceiling or windows.

Both of us called our insurance companies to file claims and we were both offered to have someone come out and help us dry up the water. And they could be here within four hours! WOW GREAT!

Now that would be wonderful if we could figure out where the leak was coming from first, don't you think?!

Tonight, my neighbor texted to say they now have water coming into their garage ceiling from just under where our closet windows are.

We checked our garage and we do not .... Yet. And our carpet is getting wetter. Yes, we've had a fan on it all day.

They have 2 contractors coming out tomorrow and will send them here - they're really nice people.

Sooooo we wait.

In the meantime, I ran to Mokena to pick up some books - STILL COLLECTING CHILDREN'S BOOKS K-high school - pm me.

I've always said that people come into your life at the right time for a reason and you find commonality.

The woman that I met up with just happens to be a speech therapist who works with autistic children.

We had a great conversation in the parking lot comparing notes of this past unimaginable year that we've had. She said she's retiring in a couple of years and will contact me as she comes up with more books from her collection.

What a kind-hearted woman.

I decided to hike it home when the snow started falling, once again.

I was pleasantly surprised by a speedy delivery of homemade gluten-free Paczki from the amazing Lucie. I thought the rum she borrowed this morning was for cocktail hour.

Suffice to say that they were quite delicious and passed the William taste test of approval!

A photo op of a tired Batman sporting ASTOUNDING pecs, cuz he's cute.

Boston had a trip to the ER to have an infection on his finger looked at. I'll say they got the infection out and for the squeamish I'll spare you the details.

Since I've been wanting to clean out this closet forever, I'll say this happened FOR us - although "right now" was not a great time for mandatory decluttering!

Just hoping nothing collapses.

We do not live a dull life here my friends!

Every day is a freaking joy.

Namaste 🙏

2/23/2021

Mindful Moments ....

These two ... buddies this afternoon - Gypsy actually didn't run away from fear of personal space invasion! Progress!

So, it was 40 degrees today - who put on shorts and a t-shirt, rolled the windows down and went for a cruise?

Well not me, but it was really bearable today! And I DID see a couple of drivers with short sleeves, no coat, window rolled down enjoying the break from frigid temps.

Everyone has been hungry for a beautiful day and today was their reward!

I believe I saw grass appearing around the melting snow and a white salt covered driveway sans ice!

Spring is right around the corner. New growth, new beginnings, fresh starts.

Contractors are taking messages, putting clients on waiting lists and insurance companies are booking out a week to send out an adjuster. Everyone is swamped, pun intended!

I hesitate to complain. My southern friends are dealing with so much worse. Displaced from their homes due to complete water damage, burst pipes and water boil orders. It's not all relative. Thinking of you Jody you are a tough cookie my friend.

We've come this far it's been quite a year and I don't mean since January. I mean since last March.

We are survivors. We will persevere despite our challenges and differences.

Those who choose to put the past behind, learn from its challenges and create acceptance of all will be the forgers of change. Renewal and growth - possibilities and commonality.

Let your hopes, not your hurts shape your future.

Namaste 🙏

2/24/2021

Mindful Moments ....

I really do! I live a little outside the box and march to the beat of my own drum.

I'm not everyone's cup of tea, but then not everyone is mine - and that's ok! 🫶

I love when someone has the stones to be unique in a world where we're always supposed to fit in, be "normal" (whatever that is!) or be judged - you are my people.

I love when I see someone, especially a young person, unafraid to lead instead of follow. To create passion and inspiration just by being, you!

To wear bright colors and stand out proud in a sea of typical.

You never know who you touch or how you can change someone's day with a smile, a compliment or a kind gesture - never hesitate to take that chance - you have nothing to lose, only something to gain.

I love genuine, shoot from hip people. Say it like it is and don't mince words people. You never have to guess where they're coming from! I respect that. Just choose your truthful words carefully and be kind.

It's not what you say, it's how you say it.

Today I saw a genuine Illinoian - 40 degrees, snow still piled high at his sides, walking his dog in shorts, a t-shirt and hiking boots ... gotta keep those feet warm and dry.

Made me smile.

I am inspired by art and all of its forms.

I have several incredibly talented friends and family who can take their given talents and create on canvas, through words, in photos, crafts or music - you get a glimpse of someone's soul through their art.

With perspective and an open mind, you gain understanding.

Namaste 🙏

> I like people who begin by blurting out something overly personal. I like people who aren't afraid to walk around with a stain on their shirt. I like people who ugly laugh at their own jokes. I like people who give compliments to strangers in the grocery store and make friends when they're washing their hands in the bathroom. I like people who get passionate about ideas and excited about others' success stories. I like people who live a little outside of the box, who march to the beat of their own drum, and who make it a mission to help those around them.
>
> *Amy Weatherly*

2/26/2021

Mindful Moments ....

We have a lot of "hard" in our house that isn't posted here. Especially evenings ....

The only reason I would post that is to bring awareness to the struggles of Autism and severe anxiety but we don't want sympathy, especially for William, or me.

Maybe on a special page one day.

It's moments like these that make every challenge worth fighting through.

I've mentioned before that Williams yearlong remote experience has had many facets.

Some positives are the amazing progress he made in academics as rewarded in his certificate.

Note his acceptance speech.

William is smart, very smart but gets stuck on things and struggles, sometimes a very long time, to work past it.

But when he does, look out world!!

When he was 11 mos. old he handed us his bottle and refused to drink from a bottle again.

One day he woke up, handed me his pacifier and refused to ever use it again even though he couldn't fall asleep easily without it.

On New Year's Day, a week after his 4th birthday and loooots of potty-training work, he woke up and said "I want to go on the potty "he never had an accident or wet his bed after!

He'll work past any struggle he has because he can, in his time not ours - it's just harder for him to bring it out!

Another positive of remote is getting to see him learn, see how he learns, watch him "get" something and know he has a bright future!! Pride!

For the first time at an IEP meeting Wednesday, I heard the words "talk about transitioning" - a bit down the road of course, but I never thought we might possibly get to a point where public school could be a possibility!

My cousin posted something about kids during this last year and I'd like to end with this ....

take the time to read it, it really hit home, I did lose a whole year, especially those with kids who've been struggling through this past year it will give you a different perspective to gain more understanding of our kiddos and what they need ....

This has been a HARD year for our kids ... so proud of Williams strength and perseverance. ♡

Here is the story ....

I've lost a year with my kids battling over school and I'm done.

My seven-year-old and I were in the midst of our usual asynchronous day battle. I had his writing homework in my hand from school. He'd written several full, well-thought-out sentences.

But he won't do the same for me, at least not without a fight.

I told him he didn't have to write about his best day like his teacher asked, he could write about his worst. He could write about whatever he wanted as long as he wrote a few sentences.

He said he'd get in trouble. He said he was doing a bad job in first grade. He was on the brink of tears but didn't know why.

And it hit me.

Instead of getting frustrated and pushing the assignment, I sat down with him at his desk in his superhero bedroom.

I said "you won't get in trouble and you can't fail first grade. In fact, you're kind of a superhero yourself."

He sat up in his chair just a little and looked at me with disbelief.

I said, "Do you know that no kids in the history of kids have ever had to do what you're doing right now? No kids in the history of kids have ever had to do school at home, sitting in their bedroom, watching their teacher on a computer. You and your friends are making history."

A visible weight lifted from his seven-year-old shoulders, "What does that mean?"

I told him it means I haven't given him nearly enough credit for rolling with the punches. I told him how proud I am of him and his friends. That kids this year are doing the impossible and they're doing a really great job.

I apologized for not saying it sooner and more often. A little tear fell down his cheek.

We've thanked everyone from healthcare workers to grocery store employees but we haven't thanked the kids enough for bearing the burden of what we've put on their shoulders this year.

We've said kids are resilient, and they are. But they are the real superheroes in this whole scenario for having ZERO say in their lives but doing their best to adjust every day.

We closed his school-issued laptop and spent the rest of the day playing. This was supposed to be temporary and here we are a year later still trying to hold our head above water.

This is our home and I won't turn it into a battle ground anymore over something we can't control. Something that no longer makes sense.

Hug your little superheroes today and don't forget to cut them the slack we've given everyone else."

Namaste 🙏

2/27/2021

Mindful Moments ....

Full moon ... nuff said ....

After the frigid polar burst the temps hit 50, the sun is shining, the snow is melting and it's time to get outside and enjoy some fresh air and sunshine while we can.

The squirrels were playfully using our lattice as a climbing wall and scaling the deck and trees like Olympic gymnasts.

A great day for a cruise to pick up more books for Williams school library.

We are up to over 360 books and 68 books on CD!

ALL DONATIONS, K-8, CONTINUE TO BE MUCH APPRECIATED!!

While enjoying the sunshine warming through the windows and music filling our ears William broke into songs of his own.

He can carry a tune and has a pretty decent voice with some training we could have an American Idol Contender.

Uncle Jeff would be proud of his ability to fill in absolute unintelligible words during forgotten lyrics.

Makes me happy to hear him singing. 💭

I can't remember the last time we played outside in comfort!

While William was tooling down the sidewalk on his pedal cart, Cody created what we used to know as a snowman.

Was more of a cyclopes alien of sorts - interested to see what the warm temps transform Mr. snowman into tomorrow!

Although winter has not yet left us, Spring is showing her tiny first sprouts.

Sunshine and fresh air is nourishment for the soul and has the ability to turn sadness to hopefulness - take some time to soak it in every chance you get.

Pay it forward.

Namaste 🙏

3/2/2021

Mindful Moments ....

Ending the day once again with some signs of Spring and hope.

Sunday Boston quietly listened to me ranting about too much work, remote teaching, trying to keep up with home responsibilities, insurance, contractors, isolation, trying to fit in needed appointments with only one or two days to do it alone, no time for self-care blah blah blah - so he brought me flowers.

It's not the flowers I appreciated as much as being heard - I try to keep it positive and try not to complain much but hell I'm human and this year has stolen so much from everyone! Sometimes you just need to really be heard!

William was unexpectedly home from school yesterday for Casimir Pulaski day. I say unexpectedly because I didn't know he was even off until last Friday.

Why are some schools off and some not? My friend had her 1st grader home and her high schooler in school wth??

Williams bus drivers weren't even told that he was off until they saw a crazy woman in her pajamas with fuzzy slippers and unkempt hair running out to the bus at 7:30 AM on Monday to tell them that there was no school that day - no idea who that was.

Am I the only one that feels that holidays like this and Presidents' Day are better spent at school learning about the reasons that the day is to be recognized rather than having yet another day off and not having a clue as to why? Or it being left up to the parents to teach a history lesson on that day as well? Sigh!

Well, we made the best of it and played checkers, ran some errands, William folded and put away his laundry and we played some riveting imaginative scenarios with myself as Lego Batman and William as all the Lego Star Wars characters hunting down and incarcerating the Joker. (Thankfully we have ALL the Lego buildings, vehicles and mini figs we needed.)

After the exhaustive hour long chase the green haired little bastard escaped while I was upstairs!

Sunday was so filled with work, work, work I made it a point to put things aside and be a kid with a kid for a while Monday.

Sometimes you have to step away from technology and be in the moment. It has been way too overwhelming these past several weeks!

Today was a beautiful day for a drive out to moms for a chat with her and her homies.

It's incredible what amazing things the sun can do to uplift your mind and heart just by being present.

It also felt good to drop off over 360 books and 68 books on cd at Williams school today. It's merely a dent in what is needed but the beginning of a wonderful library for these kids!

Donations are needed to drop off hundreds more even if collected one by one.

Making great things happen one page at a time.

If you've indulged me this far, thank you.

Warmer days ahead and hope around every corner.

Namaste 🙏

3/32021

Mindful Moments ....

So, I pulled up at a stop light in the van ... next to a police officer parked at the side of the road ... in a SUV (note the equal height view) with the bag top left on my console.

As I reached in the bag I looked to my right and locked eyes with him.

I rolled down my passenger side window as I put some of the contents of that bag in my mouth and asked if he'd ever had kale chips and would he like to try some - no response ... just a head shake - no sense of humor?!

They really are kale chips and they're delicious!

There's nothing more satisfying to a groomer than transforming grinch paws into pretty feet.

Bohde LOVES his grooming's (insert sarcasm) and he's such a good boy! Thanks for the coffee boost, Terre next we go out for some coffee and catch up more!

Tasha and Lady are always willing participants in their pedicure day – Leslie, don't let them fool you with their baulking, they are perfect angels for me and Tasha is quite protective of Lady, in a loving way!

Bella the Catahoula refused to make eye contact after her grooming but certainly doesn't turn away from her well-deserved treat - she's a sweetie.

Wolfie, not pictured, the semi vicious GSD did not draw blood today so it was a successful grooming and as always, we ended as friends with treats! He loves to be snuggled just DONT touch his feet, or de-shed him, or blow dry him ... he always earns a muzzle for his safety and mine - he bites when he's not pleased.

The sunshine and no coat are a welcome break from the past few weeks! A breath of fresh air so to speak.

We haven't seen the last of cold and snow but I will take in every beautiful day we're given in between!

Another challenge for tomorrow to pay it forward - hold a door for someone, lend a helping hand, give an unsolicited compliment you just may change the course of someone's day with a simple, kind gesture.

I learned to give not because I have much But, because I know exactly what it's like to have nothing.

Pay it forward ....

Namaste 🙏

3/5/2021

Mindful Moments ....

Back to remote learning this morning after workout, with coffee and a smile!

*****I forgot the most important part of the day!! Check out the report card at the end!

The teacher showed us all some mercy by making it a short day!

They got the news the same time we did about 4:30 yesterday afternoon and now they have to re-plan the entire week.

So do we families.

So, it gave us all a day to adjust and gave them a day to get planning done. Win – win!

I wasn't able to get things done as I had planned today but what we did get to do was go out for a nice long walk in the sunshine this afternoon!

Gypsy and I walked - William hovered.

It was great to get some fresh air and Gypsy hasn't had a walk-in month because of the cold weather. I think she was more excited than me!

We saw some fun things while cruising around the neighborhood.

I believe there are messages everywhere throughout our day we just have to be mindful of them.

Most times we're so busy rushing through our mundane days that we miss out on what's important.

What I did notice was this sticker on a car "choose kindness."

What a great way to pay this message forward day after day!

CHOOSE KINDNESS!

Another hawk was soaring overhead today. ♡

William loves his hoverboard and is quite good at it! Maneuvered some sidewalk uneven spots like a pro - stayed upright the whole ride! Me too!!

I got on it once ... once - I don't need any more injuries holding me back! I'll stick to biking, hiking, swimming and home workouts! Those are dangerous enough for me.

The fresh air was a great way to regroup!

I LOVE being out in nature it's peaceful, renewing and I feel at one with it - it's my happy place.

The next 5 days are going to be gorgeous - make sure to take some time to soak it in and let it soothe your soul.

Namaste 🙏

3/7/2021

Mindful Moments ....

Today we headed out west to Rochelle for what proved to be a fun filled, adventurous, relaxing, history guided tour of Oregon IL by Cody and Caitie.

Of course, it has to begin with my grand kitties getting their treats. It was more of a feeding frenzy that poor Harvey missed while hiding out somewhere in safety and terror.

When I hit the facilities before we ventured out today Midas thought it would be fun to follow me in ... until I closed the door.

Apparently, unbeknownst to me, he gets a bath in that room so panic ensued and if he only had thumbs that door would've been open!

So, our first sightseeing destination was the nuclear power plant not far from their home.

Quite a sight to see! Massive silos beaming halos of hot steam into the atmosphere. Seeing them roadside is quite incredulous as compared to the far-off perspective.

Our next stop was the massive Stronghold Castle standing high over Oregon with its stone construction, secret passageways and incredible grounds.

Full tours are not currently available and there was an engagement, like literally someone was proposing, to happen inside today so we shall return for the full tour at a later date!

Next stop the incredible Black Hawk statue proudly displayed and recently renovated up high overlooking Oregon and its people. It's a sight to behold with its massive strength, pride and leadership.

Our tour guide, Cody, told us that in the past you could crawl up inside Black Hawk to the top and look out through his eyes.

A quick grab of lunch and off to the Dam Tour.

The roaring flow of energy trailing along the river and over the dam was filled with power, yet soothing sounds of nature.

The boys sought out flat skipping stones and tried their hand at skating those suckers over rippling water while a lone goose made an attempt to swim toward the flowing water.

We hiked hundreds of stairs to the Overlook. We are honored to be introduced to the special location of Caitlin and Cody's engagement.

What a beautiful background and scenery for the remembrance of such a special moment frozen in time.

Our last stop to check out the Bison sanctuary. It's a beautiful vast area where farmers gave up their land to give the Bison a place to roam and local wild life and foliage to rejuvenate.

Apparently, the Bison were busy keeping social distanced today so we didn't get to see them but we did get a picture of their hospitality style should we meet face to face.

William found a working fountain and helped himself to a much-needed drink, dragged his weary body out to the car and begged for home.

He actually did really well for all the sightseeing and walking we did in 3 hours today.

Thank you, Cody, for sharing Oregon's amazing history and your childhood memories from this quaint little town with big shoulders.

Side note - every year when Caitlin goes to Ren Faire, she brings me a metal rose, always different, different color, scented.

Last year it wasn't open but today I received that metal rose hand made by Cody's brother Caleb! I absolutely love it! You are an artist, Caleb!

My perfect day has ended with watching The Walking Dead and the Harry and Meghan interview with Oprah being taped.

Tomorrow back to putting my teacher hat back on so a good night's sleep from today's fresh air and joyful moments is a must.

Soak in the moments that bring a lifetime of memories.

Namaste 🙏

3/8/2021

Mindful Moments ....

Gypsy had her grooming today after remote!

The poor old girl is so exhausted she looks like she's run a marathon!

She's like a pudding puddle.

I would add that if she didn't spin in circles, only try to face in one direction and try to jump off the table while I'm working on her we'd be finished faster and with less of a workout, for both of us!!

She's 12. Has always been my most challenging client and is too old to give up the fight - she just might win one day.

That's ok it's my turn tomorrow and I promise not to jump out of the chair or spin in circles.

I look forward to a solo hair appointment one day - William is awesome and I love spending time with him but 2hrs alone isn't too much to ask for and I don't feel guilty for it! Side note, he's tired of being with me 24/7 too, and that's OK!

The current van issues are fixed and the groomer now has covid ... and so it goes ....

If nothing else great happened today, and it didn't, then being emailed to sign up for Spring Miracle League Ball then it was a perfect day!!

We are signed up for Spring and Fall ball - covid precautions on and off the field in place and I'll be his buddy this year!

Couldn't be happier than to have a bit of normal to look forward to!

Gypsy looks comfortable and I want to be comfortable too! It's been an eventful, full day - Time for some Zzzzzzzzzz's!

"Never lose hope. Tomorrow could be the day you've been waiting for."

Namaste 🙏

3/9/2021

Mindful Moments ....

Since William willingly accompanied me to another blood test and a long overdue hair appointment today - I reciprocated and we played outside.

It was a beautiful no coat, no sweatshirt day. 🤍

Of course, we completed school work first, but compromise is needed to get through our remote learning days as amicably as humanly possible!

A bike ride for William and another afternoon walk for Gypsy started our fun.

William gathered up his friend from down the street and we played badminton.

Grammy Barb and Auntie Lucie are kind enough not to chase us out of their yard so we can play outdoor games.

Our yard is basically pool, vegetable and flower gardens and patio - not much room for baseball, soccer and bad mitten!

It was very windy so bad mitten was challenging but the boys and I didn't give up with getting that little plastic bird to fly!

Was a bit of functional fitness, some cardio with lots of squats were accomplished picking up the birdie more often rather than connecting with a racket.

Sirens in the distance grabbed our attention as our road behind the berm, behind the house is often used to get to the highway faster than Weber Rd. traffic.

I was hoping for a Gypsy siren howl but she decided to bark at them instead.

There must have been something big going on with 4 fire trucks, 2 ambulances, fire chief and commander vehicles loudly screeching by.

It brought the boys enjoyment especially when they got a loud "HOOONK" from the last fire truck.

However, I don't imagine the purpose of their parade was anything to be joyful about.

For me, nature is peace.

Fresh air, breeze and signs of Spring surrounded us.

Some tiny purple flowers peaking their little heads up through the grass to check for an opportunity to arrive without snow.

A bunny shyly sheltered behind some lattice away from the peering eyes of inquisitive youngins.

Take some time to get some nature when you can.

The work will wait for your return. 🖤

Namaste

3/11/2021

Mindful Moments ....

The day the world changed ... one year ago.

A year ago, it was China and a cruise ship kept off shore with passengers sick and dying.

Suddenly it was the world shutting down for "14 days to flatten the curve."

Schools closing.

Businesses shutting down.

Restaurants, Museums, theaters, parks, zoos, movie theaters, bowling alleys ... closed.

Empty streets.

Falling stock market.

Toilet paper became extinct.

Life as we knew it ... closed.

The panic of uncertainty and the unknown at our fingertips.

Here we are, a year later.

Mourning lost loved ones.

The loss of hard work and life savings put into businesses that couldn't survive the strain.

The gain of some business whose offerings were a beacon in uncertain times.

Still trying to survive.

Still wearing masks and social distancing, well some of us.

Who knew the challenges we would face?

The courage and strength we would need to muster.

The overwhelming responsibilities and worries put upon on our plates.

The unimaginable losses.

The incredible gains.

Friendships have ended.

New friendships have flourished.

People come into our lives for a reason, a season or a lifetime ....

We've all learned something about ourselves this past year.

We learned that we are vulnerable, yet strong.

We learned that we can look within ourselves.

When we are forced to come to a halt and lend time to reflect, if we choose to.

Many have rethought their careers ... relationships.

Some have learned that the simple things in life are the important things in life.

That "things" don't matter, making memories does.

We have found creative ways to entertain and occupy ourselves when what we took for granted is taken away.

We are forced to use our imaginations like a child discovering everything new.

We are such a busy nation that we don't allow ourselves time to soul search by keeping the wheels rolling and running through life -

This year has allowed us that time.

If you used it wisely you may have made positive changes/plans for your future.

We've learned so very much.

We've turned a corner and can see the light at the end of the proverbial tunnel.

Things happen FOR us, not TO us.

If you choose to see it that way. 🖤

Namaste 🙏

SHE BELIEVED SHE COULD AND SHE ALMOST DID, BUT THEN A PANDEMIC HIT AND SOMEONE ASKED HER TO DO DOUBLE THE AMOUNT OF WORK WITH THE SAME AMOUNT OF HOURS IN THE DAY, AND SOMEONE ELSE ASKED HER TO BE THE BEST VERSION OF HERSELF WHILE RUNNING ON FUMES, AND SHE LOST TRACK OF REALISTIC EXPECTATIONS UNTIL SHE HEARD ALL THE WOMEN TALKING, REALIZED SHE WASN'T ALONE, POURED ANOTHER CUP OF COFFEE AND DECIDED HER BEST WAS ENOUGH.

3/15/2021

Mindful Moments ....

For the love of a boy and his fur baby.

I've lost track of time but for well over a year now bedtime has been more than a challenge for William.

It hasn't always been just bedtime.

It's been any transition whether from playtime to a meal, leaving a preferred activity or going to bed.

That's Autism. Transition defiance - their brains can't manage transition without years of training: therapy with consistency and patience.

I'm so proud of this young man and the progress he has made over the years - nothing comes easy for him but he perseveres until he gets it.

Bedtime is something that used to be pleasant, calm and relaxing - my favorite time of day with him because the days were so challenging when he was younger.

I have a hunch, but not exactly sure what happened, but now it's met with nightly defiance, sometimes meltdowns, always frustration and sometimes self-injury.

I've done TONS of research and picking the minds of therapists.

I was doing most everything right and just couldn't figure out how to shift this behavior.

But something HAD to give.

Last night was one of the toughest nights we've had so when he finally allowed his mind to rest, I dove back into more research for his sake and my health.

I kept reading the same things and the only thing on these lists that I could try to change would be his environment.

I suggested a few things to him that didn't go over very well.

This morning I had an AHA moment!

I told him that tonight while he was relaxing and watching TV after dinner, 6-630 is when everything usually falls apart, that I was going to get one of his guinea pigs to snuggle with. He loved that.

They soothe and comfort him or at least Rocket does the other two are curious adventurers that would sooner fall off a ledge exploring than lay still.

So, after 15 minutes of snuggling, I had him carry Rocket upstairs and into the bathroom where we traded back-and-forth with her until he completed all his bedtime routines and got into bed with her without a peep.

She wasn't allowed to watch him pee.

No screaming, no yelling, no aggression, no engine revving, no injuring - nothing other than a little trouble falling asleep.

In many difficult instances in life the answer is just so SO simple that it's right in front of our faces and we don't even see it.

So, when you're struggling with a situation, you're frustrated and you think you've exhausted everything ....

TRY HARDER.

Ask questions.

Research.

Some are private. I believe in transparency. It's everyone's personal choice and journey.

In being transparent you may just help someone along the way, someone in your same situation, or with a challenge they're struggling with, giving them hope, most times without even realizing it.

Pay it forward.

You find your people being true to yourself and you lose people who were kind to your face but have judged you from afar and that is beyond a good thing.

Stick with those who are truly good people, behind your back as well.

This may not work every night.

But today it did and I call that success.

Thank you for your patience, Rocket, you have more compassion than many humans.

Tonight, we lay our heads to pillow in peace. ♡

Namaste 🙏

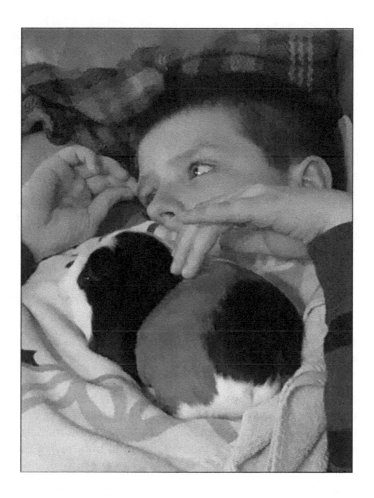

3/16/2021

Mindful Moments ....

Successful evening #2 with bedtime piggie therapy! Rocket seems to be our snuggle girl so we're sticking with her for now.

It's a year today that a national emergency was called.

It'll be a year tomorrow that kids began remote learning, and still are.

A HUGE special thank you to the Chicago Angel Mamas for organizing a Will County only special needs person and caregiver vaccination clinic next week.

And thank you to the Special Needs Mom Squad of Plainfield for reposting the information!

I have my spot for Pfizer on the 27th and the second dose on April 17th. So well organized!

Most have no idea how emotional this is for me.

When someone relies on your every moment, every breath you take, you're their constant sense of security and presence in their life, you are literally their person who they live, eat and breath for, you do EVERYTHING to keep yourself healthy to be there for them as long as you humanly can.

Losing you, for them, is the most devastating loss they fear.

This past year anytime I sneezed or coughed I was immediately asked if I was ok in a concerned voice.

I lost sleep knowing that there were hundreds of thousands of people, many healthy, losing their lives from a virus that was out of control and not respected by those who felt invincible ... and still do.

I knew that I would and still will do everything in my power to keep myself and my family safe in spite of the judgement I've received for it and the very sad posts I see of sarcastically boasting about "are you a miracle like me? Not wearing masks, not social distancing, going to and having parties and we haven't gotten sick?"

I saw this yesterday and it made me sick. The disrespect in this statement to all the lives lost this past year, all the lost businesses, the financial losses, all the suffering and heartache being met with such arrogance. It's just sad.

Someone I know has this attitude ... she traveled out of state by plane, spent time with a lot of people, she got Covid afterward and has been sicker than she's ever been, missing work and losing money with children to feed.

Your luck may run out or you may make it through this without being a victim or casualty- I choose not to take that gamble for my family.

I am so incredibly grateful to the work put into organizing this clinic and the peace of mind it will bring to so many families who are special needs and whose special needs children rely on them so very much.

My heartfelt gratitude to those who walk the walk, have seen devastation from this virus daily and yet continue to show up to work every day to do it again and care about others more than themselves.

The light at the end of the tunnel is getting brighter and I can see it!!

So I'll be wearing my mask, sanitizing and keeping my distance as long as I have to - we all have choices, those are mine.

Negativity is not welcome in my feed, you know how to scroll, please do so.

I wish everyone a speedy end to this, good health and a return to whatever "normal" is going to look like for us a year from now.

I'm going to open a free hugs booth to make up for lost time.

Namaste 🙏

3/17/2021

Mindful Moments ....

And a Happy St Patrick's Day! 🍀

Every year I plan the usual corned beef, cabbage, carrots and potatoes in the crock pot.

This is year I was too tired to cook so McWethy's Tavern via Uber Eats supplied us with lovely Reuben Sandwiches and for the boy's garlic parm fries and cheesecake.

Williams been trying new foods so a Reuben was a new, surprisingly wonderful addition to his repertoire even after mentioning the sour kraut!

Delicious!

It was an emotional roller coaster of a day in strange ways.

My day began wonderfully with an early rise for coffee and 30 minutes of me time, a lovely text chat with my soul sister Paula before work and finding a nice stimulus deposit.

I then walked into managing a disturbing bus situation for William with the district that ran an early day behind a bit.

Upon traveling to my 2nd appointment "Brown Eyed Girl" came on the radio.

I smiled and then started to cry, then laughed. I haven't heard that song in a long time - it means a lot to me.

Do you ever have those moments that take you back to a place and time of such fun and happiness long ago?

Then suddenly you're reminded, again today, that who was a huge part of making those happy times is no longer here?

and it would've been his birthday today.

Tom T was a party planner. He always had some fun party in his parents' basement in high school, concert road trip, pig roast at Farm Stock, complete with live band or St Patty's Day pub crawl with a full-sized bus ... and bathroom of course.

Each stop planned and researched to look for deals for his private party of 20ish.

The last pub crawl he planned, in 1998, was a birthday St Patty's Day crawl. It was the last because it was so much work planning them so he decided to move onto other things.

It was a second date I believe for Boston and I, the first time we dated and what a night it was, right Boston?!

We even all bought matching sweatshirts listing our stops like a popular concert tour - I still have that sweatshirt.

We walked into a bar at one of our stops, Tom walked to the juke box, played Brown Eyed Girl, pointed at me from across the room, smiled and mouthed "that's for you." ♡

I was taken aback by such a sweet gesture from a great friend.

This is what brings a smile, tears and laughter - a moment I'll never forget along with many others with a friend who was like a brother for 40 years and gone too soon.

Happy birthday from afar my friend ... I know you were there today, if only briefly ... the memories will forever be etched in my heart. ♡

"We all have jobs" yours is to finally rest and ours is to carry on your sense of humor and love of life.

Don't be a stranger.

Namaste 🙏

3/23/2021

Mindful Moments ....

Nature is my favorite place to be.

Spring is a time of renewal.

This past weekend with Spring sunshine and warmth those two things came together.

Nature with all its fresh air, budding trees and busy wild life.

Turtle Lake, a favorite nearby, peaceful haven seemed different Saturday.

Different in a good way, not that it isn't always good.

Maybe it was the freedom outside the four walls of winter and a pandemic.

Maybe it was being with Caitlin and William with no demands, no work, no worries.

So many happy, content faces so welcoming and open to a hello, some small talk and "Hi I'm William! Can I pet your dog??"

I saw gratefulness for life, community, real faces without the separation of a screen merely making an attempt at staying connected.

Real humans making eye contact without looking down at a phone.

Kiddos climbing, running, jumping, strollers - riding bikes, electric skate boards and hoverboards. Wind blowing in their face taking in a feel of normal.

I could've stayed out there all day connecting with people in a safe place, in the fresh air.

The Spring brings the return of our pool ducks and yard doves.

Every Spring these feathery couples return and every year I get just as excited as the year before to see them!

I know it's a sign of Spring.

The Ducks for a cleansing and swim in our pool cover while safely guarding their nest behind the yards fence.

We've made our neighbors aware of this sneaky stinker ever so carefully building a nest in their kitchen vent. I watched 3 of them flying in and out one day, sticks in beaks and swiftly prepping their nest for a family - Perhaps a better location is needed?!

Nighttime Guinea pig therapy is going quite well although Rocket has become the target of our tomfoolery.

I don't believe she was pleased with our shenanigans but her patience and calm were appreciated.

William was a bit under the weather yesterday and today so "out of an abundance of caution" which seems to be another phrase of the year, I took him for a Rona test - negative, as I suspected.

The difficult thing is the early signs of Covid are also allergy and head cold symptoms.

Stuffy nose, sore throat, fatigue, sneezing, slight cough, no fever, has taste and smell - allergies.

Library book pick-ups are slow but steady.

I have 15 more boxes in my Jeep waiting for drop off with the other 330 books dropped a few weeks ago.

A big huge thank you Ali and coworkers for your hand in this current collection and to the Woodridge Public Library for another donation of 6 boxes!

Still collecting - keep these kiddos in mind when you're Spring cleaning! I will happily pickup any and all donations!

Morning comes early and slumber is sweet!

Happy Spring to all, and to all a good night.

Namaste 🙏

3/26/2021

Mindful Moments ....

The doorbell rang at 2:10 today. William was at school but I knew who it was - he's very timely.

It was Williams 7-year-old friend from down the street. In nothing but a t-shirt, shorts and flip flops, no socks - it was 45 degrees - that's the mom in me.

He felt he needed to stop by and let me know that my outdoor Easter decorations were displayed prematurely as "Easter is not until next Sunday."

I felt the need to tell HIM that it won't be 64 degrees until this Sunday, today it's 45 and yet he's wearing shorts and a t-shirt so perhaps we both should rethink our decisions.

I believe Mr. and Mrs. Duck have repaired their differences and agreed to disagree as they are gone now.

We'll see what body language reveals tomorrow! Maybe he left the nest seat up - assuming it's his fault of course lol.

Hold yourself back I lead a captivating life, don't I ?! - perhaps the doves will make a reveal tomorrow as well.

It's actually the simple things like these that make me happy.

I find enjoyment and appreciate the little things - it makes the big things easier to manage - find humor in your struggles and they will feel lighter.

Oh, and don't get it twisted.

Namaste 🙏

> Listen, drunk me, work me and mom me are NOT the same person. Don't get it twisted.

3/29/2021

Mindful Moments ....

A friend posted a quote tonight ....

"It takes courage to be yourself in a world where you are constantly told that who you are isn't good enough. Being yourself is the biggest gift you can offer the world."

This quote spoke to me, loudly.

I spent a lot of my life feeling that I didn't measure up, wasn't good enough, trying to please everyone. No sympathy, just facts.

I don't feel that way anymore.

I learned the hard way that trying to please everyone else, be who everyone else wants you to be or how to act leaves you unhappy and no one is pleased in the end, least of all, you.

I encourage William to be his true, beautiful, unique self no matter what anyone says, because you'll never make everyone happy and those who love you for who you are will be true to your heart.

He's not afraid to ask questions - no matter how much the question makes me cringe.

We went for walk today - he drove of course.

His true self is social, inquisitive.

He loves cars.

We hit the jackpot in the neighborhood with a few of his favorite vehicles.

Not to mention that the Mustang owner was out waxing his ride and William struck up a conversation.

Asked if he could sit in his car - owner said sure go ahead - and this where I start sweating.

William looooves pushing buttons, shifting gears - HARD- and jamming on breaks.

He did well, PHEW!

I hope the sweat pouring down my face and the mild anxiety wasn't noticeable.

I get anxious because you'd be surprised the number of men, we've run into at cruise nights who have been down right mean to him if he got too close to their car, asked to sit in it or see the engine.

We've talked about respecting someone not wanting him to touch or get in their car because they work hard to keep them nice and that's their choice but I teach him to politely ask, the worst that can happen is they say no and politely say thank you anyway and walk away if they say no.

Their response to his questions is often unkind. He's more mature than some grown men who forget that they were an inquisitive, car loving child at one time.

He asked to see under the hood, the owner obliged - the owner was thrilled to be talking cars and bragging about his ride to an interested audience, thank goodness.

I thanked him for his kindness and patience with William - he said he loved it, and his son has a Mustang also.

After about 15 minutes I encouraged William away and we saw 2 more cars he needed to take pause and one photo op to grab!

I'm proud to see him just being true to himself and his curiosity, asking questions and learning that some people will be unkind but most will take the time to show interest and that's the important thing.

Look for the good and leave the negative behind.

Be true to yourself ... you are worthy, powerful and loved.

Namaste 🙏

4/2/2021

Mindful Moments ....

We lit it up blue today!!

Autism awareness is great but ACCEPTANCE is what we strive for.

We celebrate every little win every day!

Autism creates a lifetime of advocating ... for everything!

We are not called mama bears for no reason.

This guy is an amazing complex bundle of wonder!

He's taught me how to see the world from a different perspective.

Not to sweat the small stuff, there are always bigger fish to fry.

Never to hold a grudge.

We don't want to change Autism; we want to understand and be inclusive.

We can NOT expect them to understand US ... But to get into THEIR world while methodically introducing them to ours.

We are all human beings with feelings, our brains are just wired differently.

A blend of perfect worlds. ♡

What may take you or your child a month to learn, may take our autistics years or a lifetime ... but with constant repetition, practice, practice, practice, positive reinforcement, "this then that", therapies, strategies and damn hard work they get there!

This world was not made for these amazing individuals and yet they are thrown into it and expected to conform from a brain that is wired to see the world in a different way.

Acceptance.

Accept us when we are overwhelmed with a crowded festival and hold our ears and cry.

Accept us when we are triggered by bright lights and busy sounds in a department store and we lay on the ground and make noises you may not understand or run from our person - fight or flight is how we operate.

Accept us when we shoot from the hip with blatant honesty whether it makes you uncomfortable or not.

Accept us for our intelligence that doesn't always present in a conventional way.

Accept us for our curiosity and inquisitiveness as it helps us learn and understand ... and you can learn from us.

Accept us when we're spinning in circles or repeating a phrase ... it makes us feel comfortable inside, when we are not on the outside.

Accept and embrace our differences, learn from us we can teach a thousand lessons about judgement, fear, exclusion, hate and bullying ... we've been there because we're different.

Accept our beautifully, outstanding uniqueness, watch us as we take in the world from a different point of view.

Understand when our caregivers are drained and exhausted - they spend their everyday being our therapist, our teacher, our cheerleader, our supervisor, our mentor, our behavior strategist, our constant guide, our chauffeur to never ending therapies and Drs. while working full time jobs and trying to manage a household - self-care is when we're lucky to take a shower - most times they just want to be alone in a quiet room to recharge to do it again the next day, not to go out to a noisy restaurant / bar or have a party - their brains need calm and peace too.

Get to know us - ask questions - we are HAPPY to educate to create acceptance.

We are intelligent beyond what you see.

We are loving, compassionate and empathetic - we feel your emotions as much as you do.

We are learning to express emotions verbally above behaviorally. Sometimes we don't know the words to attach to our feelings.

Excitement can be seen as anxiety and come out in perseverating or unusual behavior. Holidays can be overwhelming with its decorations changing our norm and festive planning creating uncertainty - we crave routine.

Processing feelings can be hard for us.

Don't assume that an older child with younger behavior is undisciplined or "bad" they just might be having a hard time in their environment or their routine has changed - be kind.

You don't outgrow Autism; you learn to manage it the best you can with an amazing village who gets you and pushes you to your greatest achievements.

Don't abandon us and our families because we can't go to every function, it can be exhausting and overwhelming for all of us.

Please Be Kind.

Get to know us.

Love us.

Learn about us.

Accept us.

Today we celebrate the wonderful uniqueness of Autism - please teach your children about ours.

Be kind.

Namaste 🙏

4/5/2021

Mindful Moments ....

Last year when we spent Easter without our extended family, we said "by this time next year we'll be altogether"!

It's "next year" and still too many missing faces and missing so many hugs. Dave, Robert, Trina, Jeff, Oliver, Evi ... mom. We missed you all so much!

We made the best of it and went nontraditional ... or maybe a new tradition.

No ham, Hungarian sausage, veggies, potatoes, whipped jello forgotten in the fridge but plenty of bacon, onions, green peppers, tomatoes, hot peppers and maybe a couple of grease cutters.

A bacon fry didn't hurt. 😊

A delectable meat filled charcuterie with crackers and a side of fresh fruit helped to dull the hunger pangs in between the bacon breads!

Thanks to vaccines and rapid tests a few of us were able to enjoy a beautiful 75-degree, sunny day under a cloudless sky with a light warm breeze ahhhhhhhh

A welcome break after the frigid end to winter.

Looking back at last year and to where we are now is pretty darn amazing for such an unknown situation. The light is getting brighter at the end of the tunnel - I know we'll all be together again soon.

We had fun with Lesa's Breakable Goody filled chocolate eggs, Legos, music and some archery!

We introduced our new neighbors to the delight of a bacon fry with an over the fence handoff, inhaled, then enjoyed a second!

I have yet to meet someone who doesn't like it!

We hope that our loud singing and off pitch lyrics didn't break any crystal in our neighbors' homes but there isn't a cookout without favorite classics being belted out in somewhat unison!

The Easter Bunny delivered well - William is a loved young man with special gifts from family - the Batman Shuttle was finished today - we need to build that addition to display all of these really creative Legos!

Cody love ya sweetie but the deck, house, carpets and floor have glitter all over them for some reason - hmmm wonder how that got there.

Days of anticipation and excitement brought a sleepy pajama day for William and good day to catch up for me.

Back to reality with remote learning tomorrow ho-hum.

How swiftly a year goes by.

As you lay your head to pillow tonight find something to be grateful for ... there is always something to be grateful for.

Namaste 🙏

4/8/2021

Mindful Moments ....

Today was Duck bros night out at the watering hole lookin' for chicks.

This is a first - I've not seen 2 males hangin' at the pool.

Wife and kids must be making them quackers!

The Lego projects are being pumped out like Christmas at Amazon!

Presenting Williams latest project, the Ice Cream Truck.

I tried to order a frozen yogurt but was informed "this isn't a health food truck MOM, it's an ice cream truck!"

Zesty!

I'm very excited about my veggie plants! Thanks to Leslie gardening advice you can literally watch these seedlings grow!

They were just planted in the seed pods last Friday and a few of them need to get into larger pots tomorrow. Some are just popping through and some are reaching for the ceiling!

The only ones not peeking through are the Hungarian Banana peppers.

They are either old seeds or just as stubborn as human Hungarians and will come out when they darn well please!

If all goes well, we'll have butternut squash, spaghetti squash, radicchio (for the piggies), yellow beans, peas, zucchini, tomatoes, green beans and red peppers.

May throw in some strawberries too, we'll see.

William and I finished school work and spent a quiet afternoon doing our own thing, no tv just Lego building, searching for more donation library books and still dealing with the bus issue.

Gypsy, on the other hand, was in a naughty mood today!

She was busted eating William's candy from his Easter basket and taking wash clothes out of the hamper and shoving them under my pillow!

I hope she enjoyed the last of the malted milk balls and I give her kudos for carefully unwrapping mini nestle bars without tearing or eating the wrapper.

She didn't eat enough to get sick, just to make a mess and send William reeling! NO ONE eats his candy!

He felt bad later for getting mad at her when he realized that she has zero self-control and could've gotten very sick. He hugged her and apologized - all is well in 12-year-old land.

The torn-up padding was what was found last week when I removed her old bed cover to wash it - that's what happens when your fur friend tries to "fluff" the bedding to make it more comfortable.

I'm tired and I have much bedding fluffing to do before I can settle in for the night.

Sleep well my friends and find humor in your day.

Namaste 🙏

4/11/2021

Mindful Moments ....

Every day is a new day to start fresh.

Today we went to Rochelle for furry snuggle therapy.

This boy is an animal whisperer and feels calm and serenity with a warm furry friend in his arms and they are attracted to him.

Caitlin and Cody are foster parents for mamas and their kitties until they are well enough and old enough to adopt out to forever homes.

These little darlings are getting their snip snips end of the week and back to the rescue to be adopted out - anyone want one of these 5 adorable fur balls or their mama??

It was the perfect opportunity to socialize them and find peace for William.

They are the sweetest little angels, ok not always "angels" I mean they're kittens but so fun to cuddle with and watch play.

Mew, Caitlins cat, crawled into William's lap for smooches and snuggles as always.

Mama kitty is about done with her babies and looking for some human love from him.

Animals have an amazing connection and calming effect.

They take away anxiety and stress with a warm snuggle and gentle purr.

They are therapeutic whether they are specifically trained to do so or just being themselves.

Give it a try when you need some unconditional love.

Thank you for sharing the babies with us before they go to their forever homes. ♡

Tonight, was calm and early to bed.

Every day is an experience.

May you have sweet relaxing sleep with little furry toe beans scampering through your dreams.

Namaste 🙏

4/13/2021

Mindful Moments ....

We needed to get out of the house after school work today so the 12-year olds and I went for walk / ride through the neighborhood.

The sun was shining brightly with soooo many beautiful flowering trees and perennials opening their eyes for Spring!

The beautiful red tulips are mine gifted to me for Easter from the Dales.

They just opened up today for a photo shoot. 🌷

The sun and colors of Spring renewal brings light and hope to the days ahead and a peacefulness that normal IS out there and the seasons continue to change no matter where we are in our lives or what destiny has planned for us.

We've had some struggles the past few weeks but fresh air and sunshine always brighten the mood and lend sleepiness to overwhelmed busy minds in the evening.

Take a walk and clear your mind. You'd be surprised what a bit of fresh air can do.

I'm very excited about my gardens this year!

We are tilling up another area of the yard and adding another galvanized / wood framed 8' x 3' raised planter being made by a man in Plano.

It will blend beautifully with the others and my veggies are reaching for the stars waiting to get outside and produce healthy foods to share!

I'm pretty sure I'm late to the show but how amazed was I to find these compressed bricks of seeding soil?!!

Just add water and voila! No heavy bags to lug and store just one brick at a time as needed!

Little things make me happy.

Speaking of little things ... my Hungarian Banana Peppers have finally decided to make an appearance! The last to push through the soil - I'm so proud of their perseverance!

That's a Hungarian for you!

Be mindful and notice the little things we are gifted from nature.

They are lent to us for our enjoyment - sometimes for just a short time but they bring beauty and light up dark days.

Spring: A lovely reminder of how beautiful change can be.

Sleep well.

Namaste 🙏

4/14/2021

Mindful Moments ....

Brought to you by my models of the day.

First we have Cyan my very vocal/talkative, especially during bath time, husky friend who although hesitant to leap into the van will jump on the table obediently.

Bottom left is Phoebe the Westie sporting her summer cut for bikini season - she's trying to shed those last few winter pounds with a haircut, aren't we all?!

Center - Leah - shepherd/Dane mix graduated doggie boot camp after pulling her mama down in the garage and splitting her head open – sweet, but was over zealous. She is a perfect angel now.

Bottom right - Fisher - still a puppy standard poodle ("StaPoo" as we call them in the trades) strapping young lad preparing for a future as a super hero.

And this is what happens when you're alone with dogs all day.

My back needs some Tylenol and my brain some sleep.

Sweet dreams friends and ....

Namaste 🙏

4/17/2021

Mindful Moments ....

Vax #2 ☑ and to make the day even better, happily bumped into Leslie, Jantha and family at the same location! ♡ you all!!

Yes, I'm one of "those" people who is thrilled to have completed this process and not afraid to yell it from the rooftops!

It means a hug for my 93-year-old mom who I haven't hugged in over a year.

It means not missing anymore holidays with the whole family.

It means seeing 2 of my brothers who I haven't seen since a year ago Christmas.

It means being so much closer to returning to whatever our new normal will be.

It's been worth every agonizing minute to have taken every precaution to keep our families safe.

We didn't play Russian roulette with our health and that of our families ... and still won't.

The reward ... reuniting with an even greater appreciation for one another.

Thank you, special needs community of Will County for making this opportunity possible.

William has been on an emotional struggle bus for the past few days so when we left to run errands he said "It's a roll down the windows and crank up the tunes kinda day."

Weeeellll oooook with me!!!

So, we cruised, windows down and he belted out "Thriller" and did the best rendition of the video he could sitting down.

When we returned home, I made a pot of soup and headed outside for some yard work.

Without prompting, William grabbed his mini shovel and started helping to weed the gardens!

Who is this child in my yard??!

He also lugged the huge Preen container from planter to planter so I could get it mixed in.

It was nice to have a companion doing what I love so much - not everyone shares my interests, and I'm fine solo, but having company makes it more fun.

I lost him to Hess trucks and archery after that but I relished the hour of pleasantries.

Bedtime ... different story....

Find The Joy ....

Don't let anyone judge you for your decisions, your honesty, your openness, your integrity - I find them redeeming qualities.

YOU DO YOU!!

To better days ahead.

Namaste 🙏

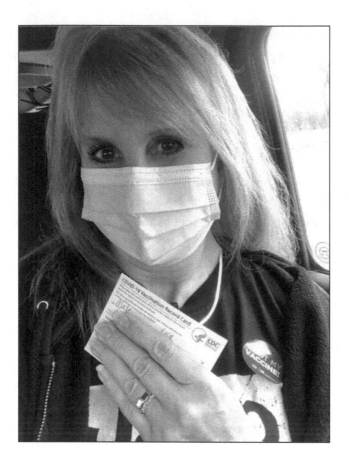

4/21/2021

Mindful Moments ....

As I opened the kitchen blinds this morning, I was greeted by this tiny fur baby nibbling on some grass beside a slight dusting of Spring snow.

He/she wasn't much bigger than our Guinea pigs and just as cautious.

I tried to sneak a clearer photo but off he scampered under the deck where the safety of his nest resides.

There are at least 2 babies I've seen and they've learned the sound of our habits and when to run home to safety, especially when the giant barking creature comes out!

They are quick and evasive, soon to be grown and off to eat everyone's flowers and vegetables.

As I continued on with my work day, I felt like I was in some sort of "gotcha" game show!

I was running late from my first appointment and instead of listening to Siri's directions as I just KNEW that the way I SHOULD go would be faster!

Nope, Weber Rd traffic jam - when WILL this massive roundabout overhaul be completed?!

Arriving at my 2nd appointment nearly an hour late I still took my time with this little old guy then headed off to number 3.

An 8-minute drive Siri reported as I was stopped in traffic by a train.

Finally free from the kids getting out of school for lunch and train traffic backup I arrived to the street of my last client only to be stopped by a flatbed dropping off a huge dumpster and blocking the entire street from passage.

25 minutes later I arrived ....

I truly believe Wolfie, my last client, sent out his canine vibes to hold me up as long as possible!!

This client's wife works for a company whose boss is a philanthropist personally.

He gives each employee $500 per year ($250,000 per year from him) and tells them to pay it forward.

He says he doesn't know who out there could use a pick me up or a little help so he leaves it to his employees to pay it forward.

They handed me $100 today, above and beyond their grooming fee, because they knew my van was in the shop a couple of weeks ago and wanted to help me out ♡ They told me about her boss and his mission.

I'm telling you there are good people out there! What you put out is what you get back - send out positive vibes!

I intend to pay some of this forward maybe to someone behind me in a drive thru as I do sometimes.

Truly humbled, heartwarming and hopeful.

To the right my sleepover buddy and "Mike" a very overwhelmed, exhausted little man. Ruuuuuufffff day for him.

Continued bus issues and more kids returning to school creating more noise are becoming too much after a quiet year at home learning without distractions.

School is ordering some noise cancelling headphones for when too much is too much - his teacher is great with making learning as tolerable as possible for everyone.

3 steps forward, 2 steps back and keep pushing forward!

Long day for both of us and nighty night time.

Pay it forward tomorrow - hold a door for someone, help load up groceries for a stranger, tell someone they look great, smile, make eye contact and say hello to a stranger - it doesn't cost a dime to be kind.

Namaste 🙏

4/26/2021

Mindful Moments ....

William is growing up, quickly.

Giving up his backyard play set was a swift agreement with promise of a "cool clubhouse" but not without sadness.

Even he feels the uneasy and exciting transition from childhood to preteen.

Not to mention his empathy and attachment to "things" which in his heart have feelings.

It comes with changes of soooo many kinds.

Independence.

Confusion.

Excitement.

Wonder.

Like most projects this tear down, screw by screw, took a good 8 hours this past weekend.

BUT William helped remove dozens of screws and helped haul wood planks to a nicely stacked firewood pile!

We finished in time for Hub Landscaping to arrive Monday to gussy up the yard for Spring and set up Mr New Planter Box!!

Welcome solid new vessel of nutritious food to come! Your seedlings await under the grow light indoors!

A random sighting of Jeep Easter egg #2 purely by accident while wiper blade changing!

Now there are tiny flip flops and a tiny Jeep - what else might there be?

We were blessed with 3 more boxes of books for the GLA library today!

In our travels to the Clarendon Hills Library for pickup I stopped at the Willowbrook Burger King for Williams lunch.

I proudly stated that this was the exact restaurant of my very first job!

His response ....

"THIS VERY BURGER KING ... THIS SAME BUILDING??"

"Yes, William this same building", I proudly replied!

"I CAN'T believe it's STILL here!!!"

Hard to believe a building could still be standing from the stone age.

Sigh!

It was also a beautiful day to get Gypsy out for a walk!

Success in getting both 12 year olds pooped out early tonight!

William even crawled into bed and went to sleep while I was on a zoom meeting ... at 630!

There won't be enough coffee for how early he'll be up tomorrow!

Landa, my friend, I've always got your back and you've always had mine - we'll figure this all out one little step at a time.

Can't wait to take you and Andrew for some Chicago Style Pizza! Maybe if I make a reservation now at Oven Grinder there will be a table available by the time you're in town ... maybe - I appreciate you more than you know. 💟

All in all, a busy, successful weekend.

Bring on the 80's tomorrow!!

Preserve each day in your memories.

Learn from mistakes and find joy in the successes - time goes by before our eyes.

Namaste 🙏

4/28/2021

Mindful Moments ....

It takes some pretty patient, clever, dedicated and engaged teachers to reach our kiddos especially during a pandemic and isolation.

William has a para professional (assistant to the teacher and providing instructional, behavioral and other support in and out of the classroom) who is brilliant!

He has developed fine motor apparatuses to help students write who struggle.

He's working on some projects with CPS and he's recently developed these cartoon videos to teach math.

The kids LOVE them! They're cute, funny and relatable. They look forward to seeing what Mr. Ryan came up with each day.

This video is one of Williams favorites!

He's also making a prototype robot of his other cartoon character "Sidekick" - had the plans drawn up and off he goes!

We need more teachers like Ryan.

It was a beautiful day yesterday, right?!

A nice day to be a duck and ....

A great day to run through some cold hose water!!

I remember those days of running through the sprinkler on a hot summer day!

I'm good with being on the other side of the cold water now and have no problem spraying down some sweaty minions!

Today was a long day ....

Last day of quarantine is Friday but I still have to work and William needs to attend zooms and complete academics.

We are resilient.

We work through the hard days and cherish the good.

For 71/2 hrs. while I groomed and drove, William attended his "dashboard zooms" and caught some fur baby snuggles in between.

We finished academics at home and at 4 we were finally finished.

If we can make it through this past year with all of its challenges, personal losses, separation of family and friends, tests of resilience, trials, judgement, creative entertainment and growing division - we can make it through anything!

WE CAN DO HARD THINGS!

BE the change you want to see in the world. ♡

Namaste ♡

5/1/2021

Mindful Moments ....

We are so excited to be back to baseball in a couple of weeks!

Missing last year's seasons were sad but understanding.

Safety was at the forefront of the league and this year they are following all safety guidelines to make the year fun and healthy!

It was jersey pickup day at The Miracle League of Joliet baseball field - another step planned with covid safety measures at the top of the list - curb side, in vehicle pickup. ♡

This year Williams team is The Angels - first game 5-15!

We needed to provide our own buddies this year due to covid so mom to the rescue!

I will be by Williams side while he runs all the bases as if he hit a home run after a single, protect him from line drives and open his routine candy from the weekly trip to the concession stand - a very important job.

I can't wait to see him having fun with his team again. ♡

We stopped for a quick outdoor lunch at B-Dubs today.

The WIND! Yikes!

They have to serve meals in "to go" boxes to avoid airborne French fries and napkins!

If not for the light pole William would be "gone with the wind"!

We saw some interesting folks at the Dubs today.

An over-served gentleman at 1:30pm happily enjoying the warm breeze and chatting with us as he said "you guys are fun, where are you from?" "we're from about 2 miles away!" I said.

"OH, I thought you were from out of town!"

Are there no fun people in Plainfield?!

One sight I certainly can say I've never seen.

A man driving his car past us in the parking lot while allowing his dog to walk on leash, held by him, alongside the car in the grass.

The grace we gave him is that he had a handicapped placard in his window and the dog seemed to be familiar with this process.

It was a sight to see I must say!

The final photo is not uncommon in our home.

William loves Gypsy's bed and, well, Gypsy loves the couch - SWITCH and sharing is caring.

A nice relaxing afternoon on the deck with our new neighbors entertaining us with their fun antics, singing, dancing, trampoline wrestling and camaraderie.

A lovely baby back rib BBQ, sweet potatoes and corn.

Beautiful day even with the gale force winds!

Reeeaaaallly looking forward to seeing my whole family again. It's been wayyyy too long, we've missed wayyy too many family gatherings! But now we can do it with each other's safety in mind.

Life seems to get shorter by the day and if this past year has taught us nothing else - life is precious, short and we aren't promised tomorrow.

Don't let another day go by without appreciating those who have always been there for you by gathering safely and with love.

Namaste 🙏

5/4/2021

Mindful Moments ....

"I don't know what you're talking about, I don't want your chicken. I just came up here to snuggle with you and protect you from intruders."

You don't "snuggle" Gypsy! You have personal space issues and your paw on my leg is cute but ... not happening!

Mooch!

Well, we made it through another quarantine.

Two days in and I wondered how the heck I did this for a year!!

Holy Moses it's been a looooong, stressful 12 days!

My plate runneth over but we're back to school hybrid again!

The constant change in routine and structure really mess with William. He struggled the first 5 days back home and the last 3 days before and after returning to school.

We go into the last month of 6th grade with hope of a better future, bus situation presented, investigated and properly taken care of! Success!

Thanks to being properly protected, Mom and I were able to spend the day together yesterday, laughed over her naughty coloring book she was gifted (David) and catch up a bit.

It was nice to finally hug her without worrying about possibly infecting her. ♡

Today after remote learning William and I took off for some errands.

The most important of which were 6 more boxes of donated books from local elementary schools for GLA's library!

A big thank you to River View and Indian Trail Elementary schools for their generous donations!

My Jeep is filled to the brim again and it's very exciting. ♡

We'll be able to tour Williams new location soon. A video was posted today and the school is big, beautiful and welcoming! He said "the hallways are fancy!" Lol

Upon leaving our last book pick up we spotted this fine fellow up in the window on a tandem bike.

He seems a bit slim to me. Perhaps a bit more food and a bit less cardio??

I'm looking forward to work tomorrow. A break from this past week and the first time I've been alone for a long time!

I will catch up with everyone who has contacted me. With school, work, zoom meetings, Dr. appointments I just haven't had the energy.

Sleep well my peeps - tomorrow is a new day.

Namaste 🙏

5/5/2021

Mindful Moments ....

Brought to you by today's models (minus Bently! I don't know how I forgot to capture him before he went in) He is ALWAYS a good boy and although he's getting older, he stands like a pro for his spa day. I'll get him next time.

Our long-time fur friend Chewbacca introduced his new Red Siberian Husky sister today ....

You guessed it .... Princess Leia.

They should've been groomed yesterday to commemorate "May the fourth be with you" but I don't groom on Tuesdays.

Chewy has always been a high spirited, high energy little dude since a pup. Full of wiggles, excitement and kisses!

Leia was just the companion he needed to have a playmate, although it took a while of playing hard to get on his part to create a friendship.

His grooming was A+ today!! Calm cooperative and adorable - he did great.

Leia, a puppy at her first beauty treatment would be expected to be wiggly, curious, distracted and teething on everything lol.

She was an angel! I only had to move the clipper cord once and take the grooming noose out of her mouth twice!

She stood effortlessly for nail clipping, ear cleaning, brushing, combing (gasp! Most Husky's who especially need brushing and combing the most, hate it! She loved it!).

She also LOVED the blow dryer - who knew?!!

Puppies find blow dryers to be vicious intrusive enemies and attack them like savages! Not her.

I believe she was performing true to her name, as any princess should!

Look at those eyes 👀!

Theeeeen we have Fisher!

Fisher, no longer a pup but not far grown from its behaviors, has decided that growling and biting is a great way to get me to skip nail clipping.

Um, no!

He's adorable though, isn't he?! Stinker! He looks like Bosco's twin doesn't he Maryann?!

Sleep is calling my name.

I must reply at once!

Do me a favor tomorrow ... pay it forward to someone, anyone - show your significant other appreciation, smile and say hello to a stranger, hold a door, give a compliment - it's free to be kind and you just may change the course of someone's day. ♡

Namaste 🙏

5/9/2021

Mindful Moments ....

I cried a little today ....

Mostly tears of pure relief and joy.

These people are MY people.

They are my everything!

17 months of separation and sacrifice to keep each around for another day together was worth it. ♡

Sacrifices made, losses endured, isolation and making selfless choices made this day possible. ♡

It almost felt like last year never happened, it felt normal.

If I hadn't appreciated my family before 2020, and I did, I appreciate and need them so much more now.

I would do anything, make any sacrifice, popular and unpopular choices to be with them for one more day, one more year, one more lifetime. ♡

Second chances aren't guaranteed but they can be made possible when love and dedication fuel them.

My sad tears were missing people who should've been there with us like they used to be.

William had an amazing day! I was able to sit and talk, laugh, relax and make new memories.

Thank you, Boston and William, for making today extra special. ♡

My family is fun, accepting, caring, loving and supportive.

We have each other's backs.

We tease.

We laugh.

We care.

We are family. ♡

Namaste 🙏

5/11/2021

Mindful Moments ....

"Flooby" is what happens when you say "Snoopy" with a mask on over the phone.

The poor vet tech was so confused and had me verify my address and Snoopy's color combo for proof of ownership before releasing her!

Dr Tracey gave Snoopy her first antibiotic dose and it's up to us to chase her down 2 times every day for the next 10 days, pry her little jaws open and get the liquid in -

We can do hard things!

Rocket needed a little TLC baby cradle before Snoopy re-entered the war zone - she's kinda bossy and alpha pig.

I'm happy to report that Snoopy dove nose first into a pile of alfalfa hay and a plate of red pepper and Radicchio while simultaneously jabbing at Rocket.

She's feeling pretty good considering! A few more days will tell if we continue as is or have to make other decisions.

I'm an observer.

I like to people watch, not in a creepy way, but in a social analysis way.

Sitting waiting in the Jeep for our appointment I watched the dynamics of pet owners, their purpose for their visit and their results.

One lady, with her dog on a leash, walked in front of us while we were on our way to ring the emergency bell so she could get there first.

She explained to the vet tech that her dog had an emergency leg injury and needed to be seen immediately, while we patiently waited.

While her dog was muzzled, growling and jumping around effortlessly on said injured leg.

We both called in to register at the same time, we were taken first.

Blood coming out of a guinea pig overrides lady who wants to get in and out of the vet quickly. 😊

I saw fur babies being picked up from surgeries and taken in for checkups.

The one that touched me the most, in my empathetic emotions, was the gurney being rolled out to an SUV.

I've been there, I know that doesn't mean anything good.

A large pit bull trying his darndest to push up off the gurney while his man human laid on him to keep him down while being rolled in.

My mind went to an injury, a run in with a car, a fall, who knew.

The humans waited in their SUV as we are all directed to do.

Soon after a I saw a vet walk this dog out the back doors of the office and watched him wearily walk for a short bit and then take him back in.

I lost track of them while getting into my own business when I later saw the humans walking out of the clinic, alone, arms around each other, heads down.

I knew.

I couldn't help but feel so strongly for them and their selfless decision.

Our fur babies bring us unconditional love, support and dedication.

I believe it's our responsibility to be there for them at the end of this life as they move into the next as we are for them at the beginning and throughout the duration of our lives together.

I wish them and everyone who has lost a fur child to always have happy memories, tell funny stories as a reminder of their friends in the best of times.

They are happy and healthy where they move onto and I believe they would want us to be also. ♡

For today, "Flooby" is home, eating, moving all plumbing and irritating Rocket.

Gypsy is slowly recovering from her ear infections, allergies and itchies.

We'll take it.

The counter in the kitchen is lined with meds for all in the morning! I think I better get up earlier!

Be in the moment.

Appreciate each day and what it has to offer.

Pages are turned quickly and stories have endings. 🗨

Namaste 🙏

5/12/2021

Mindful Moments ....

Ohhhh Gypsy Rose Lee.

It's amazing how a spa day can put a sparkle in your eyes from a drab, stinky street urchin.

Gypsy has been stinky with her ear infections and skin allergies.

Tap dancing across the floors and dragging herself around moping.

There's a sparkle in those eyes now, maybe more so because she was done!

She continues to be my most exhausting groom and after a full day of work she did me in!

But she's pretty.

Cyan reminded me that it's skunk season, I don't think I need to mention why.

Watch your fur babies outdoors and also ....

Flea and tick season!!

Odie bottom right is a new pup to an old client.

I hadn't seen his human in years and just love their family!

Her kids, older now of course, requested that I come back and groom their new friend - I thought it was really sweet to be remembered by kids. 🗨

We always clicked and after a long chat realized how parallel our lives have been most of our lives, especially recently.

It's soooo nice to befriend people who get you and accept you for who you are.

She's written a couple of children's books and gifted me these books pictured - what a kind soul!

I love Shel Silverstein "The Missing Piece Meets the Big O" a fable of quest and fulfillment and "The Boy, The Mole, The Fox and The Horse" is about love, friendship and kindness.

A couple of books to benefit all ages during these difficult times.

A bit of a reminder that what you focus on comes back to you ... keep it positive.

She told me that when she wants to learn something new that adult literature would prove to be confusing, she gets a children's book about it to read. - GENIUS!

She allows life to hold no limits and climbs all mountains to gain knowledge and understanding.

We can all learn something from her.

You know that perfectly attired person you see? Not a hair or piece of clothing out of place, everything matches and makeup is always perfect? That expensive car parked in the driveway of that gorgeous house?

One of her children's books is called "Perfekt" with a backwards "k" - it helps kiddos, and adults, see that what appears perfect on the outside is not necessarily what is going on, on the inside.

She wants me to read it before she sends it back to her publisher - watch for it!

Update on Snoopy aka Flooby - she took her antibiotic like a rock star this morning! Apparently, she liked it and with Williams loving assistance we were quite surprised at her calm cooperation!

Hoping for repeat good behavior tonight!

I have some me time to go find after showers and meds.

"Nothing beats kindness," said the horse. "It sits quietly beyond all things."

Namaste 🙏

5/13/2021

Mindful Moments ....

William and I were driving back from Channahon this afternoon.

He was giddy and relieved and I was so happy for him. ♡

I write these passages to share positivity, goodness, joy and hope.

I wanted to share our day.

The more I drove the more my mind became scrambled between our happiness and wanting to shout it to the world and yet the incredible judgement and back lashing we /he could receive.

That's our world now, you know? Everything is a controversy.

I recall proudly announcing my first and second vaccine only to see general posts to all a few days later "I don't care if you got your vaccine" "why do people post personal medical decisions on social media?"

WHY?? Because we lived over a year of isolation with worry for loved ones with underlying conditions and saw post after post of friends loved ones passing too soon, young and healthy to old and sick, but all taken unnecessarily too soon.

Worry of ourselves becoming hospitalized and not being able to care for someone who relies on us desperately.

Family and friends passing without the ability to hold their hand as they passed or honor them at a funeral.

We lived without holidays, hugs, family, friends, BBQs, vacations, evenings out and simple trips to the park.

Heaven forbid you share a story that is innocent and brings YOU happiness and relief in our day and time. It is sincerely a shame.

Seems unhappy people don't want to see others happy.

My happiness soon turned to anger.

William asked me for months when he could get vaccinated for Covid. He WANTED it! He knew it was the key to normalcy and throwing the masks to the curb.

Today was the day. Thank you, Pfizer. ♡

Before I made his appointment, I told him EVERYTHING.

Every possible side effect.

That some people had died, as they did from measles and mumps vaccine. Our population is tons higher than then which is why the ratio of deaths from the vaccine with underlying conditions can happen more often now than before.

I told him the multitude of reasons I've heard that some don't want to participate.

Why some are afraid and waiting for everyone else to be "lab rats" ... as I've been called.

I'm happy to be everyone's "lab rat."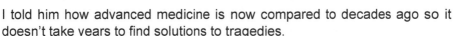

I told him how advanced medicine is now compared to decades ago so it doesn't take years to find solutions to tragedies.

I told him how people were afraid of measles, mumps, polio vaccines long ago also. He's gotten them, so has our whole family and we're fine.

I also enthralled him with the conspiracy theory stories one of which is being injected with tracking devices.

I also told him that if people really believe that they better get rid of their tech devices and live off the grid too because if "someone" wants to find them, "they will.

I told of him of every possible side effect from nothing to sore arm to flu like symptoms to death.

How I had nothing but a slightly sore arm but dad, with a different vaccine than ours, was pretty sick for one day after his second, and then fine. Everyone's reaction is different and I didn't know what his would be.

Then I said "Think about everything I've said - Do you still want me to make this appointment?"

He firmly said "Yes!"

I asked why? I just told you a lot of negative things and that people may judge you and me.

He said because I want my life back.

I want things to be normal again and I want to be a part of making that happen - not only thinking of himself but others.

WOW - a 12-year-old ....

Then I had to have the painful talk about judgement and bullying for his decision - something he's no stranger to.

He was running up to everyone to tell them his great news and I cringed in fear of judgement of him instead of allowing myself to celebrate with him.

How sad is that, that I couldn't elate with him in that moment because I've already experienced the judgement?!!!

Then I stopped myself and said:

"William, I want you to ALWAYS stand tall and be proud of who you are and the decisions you make. Be a LEADER not a follower, make educated decisions, don't listen to rumor and NEVER let anyone judge your common sense. You are an intelligent young man and made an educated decision. I held nothing back from you. I'm proud of you!!"

Sadly, I had to coach him on how to respond to demeaning judgement without the disrespect he may be shown first, and to expect defensiveness from some yet happiness from others.

Dad and I, his great uncles, Aunt and Nana are so very proud of him and that's all that matters.

Then I saw this post below on one of my Autism pages and felt validated ....

Teach kindness. ♡

Namaste 🙏

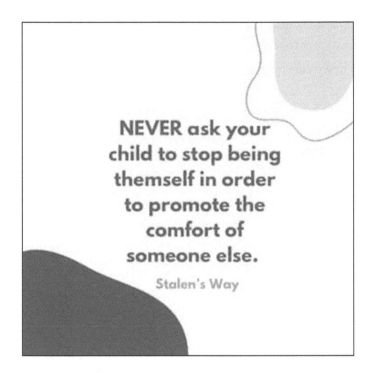

5/14/2021

Mindful Moments ....

Some of my garden Zen planted (veggies yet to get in) and positive news.

William the rock star - had a wonderful day, only a sore arm, feeling fine.

Snoopy aka "Flooby" is loving her cherry antibiotic and on the mend! No more blood. She's eating, drinking, squeaking and bullying Rocket - all is back to normal.

Gypsy, still feeling stunning in her summer coiffure, is healing up from skin and ear infections and exhausted from spending the afternoon outside with me.

I'm hearing that I'm not alone in finding this week a bit off? crazy? bizarre perhaps?

I mean we did have a new moon this week but it's things that make you go hmmmm!

We rarely have clients reschedule but we've had 5 this week - is it the weather?

One just wasn't home after much correspondence to be sure we'd be there.

Another, while she was on vacation, her husband had the dog groomed, elsewhere, and didn't tell her - She prebooked her next several appts with us.

Today some were on, then off, then later, then rescheduled, then back again!

Whaaaaat??! Insert photo of a minion.

While planting, my neighbor quickly opened his patio door and said "Lili !! did you see THAT???" (He calls me Lili - lee lee)

Um, what??

He said his kids' basketball net pole slid straight down with no one there - freaked him out, he said "someone's out there" and hurriedly went back inside.

I said "probably because my spirit friends are always with me and into shenanigans, nothing to see here." ☺

So, I spent the last few hours of 'me' time regrouping in nature before bus arrival!

The pool cover is draining and the yard is coming into itself and looking lovely.

I had a relaxing chat with my friend Lucie while we took a break from chores, talked over lawn care and neighborhood doings.

I look forward to planters filling in as the sun shines and rain falls to nourish their existence.

Veggies going in this weekend.

A little bit of everything today!

Very excited for tomorrow's season opener of Miracle League baseball! It was cancelled last year - better safe than sorry.

William is playing for the Angels this year and I shall be his buddy and run with him while he breaks every rule of baseball on the field and around the bases.

They're allowed - the league wants them to have fun and create inclusion and teamwork. ♡

Dusk falls, as are my eyelids - fresh air is good for a relaxing evening.

Take time to stop and smell the flowers.

Namaste 🙏

5/16/2021

Mindful Moments ....

Yesterday, although quite disappointed about baseball being cancelled due to rain, we carried through with our Yogurt Beach opening day tradition.

I have to say that William's choices for his cup were quite eclectic to say the least!

His cup, pictured, is Watermelon sorbet, chopped up Reese's Peanut Butter cups, cake balls, gummy worms and some sort of cake sprinkle - all his favorites in one cup!

Caitlin, Boston, William and I had a fun day spending time hanging out and just enjoying each other's company.

When your kiddos grow up and move away is there ever really "enough" time with them?

Today was outdoor catch-up day as the weather was much more cooperative!

Our goals were all met.

Aside from a pool filter out of stock the pool is hooked up, 1/2 filled and ready to fill!

William was in charge of pool floatie blow up, land mine pick up and general helping out with everything unpreferred task he absolutely hates.

While our neighbor wouldn't start up his lawnmower so he wouldn't wake his 21-year-old son ... at noon! HA

My parents used to vacuum outside our bedroom doors on Saturday mornings by 10 if we weren't up yet! Maybe "accidentally" banging into the door for effect ... ooops not!

On school mornings there wasn't a traditional alarm clock ... mom walked down the hall loudly singing "UP, UP, UP!"

We had chores to do and general responsibilities to uphold as members of a family, without allowance!

Although not followed by all parents, it's in the parent rule book to raise independent, responsible future adults, whether they like it or not.

My personal favorite part of the day was getting my vegetables in their planters… Finally!

We have a multitude of tomatoes for the future of the making of spaghetti sauce, Better Boys and Early girls, sweet peppers, pole beans, peapods, butternut squash, zucchini squash, yellow beans, eggplant and rhubarb (which we probably won't have until next year).

Strawberries will be planted soon when I have the right container.

William had a bit of a rough day and one of his perseverations was to get in the pool while it's filling.

So, I sprayed him with freezing cold water from the hose! That did the trick for a while!

Fresh air and lots of activity have me warn out and tired.

Hope to have plenty of veggies to share.

Fruits of the earth grown in your own backyard, are so beneficial to a healthy unprocessed diet.

Sleep well friends, tomorrow is a Monday!

Namaste 🙏

5/18/2021

Mindful Moments ....

Oh how hard it is to wait for warm temps to dive into summer - pun intended!

Ahhh to be young, courageous, strong willed and freezing but won't admit it!!

Temp at 70 today but windy, cloudy and just finished filling the pool this morning with cold hose water!

I swore he'd only hold out 30 seconds but he made it 13 minutes and 40 seconds, strong willed is an understatement!!

He wanted to ride his motorcycle floatie so badly it was worth the ice bath and red back to prove it!!

This pool saved our sanity last summer with nowhere to go and not much to do!

This summer we'll be free to go to plenty of fun places safely AND use the pool!!

I was out watering today - it threatened to rain but just wasn't givin' it up!

This dove landed right above my head, sat and watched me water.

Later came back with a smooth landing on the deck railing while I was making dinner and watched me inside the house then flew to the deck and strolled around the patio.

Their appearance carries a message to their host that no matter what is happening, peace will always follow.

A much-needed message today as William is having a tough week.

A timely reminder that "this too shall pass" - as it always does, in its own time.

Gotta make the donuts in the morning!

A pleasant, peaceful slumber to all.

Namaste 🙏

5/19/2021

Mindful Moments ....

Perspective.

This planter is a perfect example of perspective.

To some, it's imperfections of chipped pieces, a crack and broken handle are cause for abandonment.

For me, I love its character.

It's a little broken like we all are but its strength holds it together and produces beauty like we are all capable.

Perspective. Positive or negative, you choose.

Top right - this little old man wasn't doing very well several months ago. He was thought to be nearing the end of this life.

His owner is a never give up kind of human.

He changed his diet to protein and gets him monthly shots for arthritis.

Gibbs has been groomed on the living room floor for months and today he was quite playful and strong enough for a full spa day in the van.

His human is also a great guy who I have become friends with. We talked everything from firearms to long distance biking to Covid to fur baby care - it's nice to have adult conversations with an open-minded person.

Teddy, Beasley and Grievous were not into posing for a family photo like kids being forced to sit still and smile - but they are all earned A+'s for their behavior and patience today.

Their mama is a good friend of mine of as well. She is a kind hearted, selfless woman and our like-minded conversations and shared interests have become a mainstay in my life.

That's what I love about my job.

I love pooches and have made some lasting friendships with really amazing people that I may have never crossed paths with, without my career.

The universe brings people together for a reason, a season or a lifetime. ♡

I've had many "reasons," several "seasons" and a few precious "lifetimes."

The past year and half has thrown me some curveballs with some people but I'd rather find out sooner than later their true character. Life is too short to waste on those who aren't genuine - I don't have time or energy for disingenuous folks!

While William enjoyed another dip in frigid waters, I noticed these growing baby doves resting from a test flight on my unplanted tulips.

It dawned on me that mama dove came by yesterday to be sure I knew they'd be there and to keep an eye on them, but allow them their time to fly.

When you change the way you look at things, the things you look at change ... perspective. ♡

Namaste 🙏

5/23/2021

Mindful Moments ....

Opening day double header yesterday with The Miracle League of Joliet.

I am always humbled watching these kiddos living their best lives with their special abilities. ♡

Their pure innocent elation at being included, treated with respect, kindness, having fun and being shown compassion. ♡

I'm proud of William for sticking it out in the hot temperatures - he doesn't do well with the heat and wanted to skip the 2nd game.

I don't blame him.

It was uncomfortable wearing masks, running bases and retrieving balls - but he pulled up his bootstraps and made it happen.

You see most of these kiddos are at high risk with Covid - we keep them safe - we wear masks and we get vaccinated - it's not always about ourselves.

I'm so very grateful for these special needs' organizations!

Without them our ND kiddos wouldn't have the opportunity to experience everything NT kiddos do.

Coach George and his wife are dedicated, involved and caring with their own child and all of the teams' members and their families. ♡

William played 1st, 2nd, 3rd and short stop yesterday and managed to connect at a few at bats.

Off to Culvers for ice cream and home to "chill" in the pool for the afternoon.

Gypsy was so exhausted from our active day, that she stayed home for, that she managed to get in a serious nap.

Then Boston and I snuck out for a few hours of adulting!

A bit of normal sure feels good after this long year!

Can't wait to see what's ahead!!

Namaste ♡

5/27/2021

Mindful Moments ....

Today was the LAST DAY OF REMOTE LEARNING!!!!!!!!!

WOOHOOOOOOOOOOOOO!!!!!!!!!!!!!

On March 17th, 2020, when we thought we were shutting down for "14 days to flatten the curve" we never would've dreamed the year and a half we would survive!

The challenges we would face.

The kindness and positive messages we would witness.

The loss of life.

The absence of family and holiday gatherings.

The concern for high-risk family and friends - that hasn't changed.

Drive by car shows, to replace cruise nights.

Drive by birthdays, to replace family and friend gatherings.

Lack of human contact and hugs, oh man missing the hugs!

Everyone finding ways to experience life, stay positive and create happy memories in uncertain times.

We learned things about people we would've never guessed, both good and disappointing ....

... and survived isolation, an unbelievable toilet paper shortage and mostly ....

We learned that we are survivors in unpredictable times.

And the KIDS ... how resilient and strong have they been?!!

ESY (extended school year) brings regular days and hours and moving into August ... a normal in person schedule.

As difficult as it's been remote learning, and with special needs kiddos, I'll miss his teachers in my living room albeit virtually.

Watching him learn and how he does it and watching him excel at home - who knew?!

I have been reminded how much math is not my strength!

I've always appreciated Williams tribe but that appreciation is tenfold after this year!

With the last school day of this year upon us tomorrow, we keep our sites ahead to brighter, safer days and a return to whatever our normal will be, sooner than later.

Namaste 🙏

5/29/2021

Mindful Moments ....

First and foremost, I am so grateful for this beautiful day!

We started early today with an 8:45am Angels vs Cardinals Miracle League game with a cool breeze, blue skies and warm sun.

Very competitive team today! Hard hitters on the Cardinals!

Although William loves his baseball games, he wanted to stop half way through to get to our next event today!

But we don't let our team mates down ... nope! AND it was team photo day.

A quick stop home for warmer clothes then headed out to the Chicago Bow Hunters Club for some archery fun with Uncle Tree and his dad.

I can't thank you and your dad enough for inviting William to shoot with the boys!

He held out much better than expected with 30 targets and did quite well!

2 hrs of hiking through the woods, searching for 3-D targets and getting tips from the pros was great for his self-esteem, which can use a boost.

His favorite targets were the dinosaur, crocodile and cobra (most favorite)- he loathes snakes.

Soooo much outdoor fun and fresh air today, great for the soul - he was passed out by 7pm.

It's not often you meet people who will give a special needs kiddo with special abilities the opportunity to be included.

Quite often they are not included at all, invited to parties, sleepovers, play dates ....

But that's what we work for ... inclusion.

To treat him as if he's "one of the guys"!

He had the best time!!

Tree and Jeff took their time to explain details to him in terms he'd understand, demonstrate and encourage!!

Outside of our backyard, William hadn't shot since his lessons 1 1/2yrs ago.

He was so proud of himself and although fatigue set in, with a short break, he'd jump back in for more!

Great to see him out of the house, away from technology and showing his skills.

I could hike all day in nature.

It's peaceful, calm and renewing.

Thank you for this beautiful day filled with kindness, friends, patience, fresh air, fun and love.

Namaste 🙏

5/30/2021

Mindful Moments ....

This morning I took a quick stroll out in the backyard with coffee in hand, of course.

The air was cool, sun bright and nature alive!

My roses are blooming for the first time in a couple years - beautiful.

Mrs. Duck was quietly bathing in the cool pool, flapping her wings and enjoying some "mama duck me time."

I later ran to the store for a few more flowers and ran across this adorable truck planter, of course in blue, perfect for William to do a little planting!

Getting his hands muddy can be sensory overload therefore gloves to the rescue to help him join in on my favorite activity!

The truck has a solar panel that allows the headlights to illuminate after dark. Very cool!

With Caitlin joining us we had a delicious BBQ of rib eye steaks, sweet potatoes and corn on the cob! It was spectacular!

William decided it would be a good idea to DRINK down some hot sauce.

I went with the "Cody school of parenting" ... let him do it.

I had to pull the bottle away before he drank the whole think !!

After much agony William muttered "my colon isn't happy! I shouldn't be so impulsive. My throat is burning. My farts burn. I have a headache. I should've listened!"

Mhmm yep! All of the above!

Once William groaned himself to sleep ... the adults, and I use the word loosely, had a bon fire!

First of the season.

It was a perfect cool Spring evening to sit by a crackling fire, listen to music and laugh away our troubles.

A great way to put everything away from the day, relax.

With everyone tucked in soundly I hope for an uninterrupted slumber, quiet colons and peaceful regeneration.

Namaste 🙏

6/3/2021

Mindful Moments ....

Thursday ... in reverse.

A walk around the garden after a long day was refreshing. 💬

Everything is so green, blooming and alive.

Even Mrs. Cardinal flew by for a quick check in.

It's like letting out a huge cleansing breath you've been holding in for a long time.

William and I have had ALOT of together time this week therefore a pop over visit from Lucie was a welcome break from kid-dom with some adult conversation!

We covered a lot while William played with his Legos and hung out with his neighbor friend on the deck.

The air is warming up but humidity pleasantly low making dinner on the deck enjoyable with a quick dip in the pool beforehand.

A stop at Target, mask less, after William's 2nd vaccine was very freeing! He wore his mask and for the first time, I did not!

It feels weird, just like when we started wearing them, a bit "not right" because it became our new norm for over a year but oh so liberating and much closer to "normal"!!

We have a long way to go but for our family, we've done our part and are ready to get back to living. ♡

During our visit at Target, we came upon the book pictured.

"I need a NEW BUTT!" it has a huge crack!!

I could barely read it without cracking up! I had to share.

I love these authors that make forbidden subjects amusing!!

The sequels are a must!!

Something to laugh at through the fog!

A quote from my journal this morning ....

"Surround yourself with people that inspire you and you will not only grow, you will soar" Mimi Ikonn

That I have. ♡

Namaste 🙏

6/4/2021

Mindful Moments ....

William and Lisa's excellent adventures!

While Boston is away, we will play. ☺

Our first day began at 2:20am (which is why I passed out last night before finishing this, although I got the first 3 lines done!)

William woke up and couldn't go back to sleep.

We took a quick trip to Downers Grove to:

Honey Bee Gardens Family Farm!

The fresh made, onsite, honey is amazing and a fresh dozen eggs were a must!

But that's not all they have!!

Annuals, beautiful pottery, gorgeous charcuterie boards, gem stones, artistic vases, bird baths, fire starters, gemstone jewelry, antique farm artifacts, farm animals to pet and soooo much more!

Soon to be vegetables!!

Oh, and the staff? Absolutely amazing, kind, accommodating and helpful! Cindy (sorry we missed you!).

There was a bird bath I was eyeing up ... maybe next visit if it's still there .... or one of the others.

A visit here is a must! Sign up to their FB page for Farmers Market dates and notifications throughout the summer.

Open again today at 9 to noon!

Grievous escorted us around the farm for the simple payment of a little playtime and lovins - he was happy to see me in my Jeep and not my grooming van.

After making the rounds and hanging with the animals, a visit with Rosie the alpaca is a must (oh she got a haircut cut, so cute!) her table manners need a bit of coaching.

We headed home for lunch and a dip in the pool!

Our new favorite pool toy is water balloon sling shots!

Spent the afternoon outside, William finished a Lego kit and I wrapped up a bunch of phone calls and emails. Van was in the shop for the 2nd time this week, Snoopy aka Flooby has blood in her urine again and Gypsies skin allergies are acting up - but we take action and move on - I digress.

A movie before bed and much preparation for the really packed in day ahead of us today!

William made it to almost 8pm, unbelievable!! Slept until 7 today!

Enjoy the low dew points today and 92 degrees!

Hydrate, hydrate, hydrate ... with water!

Namaste 🙏

6/5/2021

Mindful Moments ....

Our excellent adventures weren't quite as we hoped and planned for today.

My story is merely our day and how you can transform exciting plans that turned quite sour to something positive.

We were to arrive at 9:45 for a 10am baseball game.

Snoopy to the vet.

Then off to Rochelle for a fun day celebrating Caitlin's birthday.

That all changed while putting on my socks! Yes, my socks!

I slipped on my right one while standing and then the left and BAM - no I didn't fall - that would make more sense!

I had pulled a muscle in my lower left back several weeks ago that was feeling much better. The way I bent and twisted pulled that muscle about as far as it could go without snapping.

I used to compare any pain to childbirth because nothing I had experienced was more intense ... until today.

Baseball was cancelled, William was great about it. 💗

Driving 10 minutes to the vet and urgent care were nearly unbearable so over an hour to Rochelle, I couldn't do it.

Still had to get Snoopy "Flooby" to the vet - more blood in her urine and I had to get to urgent care.

The wait at the vet was 2 1/2 hrs - I expected that.

But here's where you can take this to a positive place ....

I explained my issues to the vet tech and that urgent care was right down the street.

She happily offered to take Flooby inside so I could go to urgent care and they'd call me with info! Perfect!

At urgent care there was one patient ahead of me.

A few minutes later as I was being walked into the exam room the vet called, that was quick!

They x-rayed her and found her insides very good, no stones, so we're still dealing with a bladder infection as far as we can tell - hard to get a urine sample from a cavie! A different antibiotic for 14 days and more apoquel for Gypsy's allergies.

I was looked over, given a shot of lidocaine in my muscle (which didn't work, made it worse actually) steroid, muscle relaxers, back brace and lidocaine patches and sent on my way to pick up Flooby and prescriptions.

We're a mess.

I took the steroids, Tylenol, iced and heat, lidocaine patch ... nothing helped, walking is the worst ... so I cried all day since the pain wouldn't let up and how I felt I was letting down my kids - I know, it's not my fault, but they're my feelings and I own them - cuz that's all I could do.

So Flooby is ok.

Gypsy is being treated and plugging along.

Me, I'll be fine in time and William was happy to lay in bed and on the couch all day even though we were both so very disappointed we didn't make the party, baseball game or go swimming, mostly the party ....

I used my rest time to get my mind off of everything and listened to all of my week one videos from a group I start on Monday. ✅

A big thanks to William for being so cool about the disappointments today, hugs and telling me not cry that he doesn't like to see me cry, jumping in to help me out, picking things up off the floor, bringing in packages, getting the mail etc. etc. he truly steps up when he needs to and Lucie for bringing up our garbage cans and watering my very thirsty plants tonight, Caitlin for being so understanding that we couldn't make it for her birthday (that was the worst

427

for me!) and calls from Boston and my wonderful mother in law wishing they could help.

So, my takeaway today ....

Don't be afraid to talk about your needs you'll be surprised how many giving, helpful strangers, friends and family you have.

Most important ... Sit down to put your socks on!!!!

*Dinner courtesy of Uber Eats @ Noodles and Company (I had cauliflower gnocchi with shrimp and a yummy tomato sauce with a kick!)

Coincidentally this was the quote in my journal today:

"Train your mind to see the good in everything. Positivity is a choice. The happiness of your life depends on the quality of your thoughts." Unknown

Tomorrow WILL be a great day!!

Namaste 🙏

6/6/2021

Mindful Moments ....

As I decided last night, today WOULD be a GREAT day!

I slept well and when I woke up the severe pain from yesterday had subsided and my left leg was numb.

I've also decided I'm referring to FB for a back pain diagnosis as April hit the nail on the head - sciatica!

I did some research on it, cuz I wasn't moving anywhere, and found that after severe sciatica pain decreases, the leg affected becomes numb and tingly for up to a couple of weeks -

Yup, numb left thigh and tingly toes - sooo weird!! But I'll take the numb and tingly over yesterday!!

I felt good enough to get William to Clow Airports Air Show this morning!

So many things we frequent that we missed last year!

I won't bore you with details here - each video or photo is captioned.

I wanted to put him on the Lady Bird for a ride since the Ford Triple Engine that we usually ride wasn't flying this year BUT

It was single passenger and $350 pp - nope

Soooo helicopter ride it was!

We met a mom with 3 kids but just her son was waiting to ride with whoever else he could fit on with so we invited him with us.

His name is Nick and he and William were so excited!!

Two hours was enough for my little man - very overwhelming with loud noise and he asked to leave.

The downside of Autism is that loud, crowded functions get overwhelming and overstimulation quickly increases especially after a year away from managing it all ....

The upside is he's learned to know when he can't take anymore and we've learned to leave and not push him - it's best for everyone

He knows what he needs even though he's disappointed that he can't hold out longer ♡

We swam a bit at home and decided it was time for William to try sushi!!

He's been asking!

We ordered from Otobo Sushi and Bar / soooo good and has food we would all eat ♡

Thanks again Uber Eats for a speedy delivery!

He has found that he LOVES sushi !! woohoo!!! I'm so happy!

I didn't tell him all the deets of each roll - he doesn't know he ate eel and avocado

I love it too but rarely get it because it hasn't been a whole family favorite -

Anyone who truly knows me, knows why I had to get the "Unagi" roll!

Otobo has something for all of us!!

We are exhausted.

William is snoring.

Gypsy loves her pill in cheese.

Snoopy hates her new medicine.

I need to lay down and The Fear is waiting for me!!

I read all of your comments from yesterday and today - I can't thank you enough for your kindness and support!!

Hoping this passes quickly but now I'm afraid to move!!

Turn up your volume if you like to hear plane engines! Very exhilarating!!

Much better day today!!

Namaste 🙏

6/10/2021

Mindful Moments ....

It's hard to believe it's been 4 years since we put in these Arbor Vitae.

They've grown well and now need trimming into a natural privacy fence as they close in together and join "arms".

As far as the yard, last year was a total wash for me. Or keeping up with anything for that matter.

Remote learning was full time all year so having time to tend to nature was slim at best.

My planting choices were nothing more than necessity, not enjoyment.

Those emotions reflected all summer.

I never felt fulfilled when I was outside or looking out the window.

My goal this Spring was to bring my yard to colorful and nourishing life like it hadn't been for years.

I needed to free up a little time and stop working 7 days per week never leaving time to enjoy the things that fill my soul

Mission accomplished!

This is the first year in MANY that all 3 colors of the clematis are blooming at once!

A 15-minute watering and surveillance walk around the property can bring a day's stress to a screeching halt if even for only a short while.

It has become quite pleasing to the eye and soon to the taste. ♡

I'm grateful for this space. ♡

An enormous shout out and thank you to Judy at Lincoln Elementary in Plainfield for gathering 14 FULL BOXES and 1 bag of gently used books for donation!!

A bigger thank you to the teens working this summer at the school who hauled them out to my Jeep and tetrised them in to fill every available space!!

Life savers!!

My Jeep is full across the back, to the roof and on the rack in the far back!

I believe we've hit over 30 boxes of donated books!! So excited for the kids at GLA!!

My last round out back tonight brought me to my friend busily pollinating the perennials.

For me, there is nothing that creates more peace and serenity than nature at work.

Early morning tomorrow so off to get some sleep.

I'll leave you with this quote for today ....

You can rise up from anything.

You can completely recreate yourself.

All that matters is that you DECIDE today and never look back.

Namaste 🙏

6/12/2021

Mindful Moments ....

Every Saturday, during baseball season, we pass this mural on a building in Joliet.

I'm always amazed at the talented minds that create such detailed art on a building let alone canvas.

This particular work of art brings many memories of my brother Toms 55' Chevy he proudly displayed at Tri-Chevy Association meets years ago.

This exact color ... although I don't recall him sporting these particular fashion trends at the time.

One more B-ball game next week and Spring season ends until Fall ball begins.

It's been great being back at the field watching these kiddos living their best lives!

William held out well in the extreme heat today and some rules were altered due to the temps to get these kids off and on the field quickly - 5 pitch limit, no hit? then t-ball otherwise they pitch until they connect -

Masks remain in the dugout, on the field and in line at the snack bar otherwise mask less was nice.

I love how the league always has our kids' best interest in mind!

We headed straight up to Willowbrook to Del Rheas Chicken Basket Big Bop Car Show.

Turnout was low and by the time we got there we were able to enjoy about 4 classics - plenty for a HOT day with rain headed in.

The highlight of the day was meeting my brother Tom there and sitting down for a cold beer, a kitty cocktail for some, and some appies!

As we said our goodbyes and headed back west the sky's opened up to a much-needed down pour!

These active summer days were missed last year so we soak it in.

If you learned anything from this past year it's not to take life, and all it has to offer for granted, for it can be gone in the blink of an eye.

Sweet dreams.

Namaste 🙏

6/15/2021

Mindful Moments ....

A bit late on this for sure but ya know, life gets in the way!

Missing Caitlin's birthday, on her actual birthday, was hard.

But that's in the past and spending Sunday finally celebrating it was time I treasured.

We swam, had some time to relax, good eats and her favorite dessert, homemade key lime pie - I make a yummy key lime pie if I do say so myself.

Happy birthday my sweet, many more to come. ♡

Today was Williams first day of ESY (extended school year - 4 days per week for 6 weeks) They are back on full schedule now, IM SO HAPPY! Ooops, did I say that too loud.

They will have field trips this year which is fantastic! Back to learning socialization again!

He was excited, as was I !!

I've been reflecting to last summer and how long and isolating it was!

ESY at home, no field trips, nowhere to go … but our pool!

I also reflected on how grateful I am for that pool!! It's relaxing water literally, therapeutically, guided us through some VERY difficult losses and times!

I digress .... One of the things I will miss about remote learning will be not having to wake William up and rush for an early morning bus - 7:16 bus pick up today … we made it, but I forgot to put his school supply box on with him.

I have to get back into routine! No problem!!

A quiet cool morning stroll with my Gypsy girl, a stop to get my hair done … ALONE, 14 box book donation drop off at the new location of Williams school for Fall … ALONE and back home to work, garden and trim trees …. ALONE!

Get the picture. ☺

I got a sneak peek inside this beautiful building … saw Williams room and the soon to be library adjacent to it.

The custodian who met me there and helped me was so excited about the sensory room he HAD to show it to me, I was all over it!!

The most exciting was the sensory room!! OMG! It's amazing and I want one!

Rock walls, hand over hand loops, sensory swings, slides, ladders, play house, foam pits, lots of colors!!

They should be moving over there for Fall.

To top off the afternoon, peas are ready to be harvested, peppers on the way and a pretty little eggplant flower unaware of its future sacrifice to my table.

You see there were some frustrating negatives today and I could go on about those - but what you focus on is what you get back ....

"Life is an echo. What you send out comes back. What you sow you reap. What you give you get. What you see in others, exists in you." Zig Zigler

Namaste 🙏

6/17/2021

Mindful Moments....

Roll call from Wednesday ...

Bentley - single doodle male hopelessly in love with Lady. She is years his jr and quite obviously lacks mutual interest! She's missing out, he's quite the gentleman. Jantha your grooming over last weekend made my job easier yesterday.

Tasha and Lady...not pictured... felt a quick morning pedicure and brush out would suffice for their spa day. The eternal princesses are as thick as thieves. Tasha is quite protective of Lady - perhaps keeping her guarded from the flirtatious advances of Mr. Bentley?!

Bohde- single pure bred golden male. Loves sleeping, eating and evading the big white van in the driveway. Despite his covert efforts he entered, aided by 3 people pushing and shoving - but effortlessly jumped on the table for me! He wanted a silly photo and a serious photo to show his many personalities.

Beckett - single doodle male. Beckett bears a striking resemblance to Bentley...brothers from the same mother perhaps?! Beckett finds afternoon naps, treats and strolls in the yard to be essential in his day - could take or leave companionship.

Riley - single female - the cautious, anxious little lady vacationing at her grandparents lovely Hinsdale home. Grandma tells me she loves the spaciousness of her retreat and takes a break from her tiny Chicago apartment to let loose and RUN. I'm told that at home, she sleeps all day.

Riley's grandma is a wonderful lady I've known since I went mobile some 30 years ago.

She has an adult nonverbal autistic son and is always happy to share stories and information.

We chatted for quite some time.

She is on the board at Brookfield Zoo and told me of some really great programs they have there for special needs kiddos that I wasn't aware of!

We have been members for years but I haven't had time to keep up on emails and snail mail literature.

I can't wait to look into them!

Their family also purchased a golden puppy and funded his training to be a trained support companion for a special needs' kiddo ♡

I have some pretty wonderful clients. I'm proud to know them all and their special qualities in giving back selflessly.

Helps to see that good still exists. ♡

Morning comes early with Sir William so off to sleepy land I go!

Namaste 🙏

6/20/2021

Mindful Moments ....

Juneteenth ... a day of celebration of freedom, a National Day of Recognition long overdue!

We wrapped up Spring baseball in the morning with a little pomp and circumstance with trophy day.

I know I've said it before but watching these kiddos play their hearts out, smiles for miles and experiencing the things that NT kiddos take for granted warms my soul every time!

These kids know what it's like to feel abandoned, excluded, pushed aside, to be forgotten super heroes.

For times like these, if only for a half hour, they are "one of the gang", they belong and their inner super hero shines!

Coach George is so inspiring and dedicated to these kiddos! We appreciate him, his wife and son, Williams team mate!

Arriving home, we anxiously awaited our guests for our first family bacon fry in 2 years. 💬

We missed mom but some things have become too much for her and sitting out in the heat is one of them.

She had great company! We all appreciated and felt complete confidence in Paula hanging with mom so Tom and Annika could have a day away. 💬

There was much festivizing, catching up, goofing off, overeating … can one overeat bacon??? I think not!

Caitlin your Rhubarb Kuchen was amazeballs!

William … and Boston … enjoyed the most ginormous truck floatie I've ever seen! William is in pool heaven!

He goes to school tomorrow; I may need to test it out.

There's nothing like spending time with people you love where judgement of any kind is nonexistent and the mere honor of finally being in everyone's company in person is enough to fill your heart until the next time.

"People spend too much time looking for more, instead of appreciating what they already have."

Be safe tonight my friends and family - severe storms rolling through, eyes to the sky.

Namaste 🙏

6/21/2021

Mindful Moments …

Here in Illinois, last night was quite unnerving.

As the boys were sleeping, I was watching the radar as the huge red blob moved closer to our area.

To say it all happened fast is an understatement.

Weather reporters couldn't report the areas in danger quickly enough.

Phone tornado warnings going off simultaneously with tv alarms and weather report interruptions.

We had a "minor" EF-0 go through Plainfield to Romeoville. Our only loss was yet another tent succumbs to high winds.

For this I am grateful.

I was able to remove special floaties from the pool and bring in a box of photos as the winds kicked up but couldn't get to the tents before it got more dangerous.

That is replaceable, life is not.

This morning the helicopters were reporting overhead as I watched the news and was shocked to see the carnage left in so many familiar neighborhoods.

I took William to school in Woodridge (a main area of the storm) then went to visit with mom in Willowbrook which was remarkably untouched and yet within 2 miles of devastation.

Upon seeing a post for help from a friend I headed west on Plainfield Rd toward Downers Grove.

No street close to her home was passable.

One family's house untouched … garage, just gone. No debris, nothing … just gone.

Street after street blocked by police, debris and massive downed trees.

Weary faces and slouched posture from fatigue from working through the night trying to save their homes.

What is the good in all of this you might wonder?

No deaths, few injuries.

Neighbors and friends helping neighbors and friends.

Religion, politics, race nor sexual orientation mattered!

Just humans helping humans in their time of need ... AS IT SHOULD BE.

Chain saws, rakes and water in hand walking toward devastation ... to help. ♡

It's times like this I'm reminded of the absolute selflessness and good in most people's hearts. ♡

I am so very sad for the loss of homes, belongings and the temporary displacement of so many.

However, I am so very grateful for the safety of everyone involved.

Homes will be rebuilt.

Belongings replaced.

Precious life cannot be replaced.

Reach out for help, there are many available and ready to assist.

Wishing a peaceful, restful night to all and keeping hopes high for a better tomorrow.

Namaste 🙏

6/23/2021

Mindful Moments ....

I just adore these 3!

They all have special personalities of their own.

Beasley (grey and white beardie) and Teddy (brown and white Beardie) -

These two can get dirty in a soap factory!

They are living their BEST life on their farm!

Roaming, running, swimming and playing all day! Maybe a little poking fun at the barn yard animals and dodging bees busily making some delicious honey.

General Grievous, indefinitely visiting, certainly doesn't turn away a run around the property and any opportunity to play tour host to anyone who will follow with a ball.

His sweet, playful demeanor shines through every time I see him.

Looking back, for over 45 years of my life I've worked in some form or another.

From the age of 12 babysitting, to Burger King, Kmart, office jobs, modeling to owning my own business and pulling myself off of public aide!

I am most proud of the business I've built despite much negativity and invalidation at the onset. I proved them all wrong!

I recall a few words of wisdom passed along from our dad.

Most important ….

NEVER BRING WORK HOME AND NEVER TAKE HOME TO WORK!

If you're not happy with either, do something about it but don't take it out on others.

Leave your issues at the doorstep, always!

Always be proud of your work and give 150%, no matter how menial you, or someone else, may feel it is.

You are making a difference to someone and earning self-respect.

I've recently spoken to someone who said they only work one day per week so they can continue collecting unemployment … they don't want to work.

I said I hoped they had a backup plan when unemployment goes away in August since they have several children.

Instead of saving their stimulus money and getting back to work, they've spent it all and continue to live off of the government.

DON'T turn this into something political, I won't hear it … it's common sense and self-respect - something that is lacking in our country red, blue or green parties!

I have zero respect for this attitude.

Its why restaurants can't fully open even though we have the go ahead. Not enough servers to fill the now open tables.

Its why lines are long and frustrating in stores.

It's why our working bus drivers are taking triple routes; our kids are picked up an hour late for school and we are an hour late for work ….

Shit runs downhill. This affects William and ME.

It's frustrating!

I've worked through this mess since last May 1, safely, using EVERY precaution, chastised for being so cautious which is the others persons problem not mine, and shutting down when needed.

I am empathetic to those who need the help because there are truly people in need. I've been there and worked my way out of it.

However, for those taking advantage of the pandemics financial assistance because they simply don't want to work ... Find some self-respect and support your families with pride not with handouts!

How about not blaming the government for sending relief but starting to hold our citizens accountable for taking responsibility?

What you put out is what you get back.

"Self-esteem = seeing yourself as a flawed person, and still holding yourself in high regard."

Namaste 🙏

7/6/2021

Mindful Moments ....

I've crawled out from under my rock. 💟

I spent 5 days in bed last week with pneumonia and here are my take aways'
....

I don't think I've ever been that sick.

Marrying Boston was the best decision I've ever made.

Without question, or help, he spent that first weekend stepping up to keep William busy, take care of me and keep up with his honey do list before he had to go back to work last Monday. 💟

I discovered a local ER I will not return to.

I appreciated that a week of rain is heaven sent to keep my gardens thriving when I couldn't.

I'm grateful that Uber eats and fast food can keep your family alive when you can't cook or stand the smell of food.

I learned that as much as I long for a nap and time to myself, that isn't the way I'd prefer it.

Be careful what you ask for, you just might get it!

I learned how to make moonshine, where to set up, the supplies I need and how to get around the law.

I learned that when using wooden skewers, use 2, then your food won't spin when you turn it!

I saw many episodes of Fixer Upper and can now flip houses single handedly!!

I learned how to build a smart house living off the grid in the mountains which is what I intend to do before next July 4!!

I learned that because you find endless days and hours of mind-numbing blasts that shake your house and keep your frightened dog barking for many hours disrespectful and annoying that you must not love your country or be patriotic ....

I prefer my patriotism to be respectful, in controlled environments and for a short time on a specified holiday ....

I don't think the NHL player who lost his life, the Norridge man who lost his eye, the young man who's losing his hand and those house and car fires were found to be necessary patriotic situations in the end. Sad.

The heat this weekend made our pool like an exotic resort in the Mediterranean!

Ok, well not that nice but when you can't go anywhere you can dream with what you have.

It was nice to be able to get out of the house and enjoy a little cooling outdoor activity.

Our July 4th wasn't anything crazy but we spent it together buying Gypsy a well-deserved new snuggly bed and collar after her morning grooming.

Boston got to experience first-hand what grooming is like, especially grooming Gypsy, while he helped me with her -

I believe "I don't know how you do this all day!" adequately described his experience!

A trip to Sonic for lunch.

A little father son bacon fry stool project - who needs a clamp when you have a 12-year-old?!

A refreshing swim.

A dragonfly that teased and taunted me in the pool swooping in front of me and gracefully pausing midair to lock eyes with me several times.

Then a fire to hunker down and wait for the yearly battle zone to be over.

A lovely late-night chat with Lucie capped off the day. ♡

Poor Gypsy barked for 41/2 hrs. straight and pushed her way into Williams room looking for comfort from her little friend who, remarkably, slept through it all.

She was exhausted.

This morning a beautiful blue and black butterfly inspecting my parsley.

I'm on the mend and tomorrow brings new plans to be ironed out for my next adventure.

Although there are still a few mortars going off I'm grateful this weekend is almost over and I keep the memories of happier, calmer, safer childhood Independence Day celebrations at the forefront.

Hope you all had a safe and enjoyable weekend and are refreshed to begin a new week. ♡

Onward and upward!

Namaste 🙏

7/8/2021

Mindful Moments ….

I love being able to walk out to my yard and grab the vegetables I need to cook with for the day. Organic and fresh.

I spent the day yesterday doing one of my most favorite things, cooking.

There are 2 GF lasagnas and a triple batch of Turkey meatballs in the freezer for later.

You see my upcoming adventure is a microdiscectomy next week.

It was supposed to be Tuesday but, well ... pneumonia!

I know how to enjoy a summer don't I??!!

So, I don't have to cook for a bit and the family can have healthy food, prepping ahead of time is key.

A reminder that I began this prose over a year ago to hold myself accountable for positivity during a time of difficulty and the unknown.

I've continued it for the same reasons.

A brief synopsis of the last few months, NOT for sympathy but for perspective, life perspective.

April, revisited my spine surgeon for returning chronic back pain.

I've had degenerative disc disease from a snowmobile injury at 13yo and had a spinal fusion at about 38yo. S1/L5.

The discs above had degenerated, expectedly.

I didn't want surgery ... William.

We went 7 days steroids and meloxicam to reduce inflammation and decided on this regimen for years to come to avoid surgery ... cool.

The meloxicam caused a UTI.

I then severely ruptured a disc/sciatica on June 5th that wasn't even degenerated!

MRI declined by insurance, then reinstated.

Surgery planned for July 6.

Pneumonia June 25.

Many steps of surgical clearance needed (chest X-ray, Dr release, UTI recheck, blood work and Covid test - which is now routine before surgeries) only to have surgery rescheduled to July 13 because all of the results came in after the holiday weekend despite my timely completion of each request.

Life doesn't travel in a straight line nor does it come without challenges and frustration.

Are you going to push through the failures to create a better life or let disappointment deplete you?

It's how you approach those challenges that make or break it.

I keep it positive in the worst of times and if I can't find something positive to say, I don't say much.

To quote an adorable Disney bunny, Thumper "if you don't have anything nice to say, don't say anything at all"

Good advice!

I've spoken to some friends lately who are struggling. Seems like a lot of folks are struggling in one way or another.

I am blessed in comparison.

How do you stay positive during difficult times?

You decide ... it's just that simple.

We have choices. Every day when we open our eyes, every move we make is a decision. It can be positive or negative, that's completely up to you.

What you put out is what you get back.

My village is ready for Tuesday. Every base covered.

I'm looking very forward to getting back to what my normal is. This doesn't fix the degeneration just removal of the bone pieces off of my nerve, but in about a month I'll feel my left leg again and get back to exercise as I remember it!

You never know what people are going through behind their smiles or jovial posts ....

So be kind.

ALWAYS be kind.

Namaste

7/13/2021

Mindful Moments ....

A day after check in - microdiscectomy checked off the "things no one wants to do" bucket list!

Quite a bit sore today and moving very slow but that's expected just soooo glad it's over!

Good pain killers and ice packs!

These beautiful flowers arrived yesterday shortly after we arrived home from my wonderful friend Landa - so thoughtful Landa I'm so thankful for our friendship, though many miles away, it's always strong!

Gypsy prefers smelly boy socks to fragrant flowers.

If you can bear with me, this is a fun read, the tales of yesterday are nothing short of a Twilight Zone episode and will certainly be a highlight in my book!

I will bullet point for convenience.

6am arrival at surgical center entire computer system is down. DuPage Medical Group is still down today!

Staff is hurriedly trying to transition to paper and pen everything so they could get me checked in right away.

I'm taken back to pre op where I change, do all the vitals, line in, really cute paw print nonskid socks, warm blanket etc.

Continue to get apologies that it's taking so long because they have to hand write everything - no worries for me, I'm not going anywhere!

They brought Boston in.

I'm told the anesthesiologist was coming in to chat, the nurse and my Dr. ... Cool.

An unknown Dr. comes in to verify my "left shoulder surgery." WHAT?

After fumbling over my words slightly panicked that things seem to be a bit strange, I manage to get out "um no, I'm having a Microdiscectomy".

She hurriedly left the room.

The nurse tried to smooth it over by saying that the doctors typically have a case board they look at that tells them what room their patient was in ... But their system is down.

I could see the blank board from my bed.

I get that.

Then my doctor walks in and we do a brief chat and he says "it's the left lumbar we're doing right?"

He got the bug eyes from me and I said ... yes, it is.

He said "I better mark it". WHAT?

Now I trust this guy, he did my fusion 19 years ago but the day just keeps giving, ya know?!

So, I'm figuring everyone's brains are fried because they don't have computers to work with. A downfall of our current society.

The anesthesiologist comes in. Really nice guy, great sense of humor which is right up my alley and we were talking about the computer issue.

He said a new anesthesiologist recently started and this power outage happened to them at Edward Hospital about six months ago and Mr. young new guy had no clue on how to do anything on paper. None! Not even write a script!

So, I thanked him for being our age and having the versatility!!

Fast forward rolled into the OR, Boston goes to the waiting room for crossword puzzles and a nap.

In the OR, there's a lot of people for a relatively simple procedure.

I look to my right and there's a Contortionist shaped table which I know from past experience they're going to flip me over onto face down so they can get to my back, of course.

Last time I didn't see the other bed.

The anesthesiologist starts chatting with me about my gardening as he pushes through the sleepy meds because they don't do the counting anymore it's more reliable to hear you just stop midsentence and start snoring lol.

I wake up to my name being called and I'm in the recovery room.

Out of it and groggy of course but my head felt weird.

I reached up to touch it and the right side of my head was completely soaking wet.

I asked the nurse if I had been sweating that much but honestly, it's cold in the operating room so that wasn't really possible, and it wasn't my whole head.

She hurriedly ran over to my right side and said "oh they got some blood in your hair and they were working on getting it out" - as she was lifting the right shoulder of my gown and wiping more blood off my right shoulder.

I was too out of it to ask how the heck they got blood in my hair and on my shoulder!

But whatever, I woke up and the surgery was over.

I'm hoping it's my blood!

Maybe they do a Benihana style surgery flipping instruments in between cuts for fun!

I also have a bump with bruise on my right thigh so maybe they played "toss the patient" to see who could get me on the operating table, face down, in one flip.

Now either they were in a hurry to get me out of there or they just don't mess around because surgery started at 730.

Post op by 9, surgical recovery by 9:20, get up and walk across the room to a chair.

They said I was breaking records, hmmm

Poor Boston walked into quite a site I'm sure he won't soon erase from his memory, but I hope it becomes blurred over time.

Puffy eyes, 1/2 wet head with streaks of blood as they may have thought red highlights might be fun while I was out.

They bring in my belongings bag and I ask Boston for my phone so I can contact Caitlin and then William's teacher.

It wasn't my bag, it was the ladies who was actually having shoulder surgery!

I got my bag and made my connections.

I have some juice, go to the bathroom and off we go home by 10:15 - not quite ready for all that so fast but it got me home by 10:45.

Because of the computer issues the Norco prescription they sent through for me never made it to the pharmacy as Boston found out when he got there to pick it up.

I tried several times to call the surgical center and my doctor's office but again their whole system was down so I couldn't get a phone call through.

So, Boston drives all the way back to Westmont from Plainfield, closer to Shorewood, and is sitting at the surgical Center waiting for someone to do something about getting some pain medication for me.

In the meantime, I get a phone call from my doctor's office and it was his PA, who also attended the surgery, saying that their system was still down but she phoned a different prescription over to the pharmacy and it should be ready by the time he gets back there.

So, while my extremely patient and faithful husband is driving all the way back to Plainfield from Westmont, again, I'm feeling a little hungry and make myself a sandwich.

My throat is Kermit the froggy from intubation.

I just sit down and have a couple of bites and the ring doorbell goes off and I see its someone standing there with flowers.

I set my sandwich down to get there before she left with it or put it down somewhere that I couldn't pick it up.

No BLT ya know (bending lifting or twisting)! Ugh.

You'll never guess who got at my sandwich while I was at the front door ! She's lucky she's cute!!

I decided to throw in the towel and just lay back down in the recliner and get back to a few clients when I put on my glasses and they break!

My friends, you cannot make this stuff up!

I am so incredibly grateful to Boston for putting up with all of the running around, staying by my side and not laughing, out loud, at my frazzled, stoner, murder mystery appearance.

Thanks, Caitlin, for getting William off to school, getting dinner on and putting the little monster to bed!

I had fun hanging out in bed laughing at Friends but now I need Unagi!! What a perfect episode to be on last night!

Very grateful for everyone who checked in on me!

I'm sure with lots of rest and pain management I'll be doing better in a few days!

Can't wait for my first shower!! - neither can my family!

The weirdness of yesterday is still so surreal!!

I honestly look on this all with humor, because why not?!

And like I said, it's a great page for the book!!

Namaste 🙏

7/17/2021

Mindful Moments ....

The last few days have been filled with kindness and love.

My day began with a wonderful surprise of these lovely flowers from my favorite youngest brother Dave - they're just beautiful - they made my day brighter and hopeful - Thank You!! 💗 💗

I'm a very independent person.

Through life lessons I learned not to rely on anyone and just do things for myself.

Over the years life has become overwhelming and I've learned to ask and delegate when my cup runneth over.

Recently I've been reminded of how amazing my friends and family are because there's been no need to ask for help - just daily offers and well-being check ins.

Barb, my first shower post op was made possible by your diligent dressing removal and redressing after - probably the best shower I've ever had - at least it felt like it!!- Thank You!!

Annika, I can't thank you enough for coming out for the day Friday toting meals, good company and doing little chores for me - helping me harvest the garden was the best - I hope the eggplant and green beans were tasty! - Thank You!!

Cindy what can I say - you always open your home and heart - my first day out today couldn't have been better spent than at your farm - especially for William who's been lacking in company and different things to do.

My heart was happy watching him feed the animals, herd in the goats (and Rosie), drive the golf cart and watching you both teach him to fish the old-fashioned way with bamboo poles and corn!! Amazeballs!!

I haven't seen him that focused and excited on a new adventure in a long time!

His excitement with his first catch was incredible to see!!

Of course, special mention to my filthy fur balls Beasley, Teddy and Grievous - I just love you goofballs, you're honestly living the best life - I don't think my pockets are ever full enough of treats.

Thank you all for your kindness. ♡

As grossed out as William is with my incision he reluctantly agreed to put on my clean bandage after my shower this afternoon.

A Dr he will never be!! And that's ok, we all have jobs and his is not in the medical field or with snakes or sharks.

He said the sweetest thing to me at bedtime tonight.

His eyes have been hurting him (eye Dr appt Tues) and he said "if I ever go blind, I want you to know that I can see into your heart."

I said "what do you see?"

He said "I see kindness and love."

Wow kid, I sure needed that tonight and when it comes out of nowhere, unsolicited, it means everything.

You may feel judged and misunderstood by adults at times, but when a child tells you something, believe it. ♡

Namaste 🙏

7/18/2021

Mindful Moments ....

Today, the mystery of the blood red highlights post op has been solved!

Apparently, to add to bizarro day last Tuesday, someone was supposed to tell me that there may be blood in my hair.

Why, you ask?

Well, they do neuro monitoring during spine surgery where there are needles placed into the nerves in your head, wrists and shoulder to be sure no other nerves are being affected.

This also explains the sore spots on my scalp and bruises on my wrists and shoulder with tiny needle holes in them.

Good to know ....

A week late ....

But good to know.

Any who ....

Yesterday was the best day of Williams WHOLE life!!

A car show rarely disappoints but this one at White Fence Farm was a winner - winner - chicken dinner! pun intended.

Dozens of classics and hot rods supporting the veterans. ♡

He not only got to sit in Bobs Challenger but he started the engine and revved through about 5 gallons of gas in 30 seconds!

The fire in his eyes and intriguing grin was priceless!!

Couldn't wait to get to school to tell his friends!

Thank you, Jeff and Bette, for giving Bob a heads up to our visit - he's a really great guy and so nice to William! His kindness is soooo appreciated!

You certainly can't visit the White Fence Farm parking lot and not pick up some fresh made chicken and corn fritters.

I've been to a lot of car shows, cruise nights etc etc etc but I have to say this was one of the friendliest most approachable group of gear heads I've had the pleasure of chatting with.

Just a great group of owners wanting to share their pride and joy and spectators out to enjoy a beautiful summer day, leave their worries at home and share common interests.

We sure missed these opportunities and hope they continue.

A little bit of normal goes a long way.

Namaste 🙏

7/22/2021

Mindful Moments ….

Thursday marked the end of an eclectic year.

A transition from remote learning, to hybrid, to full regular ESY schedule.

Through it all, since a year ago March, William maintained a complete straight A report card!

He met goals that were projected for February of 2022!!

His last day at his current school location was yesterday.

It was bitter sweet.

We've been there for 5 1/2 years and this August we have an exciting transition to a new location where the old Westwood College was on the other side of Woodridge.

It's a beautiful location with larger rooms and a lot of space to spread out. This is their third location. We started at their first 6 mos. after it opened.

We began at a time of incredible confusion and change in our lives.

A much-needed move from public school to therapeutic day school.

A quick cliff note education on living with Autism ….

Change and public events are beyond hard. BEYOND HARD! For those in the back.

It's filled with fear, anxiety, uncertainty that is SO overwhelming it will rob them of sleep, appetite, take an expected happy, fun event and turn it into the need to escape into a quiet, dark room.

These photos are from Family "Fun" Day on Wednesday which they have every year.

They have games, bubbles, face painting, water balloon and water gun fights, obstacle course, food trucks, sweet treats etc.

What should be fun, is torture for him and what makes it worse, he really wants to be a part of it, but can't.

They want to have fun too, but fun is the last thing they feel.

These happy smiles are masking so much anxiety and the need to leave the chaos and go back into his classroom after begging me to take him with me when I left ... all he wanted was to get away.

His teacher took him to his classroom and hung out with him ... they know what the kids need here and they don't judge them or try to change them ... they just accept them.

Acceptance ... that's what it's all about.

They're not a tragedy. Their unique brains are beautiful and have created multi-million-dollar companies, inventions and more things than I can list.

This cute kid is headed to 7th grade this year! 7TH GRADE!

Holy cow has he come far with self-awareness at 12 years old - more than any neuro typical individual that I know!

He's learned what he needs and asks for it. He has much more to learn and although he may learn differently, he'll get everything in his own time!

He's going to do great things and I cannot wait to see where this life takes him!

I wish everyone understood him like I do. It would make life so much easier for him BUT anyone who really pays attention and doesn't expect him to be a boring neurotypical, he'll teach them how amazing he is. ♡

Don't expect him to be like you, or me ... expect him to be his amazing, unique, remarkable, individual self. ♡ ♡ ♡

On to a new phase of life and new exciting horizons to reach for.

Namaste 🙏

7/25/2021

Mindful Moments ....

My heart is happy to see this guy out and about enjoying life again.

A lot of patience and doing the right things have us out and back to some human contact without the fears that plagued us for over a year.

Saturday, Williams first birthday party in years with his best buddy Jack.

Hours of fun, good pizza, candy and cake filled some empty spaces.

The crane machine was generous using minimal funds to retrieve 6 new friends.

Oscar, he gave to a lady attending the party that tried to get him earlier and Miss Pink Penguin is now a sleeping companion for Gypsy ... not to replace Williams socks in her heart.

The remaining 4 have joined the eclectic collection of stuffed animals in Williams room, his favorite being tie dye Tweety.

I hope he finds comfort in these soft, cuddly creatures forever - you are never too old for stuffed animals - I hope his boyish heart follows him throughout life.

Too many adults let life's challenges harden them, forgetting the fun and innocence of childhood, which is so very much ok to keep living.

Sunday, after chores and errands, we managed to cool off in the aluminum pond.

We've had a game for years of midair jump catches for a $1 or extra dessert for 10 consecutive midair catches.

His enthusiasm wasn't up to multiple jumps but he did nail a few - he's still got it!

My instructions for walking took us on a trip to the park, William on 2 wheels of course, walking slows him down.

We stopped half way at a welcoming bench beside the water.

We did some mindfulness, listening for all the sounds around us, seeing all that nature had to offer.

It's important to take the time to see and feel what's around you - stay in the moment and let your troubles wash away if even for just a moment.

We live crazy, busy lives ... by choice.

Running from one chore, job, errand, event to another without taking time to breathe and appreciate each day that we're given ... each day is a gift and not promised. 🤍

We hadn't realized the many wild flowers and greenery they had planted.

It was quite beautiful.

William has been re-inspired recently to explore photography - he was into it for a while but his camera stopped working - he has a surprise coming - I think he's got potential with some practice and coaching.

My favorite part of today ....

I don't like parks, well I haven't since I've seen William rejected and bullied so many times at them because he plays "different".

But today ....

He always runs to and introduces himself to kids, he wants to play with them.

I cringe but let him go waiting for something good to happen, even just once.

Today was that day - these kids were inviting, kind, chatty and full of the imagination that also drives William.

Under the slide was an ice cream stand and wood chips were their ice cream.

Today he was accepted for who he is. ♡

I hope he remembers today the next time someone is unkind to him because he deserves nothing but love, kindness and acceptance.

Today there wasn't Autism and differences, there was sweet, friendly, fun-loving William. ♡

Namaste 🙏

7/29/2021

Mindful Moments ....

What an absolutely much needed low humidity, cooler day!

What better way to spend it than at Honey Bee Gardens "Buzz Around the Barnyard" Friday with friends!

For a small fee you are expertly toured around my friend's beautiful property to explore the many animals and attractions offered to families from 10-2 every Friday.

Aubrey, I hope I have her name correct, was our delightful, intelligent, informative, very mature for her 6th grade age, tour guide - we were honored to be her first ever tour at the farm.

Cindy and her husband open their vast and beautiful private property to guests for farm stand goodies and trinkets throughout the summer, art and nature classes for kids, wine and painting, wine and yoga, paddle boats, canoes, bamboo poll fishing, quiet nature walks, lemonade, friendly animals looking for love and hugs and comfortable, welcoming seating throughout the property and at the bee house ....

So many fun things and some future events I can't wait to attend!

The boys enjoyed time together feeding the animals, running the grounds, retreating in the volunteer constructed Teepee made from wood scraps from the property, swinging and relaxing while us moms actually had time to catch up.

You're surrounded by serenity.

Birds chirping.

Paddle boats gliding through the water drifting by tiny turtles with their necks stretched high while sunning themselves on floating drift wood.

The peaceful hum of children laughing, petting animals and catching tad poles, like the "old days" of playing outside.

Enjoying nature, away from the technology that plagues so many little minds.

A reminder that unplugging, walking outside of the house and into the sunshine surrounded by smiles, friendly faces and calming animals can turn a grey sky blue without Mother Nature - natural vitamin D.

Hearts filled with the realization that there IS happiness and kindness in difficult, still uncertain, times.

It won't come to you; you must have the courage to seek it out.

Open your mind and heart and allow those gifts to be present.

You will question as to why you've let yourself slip away from the beauty with which our universe provides.

Get out and enjoy it while you can before we slip anymore backward and restrictions hold us back once again.

For today, we enjoyed friends, fun, sun and commonality. ♡

Thank you, Honey Bee Gardens, for bringing everyone back to nature. ♡

One day at a time ....

Namaste 🙏

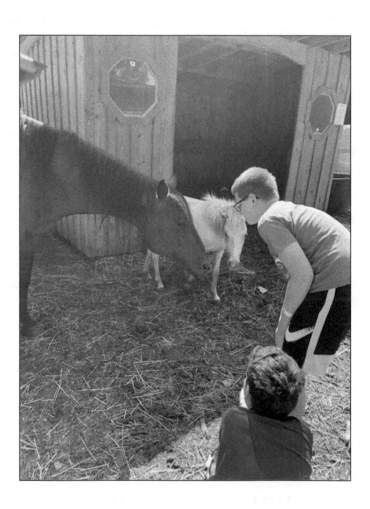

8/1/2021

Mindful Moments ....

Last night I ran away from home.

I speak very little of the "hard" of Autism to avoid pity, I don't like pity.

However, in the future, maybe on a separate page, it's time to educate on the "real" of it. I believe it's the only way to help everyone begin to see what it entails.

I'll just say for now, that as a caregiver, there is little space for self-care or anyone who can give you a break.

When your child is having difficulties, which can be daily, you just can't leave them with anyone, for many reasons.

It takes a toll. It's exhausting. Sometimes you just want to run away and not come back.

So, I drove ... far, cried, took photos and soaked in the country side that is not far from where I live but so different and peaceful.

The view was breathtaking, calming and serene.

There's that nature and fresh air again that is so renewing for the soul!

No traffic, no demands. Just miles of quiet country roads, cows, horses, crop dusting planes, blue skies and sunshine.

I drove until the sun set ... or my wine ran out ... or both ... or neither ....

But I went home because that's where I belong. ♡

So today was a new day.

I had a stress hangover.

You know, exhausted emotionally, physically fried but the weather was perfect and I had tickets to take William to the Illinois Train Museum for Vintage Transport weekend.

It was the perfect medicine for both of us.

He mentally made the purchase of a Ferrari with funds from his nonexistent job fueled by dreams of owning every auto variety he falls in love with.

I love hearing his plans and dreams. I never stop him I know one day he will accomplish what he puts his mind to. ♡

Parents, don't stop your kids from dreaming and make sure they're dreaming BIG!

We were fortunate to find a few owners who allowed him to sit in their cars and beep their horns - that's rare but not today.

Enjoying some Dippin' Dots, we watched the Steam Locomotive take yet another trip with the two of us disappearing into the smoke, downwind.

A few more rows of cars, a taco and after just under 1 1/2 hrs. it was time to leave.

Audio and visual sensory challenges allow William to be in control of when we leave events and it's usually not long.

That's ok! His emotional well-being is more important than extra time at an event.

A little over an hour was expected after over a year of isolation and the train whistle, on top of his previously escalated anxiety, was the signal it was time to skedaddle!

LOUD!

I'm proud of him for knowing what he needs and when to ask for it - adults just need to listen and avoid pushing him for their own needs.

Tomorrow will bring what it will and we'll take a deep breath and face it with heads held high, forging ahead because that's what we do.

Sometimes you need to take whatever break you can get no matter how small it is, take it!!

The weather was incredible this weekend! No humidity, warm sun, cool breezes.

Hope you got out to enjoy it. ♡

Namaste 🙏

8/10/2021

Mindful Moments ....

While Gypsy prays for a 3rd day of severe storms to pass quickly, mama reflects on the past 3 weeks.

Let's talk a little about anxiety first.

Anxiety comes in all forms ...

Excitement ...

Anticipation...

Fear...

Insecurities ....

We all have anxiety to some degree, but some struggle with it daily in spite of their best efforts to manage it.

William carries all of these.

For some, him, it can be debilitating...

-invade your sense of reason,

-cause you to over eat, under eat,

-neglect good nutrition and self-care,

-rob you of enjoyment,

The past 3 weeks this guy has had A LOT on his mind.

Some things that are exciting and enjoyable.

Some things scary and unsettling.

There have been some precious moments and days that have caused welcome distractions.

A mini golf get together and lunch watching planes at Charlies Restaurant / Clow Airport and back to our house to hang out with his best friend Jack.

Williams 1/2 birthday party celebrated with his family and especially his cousins Oliver and Evi who he loves so much.

Dip in the pool on that oppressively hot and humid day with the Mate head sweaters in full force!

A whole day with his buddy Cody hunting for Pokémon cards, fishing (briefly), playing Animal Crossing and just having together time - he's missed him terribly.

In life's great challenges there is always, always something to be grateful for ....

There is always love ...

There is always help ...

There is always kindness ...

There is always hope ...

Namaste 🙏

8/13/2021

Mindful Moments ....

On our last official day of summer break, we decided to spend it having some chill fun.

What better place to do that than Honey Bee Gardens Farm.

A pleasant day with less humidity made hiking around the farm enjoyable and, without a doubt, peaceful and serene.

With so many fun activities to explore I let William lead the way to where his heart led him.

Our first visit was over the creek and into the teepee.

A great place to be in nature and yet block out the world and its busy agenda.

A gentle swing by mom while breathing in some peace and exhaling some anxiety on the hammock.

I LOVE that William is his own person, wears all his favorite things, matching or not - makes me smile that others unsolicited opinions don't phase him in the least.

Rosie and the goats are always entertaining - in fact I really don't think they know how amusing they are just being themselves!

While sipping some ice-cold delicious lemonade on the deck we looked over all that nature had to offer.

Goats ... being goats.

Turtles sunning themselves ....

Miss Cindy gave William a VERY special rock, he's been a rock collector since he knew what rocks were.

She then took the time to sit down with him and tell him the story of stone soup. He was enthralled!

Funny thing is it was just about a week ago where I read him the story of stone soup.

It obviously did not make as grand of an impact as it does when someone tells you the story in first person in their own words.

He asked to go home and make stone soup!

With our farm treasures of hand poured honey, farm fresh eggs, cabbage and zucchini we had a final sip of lemonade in the bee house and headed out for an errand, home for lunch and a dip in the pool.

With all of its peacefulness it was the perfect end to a bit of a stressful second summer break before we head off into a new school year with positive thoughts that we'll be in person next week.

Thank you again Cindy and Honey Bee Gardens Farm for opening up your home and sharing your love of nature, organic goodness and a safe, peaceful place to escape. ♡

Namaste 🙏

8/14/2021

Mindful Moments ....

You may remember seeing my jeep loaded to the top with boxes in other mindful moments posts throughout the year.

You see years back I noticed that Williams school didn't have a library.

It's a wonderful therapeutic day school for autism and special needs children in a building that used to be a massage therapy school.

It's small.

Needless to say, the available rooms are filled with classes of students, occupational therapists, speech therapists, social workers, meeting rooms, administrative staff etc.

There was no room for a library.

Guiding Light Academy's ever-growing waiting list fueled them to seek out a larger location, their third location.

When it was announced earlier this year, I think back in January or February, that they had secured a larger building, I immediately asked the administrator again if there was room for a library.

YES! Was the answer and I was given the go ahead to begin creating a library for them.

Excited is an understatement!

Projects like this drive my spirit and fill my soul with my natural desire to help people and make lives better.

The intention behind these projects is NEVER self-gratification.

I felt very strongly about this project because I feel that books are important!

Every child should have access to literature. ♡

They open doors to knowledge, build self-confidence and are the key to success.

I immediately sent out dozens of letters to local schools and libraries looking for donations.

I scoped Marketplace.

I minimally paid for a few boxes off of Marketplace.

Most of the nearly 35 boxes of books were wonderful donations from generous libraries and schools and friends who are teachers and rallied their fellow teachers (Ali G) to clear out their classrooms ♡

William was in on this project whenever possible.

He accompanied me to many pick-ups and several drop offs at his school.

He helped haul boxes and on occasion was allowed to choose a book from those that were donated for his efforts.

And for me, secretly wanting him to read more.

New location Open House was Thursday.

I didn't think they had any time to get the library together yet.

There were so many books and they had an entire brand-new school to put together.

A couple of the staff members asked me to come with them and they took me into the room next-door to William's classroom which is now the school's library.

I can't say I didn't shed a couple of tears!

They have shelves on back order to display the other 9 boxes of books behind that 1/2 black wall that you see.

It's not finished yet, but it's a huge beginning.

So, there will be many, many more books and more shelves in the near future.

I will continue to take donations as they are offered until this room is filled to the brim with pages of adventure, history, science, biographies, auto biographies, nature ... for years to come!

I am very proud of this project and so very happy for all of the students who will have the opportunity to have a book in their hands that they can look at and read.

Mostly I am hoping that this outcome sends a message to anyone who is struggling with reaching their goals and their dreams in life.

Anything, and I mean ANYTHING can come to fruition when you just decide to make it happen, visualize it and put it into action!

Open a book tonight!

Namaste 🙏

8/19/2021

Mindful Moments ....

Yesterday, coyly from my front porch, I snuck this photo.

William had made another friend in the neighborhood and I was so happy.

He, Shiloh and this boy were having so much fun together playing with their common interest, cars.

I checked on them several times, each time found them sitting and playing contently with one another ... until they weren't.

An older boy was riding his younger brother's small electric bike and stopped by this house to see the girl that lives there.

He goes to school with her but this mom didn't know him and he had never been there before.

William wanted to ride the bike, the boy postured and became defensive, William tried to grab the bike to ride it anyway (poor choice - we're still working on boundaries).

The boy, bigger than him, punched him in the stomach and threw him to the ground several times (even poorer choice).

Let me interject here to say that William defended himself and can hold his own and I would take him into battle with me anytime ... I digress.

While I don't condone physical fighting, I also feel that one should defend themselves when attacked with no help in sight.

William has been bullied many more times than I can count in his lifetime and didn't take a stance, until now.

My point of this is a reminder that we all have things going on in our lives that no one knows about.

This situation could be approached by adults in one of two ways.

Raging, angry, yelling, finger pointing, name calling or calm and objective conversation.

While being met with calm and objective conversation, I found out that this older boy's younger brother has Autism and many other challenges.

He began crying talking about it. He's really a sweet kid.

His pain and burden was apparent.

I found that while dad is not in their lives, mom works many hours as a nurse to support them and he is care giver much of the day for his special needs brother.

I also found that this boy was attacked a month ago by someone who beat him up and stole his bike.

The pieces were coming together.

The boy was in tears, William was in tears.

The boy left his broken necklaces with me on my request so I can get them fixed for him, his grandfather gave them to him, he said.

He went home but returned with a visibly angry mom and little brother toting behind.

I braced myself and asked William to hang back.

I explained what happened, that William has Autism and challenges regulating when he's been or feels attacked.

She looked at her older son and said "that's an important detail you left out. Are you trying the play the victim?"

I honestly feel the boy felt terrible about what happened, he was embarrassed to tell his mom about William because of his own brother and related what he did to William to what was done to him.

He knew how it felt and how he protects his brother with similar challenges but buried feelings have a way of taking over our common sense.

I will say from there we had a very open conversation about our challenges living with Autism and special needs individuals.

I gave his little brother, legally blind, ASD, DMDD (a childhood mood disorder) and has had brain surgery in his 5 years of life, a tour of the van. Let him raise and lower the table.

I told the boy what a great young man he is and how lucky his little brother is to have him and his mom to have his help when her days are hard.

I validated his visible anguish over what he had done and how hard his life at home must be sometimes. He just wants to be a kid but bears the brunt of much responsibility.

Don't we all just need validation sometimes?

Continuing to cry he walked over to William, looked him right in the eyes, asked if he was ok and said he was sorry, again.

I quote his mom when I say:

"We all learned something today"

Take a deep breath. Practice the pause. Have compassion.

Everyone is fighting a battle we don't know about. ♡

Namaste ♡

8/26/2021

Mindful Moments ....

Most importantly - Happy National Dog Day to Gypsy and all our pupparoni friends!!

Perspective is really what these posts are about.

There are always two ways to look at any situation.

Positive or negative.

I'm choosing positive, as always. ♡

6:45am, it begins with a call from Septran that she's coming at 7:45 instead of 8:20 and he's still sleeping. I wake him.

He's not happy. Tired and disappointed that he's on bus driver #3 in a 2-week period and he was just getting to like driver #2.

We are grateful we have bus service, many don't, frequent change, driver and time, is hard for Autistic kiddos.

6:47am a text from my groomer that she left a resignation letter on my porch before she left for work.

Shocked, but not surprised.

Initial thought, stress.

Ten minutes later, complete peace.

I've been contemplating business changes for some time and this forced my hand.

She did give me 4 weeks' notice so there's that.

7:10am - text from my friend and client regarding need for an emergency grooming.

I just groomed the pups yesterday.

Today, after one of them, who shall remain nameless, L, killed & partially ate a possum at midnight had an explosion of the innards, to be coy ... in her crate WITH her little buddy by her side!

A beyond amusing text conversation with my "poopy dogs" human certainly broke up the carnage that was ensuing in both of our mornings!

The van is out working for the day and being dropped off for repairs tonight, so no grooming space.

7:36am - text from another client whose puppy peed in her crate and laid in it asking for an emergency bath- I just groomed her last week.

Pup #2 was on her own.

Pups #1 on deck - I pack up my "Dr" bag with equipment, my hair dryer, disposable towels and Smelly Dog shampoo.

Take William out to the bus and he spots this Downy Woodpecker.

I believe in spiritual signs; this was the first of several this morning.

I load up the Jeep and head to help out the poopy siblings.

On the way, a block from my house, I see a Hawk roadside in the grass just hanging out.

Another sign, seemed too good to be true, so I flipped the Jeep around and go back to look for him.

He's not there so I turn back around to continue with my journey and think to myself, where are you? Where did you go? Come out and show yourself.

Believe it or not he flies up from behind a tall evergreen and perches himself on top. He sits there long enough for me to stop and take several pictures.

While the pup's dad painstakingly cleans crate, floor and carpet I perform an emergency poop exorcism on the pooches in their bathroom. With blow drying and kisses, from the pups - a first for me - but we conquer and persevere!!

A brief post-poop removal laugh and I head back home.

Grabbed some water before my workout and TWO, not just one, beautiful red cardinals simultaneously land on our back fence, briefly perch and fly off.

Upon running an errand that I just today thought to do this cup jumped out at me. I don't often buy anything for myself but this was meant to be today!

"Today I will not stress over things I can't control."

My plans for today are moved to tomorrow and I lay my head to sleep tonight completely content in knowing that everything happens for reason ....

Although I don't think Rob has found a reason for their pooptastrophy this morning, but there is one!

Keep it light, positive, watch for signs and try not to stress over things you can't control. ♡

Namaste 🙏

9/3/2021

Mindful Moments ....

"We ourselves feel that what we are doing is just a drop in the ocean. But the ocean would be less because of that missing drop." - Mother Teresa

One of the biggest lessons I've learned about life is that it doesn't travel in a straight line.

We learn to live with change and adversity or we drown in emotions.

When we learn to let go of the need for perfection, free ourselves from our comfort zones and realize that life isn't perfect we create emotional freedom.

We open ourselves up to opportunity.

We take chances with confidence and perseverance.

We better ourselves, one decision at a time.

And learn that it's ok to fail, learn from it and move on.

When we learn to step into our courage zone and create change, we reach our higher selves, our ultimate destiny.

I've had some major career and life changes in the past week. Major!

When you get out of the victim mode of this happened "TO" me and flip the script to it happened "FOR" me you are free to progress!

As the detailed story will unfold in its own time ....

I am going into semi-retirement from grooming. 30 years has been wonderful but it's time for changes.

No more groomers, I've severely cut back my client base, just take care of MY personal clients! Freeing!! No worries my friends on FB I'm still here for you!

As most have seen I've launched a business I developed a year ago to employ the special needs community.

Thank you for the original idea, Shelley! You are an incredible supporter who deserves so much notoriety and love! You are appreciated.

I'm working on publishing a book, very soon.

ALL of these decisions and actions have been within the last 2 weeks. Mostly this week.

I feel excited, exhilarated, exhausted, focused, driven and a bit overwhelmed!

I've been running on adrenaline and little sleep.

I'm action and goal oriented. I get things done!

A special thanks to Paula for always being my cheerleader and right-hand lady whenever I need you - you're making this transition so much less stressful!

And to my family Boston, Caitlin and Cody for your support, encouragement, assistance and offers of helping me step into my dreams! Thank you for believing in me.

I've been awake since 3:30am putting a list of goals into play that need immediate attention - mission accomplished!

I'm very excited to share my progress and am so very thankful to all of my friends and family who support me and love me no matter how crazy you think I am!

With contentment in my heart and peace of mind I bid adieu to the past and forge ahead with confidence into a successful and fulfilling future. ♡

Namaste 🙏

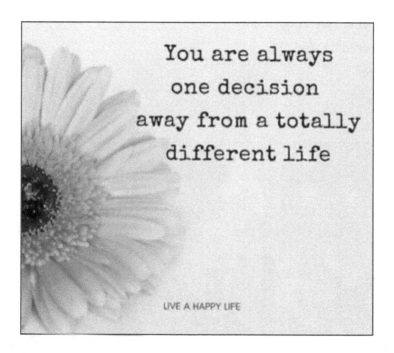

You are always
one decision
away from a totally
different life

LIVE A HAPPY LIFE

9/11/2021

Mindful Moments ….

19 years ago, tonight we routinely tucked ourselves and our families into bed.

We took for granted the normality of that day. A normality that would change with shock and devastation just hours later.

Before you put your head to pillow tonight, remember how quickly and unexpectedly life as we know it can change.

Remember to appreciate the roof over your head, your loved ones, tell them you love them - we are not promised tomorrow.

Remember to recognize the sun, the air, the trees.

Remember to appreciate our freedoms.

Remember to care about others.

Remember to be kind.

Remember ….

Namaste 🙏

9/18/2021

Mindful Moments ….

What a difference a year makes ….

Since William went back to full time, in person school in August, I've made it a point to take long walks on days I'm working from home.

I went 15 months with zero self-care - that needed to change.

As you've heard me say, nature is my Zen and walking without distraction brings many thoughts and realizations to mind.

As isolating and challenging as 2020 was it almost seems like a bad dream that's disappearing as quickly as it appeared, in some aspects.

Many reflected upon careers, relationships, living situations and made changes.

I noticed so much today that had me reflecting on a year ago.

Not only were there children at school but on the playground running, laughing and having gym class. Last year it was silent.

I've seen schools with event tents set up outside and rows of lunch tables next to their buildings taking as many precautions to keep their young attendees as healthy as they can.

And yet my neighbors school threatening to return to remote as cases rise in their classrooms, the young children who aren't eligible for vaccinations.

The brand-new playground in our subdivision open and welcoming unleashed from its restraints of last year. Available for enjoyment with less concern.

These are 2 separate playgrounds both were fenced off last year to reduce the spread of Covid.

So many people out walking, walking dogs, babies in strollers, jogging.

The sun was shining bright with clear blue skies and airplanes.

It was the little things we took for granted that went unnoticed at first.

Lack of flights, lack of traffic, lack of events … most of that in the past now.

What I do miss is the colorful positive messages written in chalk on the walking paths.

Hearts in residents' windows, car windows and front yards.

Thank yous' to front line essential workers putting themselves and their families in harm's way to care for the sick and dying.

Now I see a black American flag flown from a front porch - a prominent reminder of the divide that transpired over 2020.

I miss the days of joining arms, supporting one another, sending messages of hope and positivity.

I believe we have the ability to come together in any situation if we just decide to do so.

Every day we wake up, everything we do is a decision.

We have the ability to change the world, one decision at a time … make the right one 💙

Namaste 🙏

9/25/2021

Mindful Moments ….

A most wonderful happy daughters' day to my beautiful daughter Caitlin! You make the world a better place with your kindness, warm heart and compassion - I love you sweetie !

To add to this special and beautiful day The Miracle League of Joliet sponsored Family Fun Day.

A family fun day isn't complete without family 💙

Every week William asks if anyone is coming to watch his game. With full schedules it has been challenging for his fans to come out and cheer him on.

A big huge thank you to Uncle Dave, Cathy and Uncle Tom for arranging to be there today - I haven't seen him this excited and happy for a long time 💙

Along with special attendee surprises, fun games for the kiddos and beauuutiful weather came the opportunity to dunk Coach George in the dunk tank.

William took on the challenge willingly and coach was a trooper with upper 60's temps, cold water and a hefty breeze Brrrrrrrrrr

There's a sweet new boy on our team this year that William has taken under his wing. They hit it off at the first game.

This boy has come to rely on William's encouragement, validation and kindness.

R, as we'll call him, gets anxious and feeling uncertain before games. When he sees William and William gives him a huge hug and a smile, he hits the field with confidence!

Coach commended William for his caring nature, told him he's proud of him for taking R under his care and treated him to a hot pretzel!

Mr. W. really needed all of this positivity and validation today.

A little kindness goes a long way when we don't know what others are going through ♡

"Inspired" has a Golf outing fund raiser each year to raise funds for The Miracle League in honor of Tim Garvin Jr.

He was a player buddy years ago who passed at an early age.

This year they raised $5,000! What an incredible organization doing good for others!

Back home for pizza and catch-up time!

Our hearts are full tonight ♡

Namaste 🙏

9/27/2021

Mindful Moments ….

"I believe one of the most important things to learn in life is that you can make a difference in your community no matter who you are or where you live." – Rosalynn Carter

Tell your story.

You are worthy of love, happiness and peace 💙

Heal your soul while you give someone else validity and hope 💙

Namaste 🙏

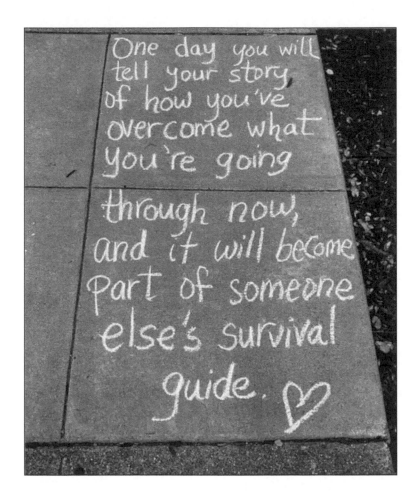

Aus: Williams, "A Feminista World of Poslavery and Crafting"

9 781647 198688

CPSIA information can be obtained
at www.ICGtesting.com
Printed in the USA
BVHW070218301121
622858BV00015B/1563